CW00690695

THE "PEOPLE" IN THE PLA: RECRUITMENT, TRAINING, AND EDUCATION IN CHINA'S MILITARY

Roy Kamphausen
Andrew Scobell
Travis Tanner

Editors

September 2008

This publication is a work of the U.S. Government as defined in Title 17, United States Code, Section 101. As such, it is in the public domain, and under the provisions of Title 17, United States Code, Section 105, it may not be copyrighted.

*****

The views expressed in this report are those of the authors and do not necessarily reflect the official policy or position of the Department of the Army, the Department of Defense, or the U.S. Government. This report is cleared for public release; distribution is unlimited.

*****

Comments pertaining to this report are invited and should be forwarded to: Director, Strategic Studies Institute, U.S. Army War College, 122 Forbes Ave, Carlisle, PA 17013-5244.

*****

All Strategic Studies Institute (SSI) publications are available on the SSI homepage for electronic dissemination. Hard copies of this report also may be ordered from our homepage. SSI's homepage address is: www.StrategicStudiesInstitute.army.mil.

*****

The Strategic Studies Institute publishes a monthly e-mail newsletter to update the national security community on the research of our analysts, recent and forthcoming publications, and upcoming conferences sponsored by the Institute. Each newsletter also provides a strategic commentary by one of our research analysts. If you are interested in receiving this newsletter, please subscribe on our homepage at www.StrategicStudiesInstitute. army.mil/newsletter/.

ISBN 1-58487-354-X

CONTENTS

FOREWORD

I am pleased that, for the second year in a row, the U.S. Army War College and The National Bureau of Asian Research (NBR) teamed up to convene the annual PLA colloquium. Over the years, this event has successfully increased understanding of China's military and the multiple aspects of its ongoing modernization effort.

Last year was no exception. On September 28, 2007, under the joint leadership of the U.S. Army War College's Strategic Studies Institute and NBR's Pyle Center for Northeast Asian Studies, approximately 70 leading experts on the People's Liberation Army (PLA) convened at Carlisle Barracks, PA, for a 2-day discussion on the Chinese military's human infrastructure. Presentations and discussions at the conference focused on identifying trends in recruitment, education, training, personnel management, and demographics within the PLA.

The People in the PLA: Recruitment, Training, and Education in China's Military represents the latest volume in the series published by the Strategic Studies Institute and brings together top-tier academic analysis and insight on the important questions addressed at the 2007 colloquium. This volume describes the advances and reforms the PLA has made in its recruitment, officer and NCO training and education, and mobilization.

As part of its larger reform effort to modernize and transform its military into a technologically sophisticated force, the PLA has implemented a number of measures aimed at training up a "new-type" officer for its modernized forces—one capable of operating effectively in a technologically advanced "informationalized" environment. This volume sheds light on such important questions as how the PLA's personnel system is adapting to fulfill the requirements of a military force capable of "winning local wars under informationalized conditions" and how the PLA is cultivating a new generation of officers and what capabilities these new officers will likely possess.

The importance of any military's "human capital" cannot be understated. A military is only as effective as the people running it. To date, certain facets of China's military modernization, including arms buildup, the development of new weapons and systems, and even the emergence of new doctrinal and strategic missions have garnered relatively significant attention. However, the critically important dynamics associated with the PLA's attempts to improve the quality of its human capital have not been as closely scrutinized, and thus, still are not well-understood.

I believe improving our understanding of the professionalization of the PLA, to which this volume makes a significant contribution, holds tremendously important implications for policymakers and military leaders in the United States and across the globe. As such, I am proud to see this important work carry on for another year, and I commend the colloquium organizers, sponsors, and participants who made this undertaking not only possible, but so successful.

John M. Shalikashvili
General, USA Retired
Former Chairman, Joint Chiefs of Staff

CHAPTER 1

INTRODUCTION

Roy Kamphausen, Andrew Scobell, and Travis Tanner

Twenty-first century China is undergoing major transformations in virtually every sphere. Decades of almost double-digit annual economic growth rates have been accompanied by double-digit annual growth rates in China's military budget. There is considerable concern over the pace and scope of this modernization of the People's Liberation Army (PLA). Such concerns are underscored by high-profile incidents, such as the January 2007 anti-satellite missile test. Public attention has, understandably, focused on the burgeoning military budget and an impressive modernization of the PLA's technological hardware. However, a state's military is only as effective as the people who constitute it—the military's human capital. This volume examines the "people" in the PLA.

ASSESSING THE HUMAN ASPECT OF THE PLA'S MODERNIZATION

Following on the 2006 Carlisle Conference's efforts to examine the "right size" for the PLA in achieving Beijing's legitimate defense requirements, the 2007 conference, again organized by The National Bureau of Asian Research (NBR) and the U.S. Army War College's Strategic Studies Institute (SSI), sought to assess the quality of the PLA's human resources; identify trends in recruitment, training, and education of conscripts and officers; and assess how these trends are likely to influence the overall effectiveness of a future "informationalized" PLA.

The chapters contained herein comprise key insights from over 60 leading experts on China's military. The volume's research draws from a rich pool of English and Chinese language sources. But, given the relatively recent start and ongoing nature of the PLA's reforms in professional military education (PME), training standards, and recruitment practices, comprehensive data and firm conclusions are by no means readily forthcoming. Conversely, the obvious importance of human capital to an effective, capable, and modernized PLA makes filling this lacuna all the more significant and this volume all the more timely. The trajectory of the PLA's professionalization holds important implications for policymakers and military leaders in the United States and throughout the world.

The chapters in this volume raise two common themes. First, each piece emphasizes the PLA's continued focus on the "two transformations," the concept invoked by then President Jiang Zemin in 1995 that underpins the PLA's efforts to transform itself into a force capable of (1) fighting and winning local wars under "informationalized" conditions, and (2) a force based on quality instead of quantity. The second major theme concerns the PLA's conception of the "new-type" officer for its modernized forces, one who is better educated and more technologically capable than previous generations. The policies of the Chinese government and the PLA have striven to cultivate a new generation of officers capable and competent in executing the PLA's evolving missions. While the modernization of the PLA's technical capabilities has arguably been a linear and predictable process,

2

uncertainty still remains concerning the development of the people within the military. This volume attempts to shed light on this development, from the enlisted soldier to the strategic thinkers of the future.

HISTORICAL OVERVIEW

Thomas Bickford provides an informative overview of historical trends in PLA education and training in Chapter 2. Bickford chronicles the development of Chinese PME through five distinct periods, from the establishment of the Whampoa Military Academy by Sun Yat-sen in 1924 to the "two transformations" reforms. Bickford highlights three key characteristics of the evolution of the PLA's PME.

First, the development of PME has been conspicuously nonlinear, with political education remaining nominally constant throughout. PME often changed to suit the PLA's shifting goals and the intensity of political struggle espoused by the Chinese Communist Party (CCP). Second, the PLA's PME has been a work in progress as the conception of the ideal officer has changed based on the political and military environment. Third, officer education and training has not only been shaped by the CCP regime's threat perceptions, but also by political, economic, and social factors.

During the revolutionary era, the content and emphasis of the PLA's educational system was politically-focused and tactically-based, with the goal of fielding a low-tech infantry force capable of sustaining a guerrilla campaign. Political and military education were fairly evenly balanced, with Soviet experience providing the template for the latter.

Subsequent to the establishment of the People's Republic of China (PRC), the PLA faced the challenge of forming a modern military force including developing a navy, air force, army armored units, and other specialized units to defend the state. A Soviet-style military academy system underpinned the new requirement for specialization, and command schools were established for various levels of rank. Chinese PME was characterized by a high degree of functional specialization through 1965. Thereafter, a break occurred with Soviet military orthodoxy, mirroring the Sino-Soviet rift in the 1960s and underscoring the unique and evolving goals of the CCP and the PLA.

Chinese PME came under intense attack during the Cultural Revolution as distinctions between officers and enlisted personnel and an emphasis on technical training were branded as "bourgeois." About two-thirds of the PLA's military academies and many more technical and regional schools were closed. Officers effectively had little-to-no training or basic education between 1966 and 1976. Political warfare was the overriding priority of that era.

The period 1977-85 saw the rehabilitation of the military education system in response to the backwardness of the PLA, which was clearly on display in China's poor operational performance in the 1979 attack on Vietnam. Equally important were the political and economic changes taking place at this time. The economic reforms increased the resources available to the PLA and the political environment tilted away from a communist revolutionary agenda and towards a pragmatic approach for national development. Each of these broad developments framed the debate over the future of the PLA.

Deng Xiaoping's "strategic decision" in 1985 called for the downsizing of the PLA and a reorientation of the PLA's strategy away from people's war to limited warfare focusing on China's periphery. These important shifts were marked by the establishment of the National Defense University (NDU), which was the first true all-service military academy. In addition, students throughout the PME system became exposed to a more diverse curriculum. Technical and command training were also vastly improved and graduate programs were introduced. All of these changes reflected the desirability of a more professional and better-educated officer corps.

Since 1995, the PLA's reforms in PME have been guided by the "two transformations" and the lessons learned from the 1991 Persian Gulf War, 1995-96 Taiwan Strait crisis, and the 1999 Kosovo campaign. The goal now is to field a smaller, technologically advanced PLA capable of waging war in "informationalized" conditions. PLA curricular reforms now encourage debate, creativity, innovation, and spontaneity. Technical training places a heavy emphasis on computers and electronic simulation. Another significant change has been a shift in recruiting more PLA officers from civilian educational institutions, reflecting both the continuing shortcomings of military academies and improvement in China's civilian education system.

What exactly does "informationalization," or "informatization," mean in practice? In Chapter 3, James Mulvenon highlights the application of "informatization" to the PLA's training practices and assesses the potential costs and benefits of "informatized" training to the overall effectiveness of the PLA. Mulvenon relies on extensive Chinese language sources to construct the principles, evolution, and types of informatized training and professional military education. The PLA has applied various technologies in diverse ways in order to improve both combat capabilities and individual educational opportunities at a lower cost. Technology-driven activities, such as simulations, virtual wargaming, and online interregional cooperation also lower the costs associated with the movement of materiel and personnel during training exercises and possible loss of weapons systems via accidents or everyday wear-and-tear. These activities also minimize the physical risks to the servicemen themselves.

Mulvenon concludes that the PLA has aggressively pursued technology-assisted training, primarily for the efficiencies the military gains in a resource-constrained environment. This technology-driven training regime also holds important implications for the United States. On one hand, the PLA's focus on simulation and virtual training may make it more difficult to assess the PLA's warfighting capabilities from a distance, as observations of physical field exercises still provide the most robust data on a military's progression. However, on the other hand, such virtual training may not significantly increase the CCP's confidence in the PLA's ability to defeat a high-technology military power like the United States. As Mulvenon succinctly states, "At the end of the day, the PLA needs to prove its combat power in the field against real adversaries, not electrons on a screen."

RECRUITMENT, ENLISTMENT, AND INITIAL TRAINING

In Chapter 4, Dennis Blasko shifts the focus from Mulvenon's technology-centered piece to address the PLA's process in training conscripts and noncommissioned officers (NCOs). Blasko outlines the PLA's overall training regimen, but devotes particular detail to the first two rungs in the process: common task training and specialty technical training.

The PLA has been engaged in ongoing efforts to find recruits with the requisite combination of mental and physical abilities commensurate with the new demands of its modernized force structure. To accomplish this, the PLA has tried to recruit more technical school and college graduates by cutting required military service from 3 to 2 years, increasing pay and providing opportunities within the military education system for enlistees and NCOs to gain professional certificates. While the percentage of college-educated conscripts has increased over previous years, college graduates still make up only a very small percentage of the overall force. The percentages are several magnitudes smaller for college-educated NCOs. Thus, the PLA has been forced to focus on increasing the educational standards of its recruits via its own decentralized network of regional and local military schools and training bases.

The success of these efforts in raising the educational and technological standards of the PLA's conscript and NCO corps is still uncertain. Anecdotal accounts highlight differences in physical fitness and obedience to authority between more educated and less educated recruits and between urban and rural recruits. Such dynamics could pose problems for unit cohesiveness. Finally the cost savings realized through the downsizing of the PLA's end strength may be offset not only by the costs of building and deploying advanced weapons, maintenance and operations, modernizing facility infrastructure, electronics, and simulator training; but also by the cost of better preparing new conscripts and NCOs to effectively execute the missions of a modern PLA.

John Corbett, Edward O'Dowd, and David Chen follow Blasko's analysis of conscript and NCO training with an examination of the PLA's officer accession programs in Chapter 5. Similar to the goal of increasing the educational and training standards for conscripts and NCOs, the PLA is actively investing in programs to recruit and train a better educated and more technically proficient officer corps.

Recognizing the inherent limitations of grooming officers through the military academy system, the PLA has tapped two new sources for officer recruits: civilian universities and promoting soldiers "up from the ranks." University-based recruitment was authorized through a joint State Council-Central Military Commission decision in 2000. Recruitment is done through the National Defense Student Program (NDSP), a Reserve Officer Training Corps (ROTC)-style initiative, and through direct recruitment on college campuses. Based on the estimated proportion of newly-accessed PLA officers, NDSP has been a success: approximately half come from civilian universities, with the other half coming up through the traditional military school system. It is projected that a majority of the PLA's new officers could be graduates of civilian universities by 2011. The implicit argument is that graduates of civilian institutions are better geared to leading a modern military.

However, military educational institutions have also made progress in increasing their educational standards and remain the primary institutions for educating new officers. Although the system contains institutions that provide both undergraduate pre-commissioning education and post-commission "pre-assignment" PME, priority has increasingly been given to the latter, thus increasing the PLA's reliance on civilian institutions to provide officer candidates with at least an undergraduate education. From this perspective, the two primary sources for new officers have both complementary and competing elements.

The NDSP was also created to mitigate the challenge of attracting talented candidates away from opportunities in the more lucrative domestic economy. Service-specific programs have also been devised to attract more young and educated people, such as the PLA Air Force's (PLAAF) "2 + 2" program, in which students are able to achieve a bachelor's degree after spending 2 years in a civilian college and 2 years at a PLAAF flight academy. Similar experimental programs are being tried by various units, military regions, and services to complement the NDSP.

The nature of officer training regimens has also shifted to place more emphasis on the development of leadership and management skills, as well as technical skills. Summer training with active units, for instance, has provided hands-on experience for recruits in the operation and effective deployment of weapons systems. While policies on recruitment, education, and training of officers have shifted to accommodate a more modern and technically-advanced military, the challenge of competing with China's rapidly growing domestic economy remains the highest hurdle.

PERSONNEL MANAGEMENT

Once recruited, trained, and fully prepared for duty, how does the PLA manage and retain its officers and NCOs? Kristen Gunness and Fred Vellucci examine this question in Chapter 6. Through revisions to the "Active-Duty Officer's Law of the People's Republic of China," and passage of the "Regulations on the Appointment and Dismissal of Officers in Active Service," the PLA implemented three specific reforms to its officer and NCO management system. These reforms were meant to build and retain a highly educated, professional, and technically skilled officer corps, reflecting the guiding principles of Jiang Zemin's "two transformations."

The first major reform entailed massive downsizing of the force, especially the officer corps. Since 1985, the PLA's manpower has been reduced by approximately 1.7 million. More recently, the "Active-Duty Officers Law" instituted mandatory retirement ages for each officer grade as well as minimum service requirements prior to retirement eligibility.

The second major reform entailed improvements in recruitment and PME (discussed above) and retention. To improve officer retention, the PLA improved salaries and benefits and standardized its officer evaluation process. Officer salaries more than doubled after July 2006 while the PLA also devoted increased resources to improving officers' living conditions, including building new quarters and increasing housing subsidies, and providing for better mess halls and meals. Similarly, the PLA took steps to reform the officer evaluation process. The "Active-Duty Officer's Law" and the "Regulations on the Appointment and Dismissal of Officers in Active Service" provide for standard performance appraisal based on evaluations by senior officers, a unit's political officer, and officer peer reviews. In some cases, evaluations combine such appraisals with objective examinations on subjects ranging from military technology to foreign languages to computer science.

The third major reform entailed retaining skilled NCOs. In addition to standardizing a 30-year career path and improving educational and training opportunities, the PLA has, similar to the officer corps, improved salaries and benefits. Gunness and Vellucci reiterate the difficulty in assessing the overall success of these reforms given their recent implementation. NCO and officer retention faces the same broad challenge highlighted by Corbett, O'Dowd, and Chen: the attraction to opportunities in China's dynamic domestic economy.

In Chapter 7, Elizabeth Hague explores the career progressions, geographic assignments, and ethnic minority representation in the PLA's officer corps. Hague distinguishes three main career tracks within the officer corps: operational, political, and technical. She subsequently sketches out the typical career progression for each track and analyzes the content of PLA policy on geographic assignment and integration of ethnic minorities into the officer corps. The careers of specific high-profile officers are highlighted as case studies.

Operators, the actual warfighters and commanders of the PLA, follow diverse and specialized career paths. They lead the PLA's operational units of submarines, tanks, fighter planes, artillery, and missile systems. An operator tends to begin his career with intensive training and education in a particular specialty. As the officer rises to senior-level ranks and receives additional PME, a successful operator is likely to possess several specific characteristics. These include some educational or professional travel abroad, experience in joint operations, experience with different geographical units, the ability to easily incorporate new equipment and procedures, and the capacity for innovation.

Political officers ensure the "political rectitude" of the PLA's personnel, meaning maintaining allegiance to the authority of the CCP, and play a critical role in promotions and other personnel decisions. Most travel a route similar to civilian party cadres, but usually have additional education and training in operational and technical issues. Many also likely start out in one of the other two career tracks before switching to the political track. A common career progression for political officers includes service as secretaries, cadres, political instructors, political department directors, and deputy political commissars and political commissars at different levels of command. Additionally, similar to operators, a political officer's career involves geographic transfers, usually occurring in the middle-to-late stages of the officer's career. The desirable characteristics for a political officer include a spotless political record, and continuous achievement through the political education establishment culminating in time spent at elite national-level institutions such as the Central Party School and the General Political Department, extensive experience in diverse geographic regions, and experience in joint operations.

Finally, technical specialists comprise those who handle roles such as logistics, maintenance, financial, intelligence, and medical support. Though not considered as glamorous or desirable a track as the operational and political tracks, the technical track has nonetheless grown to become a prominent source of the PLA's senior officers. Many officers who began in logistics, finance, and armaments issues have gone on to operational commands and political positions. Likewise, operators and political officers have crossed over to handle technical portfolios, nurturing the PLA's desire to enhance "jointness" through a variety of assignments with other services, tracks, geographic regions, and general staffs.

FIELD GRADE AND SENIOR OFFICER EDUCATION

Chapter 8 turns to changes in the PLA's intermediate and advanced command colleges and their overall effect on the professionalization of mid- to senior-level officers. Nan Li highlights major changes in various areas including missions and objectives, curricula, pedagogies and teaching, and research faculty. Li suggests four main factors driving these changes and concludes with a number of challenges remaining for the reform of the PLA's command colleges.

The basic mission of the PLA's command colleges remains fundamentally to educate and train intermediate and advanced commanding officers to fulfill the demands of the PLA. However, the content and nature of this preparation has changed along with the PLA itself. As reflected in previous chapters, the PLA's transition to a high-technology force has placed new demands on the PME system to shape a modernized officer corps. Such a corps needs to be able to employ military, political, economic, diplomatic, and cultural means to achieve dominance not only on land, air, and sea; but also in outer, electromagnetic, cyber, and cognitive space. Pursuant to this, command colleges have adopted new goals in terms of preparing field grade and senior officers, for whom the transition may be especially stressful. As a result, the changes experienced by the command colleges are somewhat deeper and more fundamental than those experienced at entry-level military academies whose curricula and objectives are more short term and tactical in nature. For senior officers, the PLA's modernization and the realities of modern warfare require a major rethink in how to think strategically.

Near-term objectives—to be achieved by 2010—include having 60 percent of regiment and higher-level officers possess a 4-year college degree and 100 percent having attended a command college for advanced training in science and technology prior to assuming command. In addition to improved educational levels, the PLA's near-term goals include a widening scope of knowledge, particularly in joint operations, and service credentials. Longer-term objectives, for 2020, seek to build on the previous benchmarks and have all high-level commanding officers possess 4-year degrees and diverse service credentials, with a majority possessing a master's degree.

Curricula have changed to reflect the shift in objectives. New subjects such as joint operations, information operations, simulations, strategic logistics, legal warfare, space operations, psychological operations, and peacekeeping law have been integrated in many of the colleges. Courses designed to prepare officers for cross-service appointments have also been added to curricula, helping to institutionalize interservice knowledge and cooperation. Colleges have also developed programs to dispatch research groups to individual units to learn and adapt new operational and management techniques and to better assess improvements at the operational level. These research projects also serve as a feedback mechanism leading to further development of curricula.

Pedagogies have likewise changed to foster the innovation and creativity among students. Instructors act more like a "first among equals" and are encouraged to serve as organizers and directors of smaller seminars, rather than as staid lecturers. Practical tools, such as case analysis, wargaming, and organization of command exercises, have been implemented to enhance student participation and hands-on learning. Command colleges are now beginning to share their resources among themselves and with civilian universities in an effort to expose their students to a greater variety of knowledge and experiences. The upgrading of teaching and research faculty has emphasized this pedagogical shift while improving overall teaching quality and research. The development of more objective evaluation standards has also served this purpose.

These and other reforms to the PLA's command colleges have been driven by four main factors: external security competition, learning and adaptation, central leadership, and technological development. With its reorientation away from involvement in domestic politics, the PLA developed into a more normal military, concerning itself with the external defense of the country. The PLA now worries more about security competition with potential rivals. Li argues that this competition has driven the PLA not only to modernize its weapons and accelerate technological development, but also to cultivate competent and adaptable senior officers to keep up with the more advanced militaries of potential rivals.

These four factors would not have been possible, Li argues, without a fifth: the support of civilian central leadership. Following the death of his predecessor, Deng Xiaoping, and the departure of Liu Huaqing and Zhang Zhen from the Central Military Commission (CMC), Jiang Zemin was able to assert himself successfully in military affairs. Using loyalty of the PLA's top brass gained from having promoted them and from providing dramatic increases in the defense budget, Jiang successfully marginalized military involvement in both domestic political and commercial activities while pushing the PLA to concentrate on implementing a modernization agenda.

Such far-reaching changes in the PLA's command colleges are not in themselves signals of success, asserts Li. Rather, the main challenge remains the PLA's actual performance under real-world conditions. Li also suggests that the command college system is not yet operating as efficiently as it could, meaning too many schools continue to teach subjects irrelevant to achieving the goal of training "new-type" officers. Courses on Marxist thought seem to be of particular irrelevance. Finally, slow progress in vertical compartmentalization of the PLA's service arms-based command colleges remains a barrier to effective development of jointness within the PLA.

Paul Godwin shifts the analytical lens upward in Chapter 9 to discuss changes occurring in the education of the PLA's senior military leadership, particularly the role of the PLA's NDU, the pinnacle of China's PME system. In order to keep up with the new military realities, NDU has taken steps to institute significant reform in its curriculum and teaching requirements.

While NDU's main academic structure remains the same, the content of the main curricula began to change in 1999 with the CMC's issuing of the "New Generation Operations Regulations." These regulations called for the PME system to focus on developing joint operations skills, which in turn led to the NDU's party committee to create five teaching priorities: improving understanding of military technological advances, enhancing student capabilities in strategic analysis, a focus on practical learning, improving competency in command of high-tech joint operations, and managing the military within the context of China's building of a socialist market economy. The party committee also developed the "Outline of 21st-Century-Oriented Teaching Reform and Development at National Defense University" in order to help guide future curriculum development.

NDU's faculty also now focuses less on theoretical issues in favor of more pragmatic topics based on the real-world experiences of current commanders in the field. As in the case of mid-level officers, greater participation is urged in senior-level courses. Additionally, students are now gaining more foreign experience through military-to-military exchanges with countries such as France, the United States, Canada, and Australia, providing them with information on foreign views on security and military affairs.

Godwin speculates that the main objective of the NDU currently is to familiarize senior commanders with the changing operational aspects of the new PLA, rather than to train them as military strategists. The latter task seems to have become the responsibility of the PLA's Academy of Military Science and the NDU's Institute for Strategic Studies. However, he also notes that NDU's reforms are still maturing, and, based on the progress made to date, it appears that the PLA's senior officers are likely to be better prepared than ever to command China's future armed forces.

TO WHAT ENDS? THE PLA'S FUTURE LEADERS

Ellis Joffe concludes the volume with a reflection on what can be expected of the PLA in the coming years. Joffe ties together the variety of reforms enacted and implemented by the PLA within the broader context of China's evolving threat environment since the founding of the People's Republic. One important point that Joffe reminds us of is that the rapid qualitative improvements in the PLA have been far-reaching relative to its low starting baseline. The PLA as presently constituted is likely sufficient for territorial defense, but the quality of its power projection capabilities are far more uneven.

A second key point is the PLA's continued relative lack of transparency. As has been noted in almost all of the chapters in this volume, specific and comprehensive data on the PLA's PME is often hard to acquire, making accurate analyses on the topic difficult. Much of this is due to the dearth of open source information available on what challenges the PLA has encountered in its transition and how it is managing them. Evaluative studies of the PLA's measures are subsequently fraught with some uncertainty.

On the national level, Joffe predicts that, at the very least, the verdict on the PLA's PME reforms will depend on the continued growth of the economy, its ability to successfully compete with other sectors for funding, and the ability of China's defense industries to produce modern weapons. These dynamics, while thus far relatively predictable, nonetheless need to be closely monitored.

Joffe succinctly restates the most important general finding of the research and analysis contained in this volume, "[The PLA's ability to continue its transformation] will require efforts to recruit 'the best and the brightest' into its ranks. And the PLA knows it." That the PLA has invested so much in improving the recruitment, training, and educational levels of its soldiers and officers is itself a telling sign of change. For the rest of the world, the impact of the PLA's commitment to fielding a force of better educated and more professional people is perhaps just as crucial to understand as the destructive potential of the weapons they are expected to wield.

CHAPTER 2

TRENDS IN EDUCATION AND TRAINING, 1924-2007:
FROM WHAMPOA TO NANJING POLYTECHNIC

Thomas J. Bickford

INTRODUCTION

Professional military education (PME) and training is fundamental to shaping what kind of officer and noncommissioned officer (NCO) corps the Chinese People's Liberation Army (PLA) has and is an essential part of China's efforts to create a modern military for the 21st century. The PLA may acquire new weapons systems and technologies, streamline its organization, receive more funding from the government, and develop new strategies and doctrine, but without a well-developed educational system, the PLA will not be able to fully implement any of its other modernization efforts. PME and training provide the knowledge and skill sets necessary to successfully conduct combat operations and make use of available weapons systems and technology. PME provides officers (and career NCOs) with the intellectual tools, structure, and technological background necessary to constantly update their knowledge throughout their careers. PME, however, can and does mean more than this. PME also provides a common military language and a common methodology towards problem identification and solving essential for joint operations. Military academies are, or should be, arenas for debate about all aspects of the military; doctrine, tactics, appropriate equipment, who is a potential enemy, how to prepare for the next war, what went wrong in the last conflict and why, and so forth. PME can function as a huge laboratory for testing ideas and conducting research on the changing nature of war. It allows officers to come together and exchange ideas and develop new concepts.

Currently, the PLA is undergoing a wide range of changes as it tries to implement the "two transformations" (*liangge zhuanbian*; 两个转变), that is, creating a military that is capable of fighting and winning local wars under "informationalized" conditions and a military that is based on quality not quantity.[1] Reforms in PME are essential if the PLA is to have the human material it needs to take advantage of its restructuring and new weapons systems and technologies. An effective educational and training system that is capable of turning out the kind of officers and NCOs the PLA wants, however, is something that takes years to build.

This chapter, therefore, seeks to put discussion of the current educational and training reforms in a greater historical context by providing a long-term overview of the development of education and training within the PLA from its origins to the present day. The chapter primarily focuses on PME, identifies distinct periods in the education of officers within the PLA, and discusses key trends within each period. The chapter also discusses factors that help account for changes within PLA education and current trends in PME.

There are three key points this chapter wants to make in discussing the history of education in the PLA. First, the development of education and training in the PLA is not necessarily linear. While there are some continuities in PLA education, such as political education, the current professional military education system in the PLA is in many respects evolving in a very different direction from that developed in the 1950s and early 1960s. Second, in some respects education in the PLA has always been a work in progress. That is, the PLA's conception of what kind of officer it needs has altered several times as a consequence of changes in the PLA's military and political environment. The result is an education system that has experienced a number of shifting, sometimes contradictory, trends in its development as the PLA reevaluates what kind of officer corps it wants and needs, and the current system is still evolving. Third, while officer education and training are obviously shaped by how the Chinese leadership and the PLA perceive China's security environment, the development of military education has also been shaped by political, economic, and social factors.

This chapter divides the history of PME in the PLA into several distinct periods. The first covers the origins of PLA education at Whampoa in 1924 through the guerrilla war period from 1927-49. The second period covers the creation and development of a Soviet-style PME system in the 1950s and early 1960s. Third, the Cultural Revolution 1966-76, which saw extensive disruption of the PME system in the PLA. Fourth, a period of rebuilding in PME that lasted from approximately 1977 to 1985. Fifth, a period of reform and readjustment, 1985-95, following Deng Xiaoping's "strategic decision" to focus on economic modernization and opening to the outside world. Finally, the period from 1995, when Jiang Zemin's called for the "two transformations" to the present; involving even greater reform and efforts to create an officer of a new type.

Each of these periods represents a different shift in the PLA's objectives in terms of officer education and training. Developments in PLA education before 1949 were driven in large part by war and the need to create a revolutionary armed force to seize power. The various shifts between 1949 and 1976 are dominated by competing visions of how to create an officer corps that can meet the needs of China during the Cold War as well as fulfill its role in contributing to Mao's vision of a revolutionary state. The period between 1977 and 1985 can be seen as a period of rebuilding and recovery from the extreme harm of the Cultural Revolution. Since 1985, there is an accelerating pace of change in Chinese PME that is taking the PLA away from a Soviet-style educational system to one more like that in Western militaries.

BRIEF OVERVIEW OF LONG-TERM TRENDS IN MILITARY EDUCATION

From Whampoa to Liberation, 1924-49.

One can argue that the history of military education in the PLA predates the founding of the PLA in 1927 and has its roots in the Whampoa Military Academy. Founded by Sun Yatsen in 1924, the academy was originally a one department operation providing basic training for infantry units, but it soon expanded to include specialist training in artillery, engineering, logistics, and other courses. Soviet military personnel provided lectures on a wide variety of topics and helped to train and educate Chinese cadets. Other instructors included two future Chinese Communist Party (CCP) leaders, Zhou Enlai and Ye Jianying. The academy trained and educated members of both the

Guomindang and the CCP until their split in 1927 and had a lasting influence on both parties.

Even though the CCP was only involved in Whampoa for 3 years from 1924 to 1927, the experience left a lasting imprint on the future PLA and helped to influence the development of the PLA's education system for many years. It was Whampoa that was invoked as a model by Mao in the 1930s when the PLA began to create its first educational institutions.[2] Whampoa was the seminal experience for many of the PLA's early leaders and it is worth noting that when ranks were introduced into the PLA in 1955, five of the ten marshals had been affiliated with Whampoa.[3] In addition, three of the ten officers granted the rank of senior general (*dajiang*; 大将) and eight of the 57 generals (*shangjiang*, 上将) had affiliations with Whampoa Military Academy.[4] This is important because, unlike other military academies in China at this time, Whampoa was initially modeled on Soviet lines and many of the early instructors were from the Soviet Red Army. Whampoa introduced several future leaders of the PLA and CCP to Soviet thinking about strategy, tactics, PME, and political work in the military and helped shape ideas about how to develop education and training for a revolutionary army for the CCP.[5] Most important, it is at Whampoa that political education as part of PME first becomes established, and while the nature and extent of political education and political work in PME has changed over the decades, it has always been an important and valued part of PME in the PLA.[6] This is not to say that the Soviet Union was the only foreign influence in the early development of PME in the PLA, Japan also had a strong impact on military education in early 20th century China, but it is to say that the Soviet model did play a role in the origins and early conceptualization of PME within the PLA and CCP.

Chinese Communist participation in Whampoa ended in 1927 with the split between the CCP and the Guomindang and the establishment of the PLA. From its creation in 1927 to 1949, when the People's Republic of China (PRC) was founded, the PLA was constantly at war; first against the Guomindang, then the Japanese, and then against the Guomindang again. As a result, a regular system of education and training never really emerged during the revolutionary period. There is little evidence for standardization of training and education across units, and military education was primarily a matter of political education, literacy classes, and the imparting of a few basic military skills. PLA officers were essentially generalists who primarily learned their business through practical experience, and the PLA was basically an infantry force for which specialized functional knowledge was simply not needed. What military education that did exist evolved as a result of the Whampoa experiences, the political needs of the CCP in organizing base areas, and increasingly the PLA's own combat experiences.

Initially, education and training were carried out by teaching teams (*jiaodaodui*; 教导队), which provided basic political, military, and cultural (literacy) training in the early PLA units. Content varied and appears to have been very basic with a focus on political work and basic tactics.[7] By the early 1930s, the CCP had set up the Chinese Workers' and Peasants' Red Army College (*Zhongguo gongnong hongjun xueyuan*; 中国工农红军学院), with several branches distributed throughout the base areas.[8] Education was still fairly rudimentary, and political education was at least as important as military education. For example, the 1935 curriculum of the Fourth Front Army's branch of the Red Army School includes the following political courses: China's revolutionary history, Marxism-Leninism and army political work, party policies, and goals of the Red Army. Military classes included the use of two texts: *Soviet Red Army Combat Regulations*, (*Sulian hongjun zhandou tiaoling*; 苏联红军战斗条令) and *Soviet Army Field Operations Regulations* (*Sujun yezhan tiaoling*; 苏军野战条令), as well as classes on small unit tactics and fighting in different types of terrain.[9]

In 1937 the Red Army School was renamed the Military and Political University of the Chinese People's Anti-Japanese War (*Zhongguo renmin kangri junshi zhengzhi daxue*; 中国人民抗日军事政治大学), and there would eventually be 10 branch campuses distributed throughout the various base areas.[10] These represent a maturation of the PLA and CCP's experiences with building political support in base areas and struggle with the General Military Department (GMD).[11] Education was evenly distributed between political and military instruction, and there were also classes to provide basic literacy for cadres. Instruction was short, 6-8 months, and included topics such as Marxism-Leninism, political economy, party principles and policies, military political work, military strategy, and infantry tactics.[12] Military education had by this time evolved to a system that put equal weight to both political and military education and stressed pragmatic experience as much as military theory. Because military education stressed the pragmatic experiences of soldiers and commanders, it was also an education that increasingly reflected the PLA's experiences at the expense of foreign influences and theory.[13] As the next section will show, differences between educational practices based on the PLA's own combat experiences and foreign (i.e., Soviet) practices would be a major source of contention and debate in Chinese PME in the 1950s.

These trends reflect the military experiences of the PLA during the guerrilla war period and the difficulties inherent in developing a more systematic education system under the conditions that prevailed at the time. But education in this period also reflects the greater political goals of the CCP. The PLA was the armed wing of the CCP, a military force for defeating the party's enemies and seizing power. It played a necessary role in the transformation of areas under its control, and in many cases the PLA was the only party presence in the area. It was an army of a new type to seize power and the emphasis on political education reflected that. The nature of officer education was driven as much by ideological and political goals as military needs, and ideological and political issues would continue to help shape PME in the 1950s and 1960s.

Establishing a Communist State and the Development of a Soviet-Style Military Education System, 1949-65.

With the creation of the PRC in 1949, the PLA faced new challenges. It needed to transform itself from a largely low tech, poorly educated infantry force into a modern military with navy, air force, armored units, and other specialized units capable of defending the PRC. With Soviet assistance, it introduced a Soviet-style military academy system that, with modifications, still exists today. Military academies were established for the ground forces (PLA), navy (PLAN), and air force (PLAAF). Within each service, specialist and technical academies were established for engineering, logistics, radar, armor, and so forth. In addition to specialized schools set up for each new branch of service, the PLA set up a series of command schools. Command schools were divided into low level (platoon, company), mid-level (battalion, regiment), and high levels (division, army) as appropriate for the rank being trained. As officers advanced in rank, they would have to go to the appropriate command academies for education and training. By 1955 the PLA had a total of 253 military academies and schools. Of these, 26 were command schools, six were political commissar schools, 72 were technical schools, and the rest focused on literacy and basic education.[14] As educational levels in China improved, schools providing literacy and basic education were phased out, and PME focused on the technical, command, and political schools, and the number of academies was reduced to between 119 and 125.[15]

Officer education was based *entirely* on the military academies. Civilian universities did not contribute to the academic preparation or education of future officers. Military academies were thus responsible for not just teaching military skills but also supplying a basic undergraduate level education to PLA officers. This partly reflected then current Soviet practice, which combined post-secondary education with military training in their PME system,[16] but it also reflected the low level of education in Chinese society at the time. The PLA PME system, therefore, had to supply basic education to bring recruits up to the standards that it needed.

As with the Soviet system, the Chinese PME system tended to be highly specialized along functional lines, and Chinese military personnel were very narrowly educated. Officers in command schools would receive little, if any, exposure to more technical subjects. For example, PLAN officers taking navigation courses would not be educated in observation and communication.[17] The fact that there were separate engineering academies for the armored and radar troops, or that armored command and armored engineering were taught at separate academies, also speaks to the high degree of functional specialization in the Chinese PME system at this time.[18]

As the 1950s progressed, relations between China and the Soviet Union deteriorated, culminating in the Anti-Dogmatism campaign of 1958, which criticized over-reliance on Soviet practices and the subsequent Sino-Soviet split. Despite the rejection of the Soviet Union as a model and the increasingly intense ideological conflict between the two countries, the PLA retained the Soviet-style system, though with an increasing emphasis on China's own military experiences as the basis for instruction and a more equal mix of political and military education.[19] PME was thus a mix of both modern, professionalizing, trends in PLA education and an increasing stress on the traditions of the guerrilla war period.

The 1950s and early 1960s thus show two rather different trends in Chinese PME: one closely based on the Soviet system, the other drawing more on the PLA's political and military traditions of the revolutionary period, reflecting the broader context of political and security issues in China at this time. On the one hand, China needed to create a more modern military force to defend its territory and national interests. This was underscored by the PLA's experiences in the Korean War, conflict in the Taiwan Strait, and the Sino-Indian border conflict. On the other hand, the PLA had its own, very successful, military experiences to draw on in developing military modernization. Both the Cold War and the Sino-Soviet split isolated the PLA from foreign military influences, further emphasizing the tendency to rely on its own experiences and practices, which emphasized being both red and expert.

The greater political context also impacted the development of PME at this time. China's political leadership was very much focused on a revolutionary transformation of Chinese society. The PLA was to be not just a national defense force but a political force for social transformation. The political context of the regime impacted thinking about what kind of military China should have and how it should be educated. Finally, China's low level of economic development also had a limiting factor in terms of human and financial resources available for military education. How these factors might have played out in the long run is uncertain, as the Cultural Revolution (1966-76) took the PLA in a very different direction and had a major impact on training and education.

The Cultural Revolution, 1966-76.

The Cultural Revolution was a period when military education came under severe attack. The academies' stress on academic credentials and professional accomplishment was the antithesis of many of the themes of the Cultural Revolution. The system of ranks and other distinctions between officers and enlisted personnel, PME, and an emphasis on technology were all seen as taking the "bourgeois line" in army building, and military schools suffered accordingly. Professors were attacked, and classes disrupted. Academic and professional criteria for promotion were rejected, and the PLA went back to its old revolutionary practices of promotion based on political rectitude and the recruiting of officers directly from the ranks. Promotion was no longer based on completing courses at higher institutions. Instead, promotion was based almost entirely on political criteria.

Of the 125 military academies and schools that existed at the beginning of the Cultural Revolution, a total of 82, or about two-thirds, were shut down.[20] Closures affected all branches of the military. Of the 13 PLAN academies that existed before the Cultural Revolution, eight were closed by 1969. Four out of five engineering schools and 23 of 25 Military Region (MR) schools were also closed by 1969, as were just over half of the logistics schools.[21] The sheer number of schools closed is indicative of the concentrated attack on the military education system, but the full extent of the damage becomes clear when looking at the details. The 82 schools that were closed down represented 97 percent of the command schools and 50 percent of the technical schools.[22] In addition, libraries and other educational resources had been destroyed, and teaching staff scattered.[23] Several years went by during which there was no effective education, officers fell even further behind international standards, and leaders were unable to keep up with military developments elsewhere. Those texts that still were in use dated back to the 1950s and were in serious need of updating. Many unfit officers had received promotions on the basis of political criteria and were woefully unqualified for their new posts. One article in *Jiefangjun Bao* claims that by the end of the Cultural Revolution, less than 30 percent of PLA units could be regarded as fully trained.[24] Another Chinese source states that in 1978 only 8 percent of all PLA cadres had college degrees or the equivalent.[25]

Post-Cultural Revolution Recovery, 1977-85.

The years between 1977 and 1985 saw renewed emphasis on building a professional military education system and a renewed emphasis on expertise. Political and military leaders were well aware of how much the PLA had fallen behind other armed forces, especially after the disastrous attack on Vietnam in 1979. There was considerable discussion of military reform, including reform of PME, which laid the groundwork for later changes. However, no major changes in the way the education system worked were instituted at this time. Rather, this was primarily a time of rebuilding and restoring education and training in the PLA, as it had been prior to the radicalization and destruction of the Cultural Revolution. By the end of the 1970s, the PLA's educational system had reopened most of the closed schools and had reorganized some of the academies.[26] The system of command schools was restored,[27] and technical academies were reopened with a range of courses from basic to advanced levels.[28] The amount of teaching time devoted to political education was reduced.[29] New guidelines were introduced to strengthen and regularize training and education and to improve educational standards for officer recruitment and promotion.[30]

Just as important were the dramatic changes taking place in the Chinese political and economic system in this period. The year 1979 saw the beginning of China's economic reforms, which ushered in decades of rapid economic growth that changed the face of Chinese society, opened the Chinese economy to the outside world, and greatly increased the resources available to the Chinese state and the PLA. Politically, this period also saw the Chinese state reorienting itself away from a revolutionary agenda that stressed class struggle and toward a program of pragmatic development. Nearly 30 years later, the economic and political changes that began the aftermath of the Maoist era have profoundly altered the greater social, economic, and political contexts in which PLA policy debates take place.

"The Strategic Decision" and Change in Chinese PME, 1985-95.

This period begins with two landmark events in the development of Chinese PME: Deng Xiaoping's "Strategic Decision" and the founding of China's National Defense University (*guofang daxue*, 国防大学, NDU). In June 1985, a critical meeting of the Central Military Commission (CMC) took place. At that meeting, Deng Xiaoping advanced his "Strategic Decision," which justified the deepening of China's economic reform and modernization, as well as its opening to the outside world. At the same time, the "Strategic Decision" rejected Mao's notion of imminent war and argued that the international system would be dominated by peace and development. This set the stage for a major change in Chinese defense policy, including a dramatic downsizing of the PLA and a change in PLA strategy away from traditional people's war and luring in deep toward a strategy of limited warfare fought at or just beyond China's borders.[31]

The "Strategic Decision" ushered in a number of PME reforms. First, in conjunction with the decision to downsize the PLA, a decision was made in 1986 to downsize the number of military academies. This resulted in an initial reduction of 19 academies in 1986.[32] More reductions were discussed, though the next major round of reductions did not occur until after 1995 (see below).

Another important change was the decision to create graduate programs at military academies. After 1985, a small number of academies were granted permission to begin building master's programs. Since then, the program has expanded, and the number of military academies allowed to grant advanced degrees has steadily increased, with most of the PLA's educational institutions now offering graduate courses.[33]

Other curriculum changes were introduced in 1987 with the Interim Regulations on academic work. One important change was to broaden the focus of technical classes to expose students to a wider range of topics, and greater efforts were made to combine technical and command training. In addition, new kinds of courses have been added to the curriculum of many military academies, including military education theory, military psychology, foreign policy, international relations, management, and computer programming.[34]

The other key landmark change was the creation of the NDU in 1985 by combining three existing academies; the Political Academy, the Military Academy, and the Logistics Academy. The creation of the NDU was a crucial development in Chinese PME because, until this time, PME was essentially single service in nature. NDU is the first truly all-service PLA academy. For the first time, 58 years after its founding, the PLA finally had an educational institution that had the ability to promote "jointness" across the PLA. This was, therefore, a significant step away from the way Chinese PME was conducted in the past and helped lay the foundation for further restructuring and reform of PLA education. As Paul Godwin notes in his chapter in this volume, the NDU is the pinnacle of the Chinese PME system and plays a critical role in the education of China's future military leaders. Almost all the senior commanders of the PLA have now gone through NDU.[35] NDU has also served as a center for developing new ideas on teaching and curriculum and has served as a vehicle for educational exchanges with foreign militaries.[36]

These initial efforts to improve and reform PME were given further importance following the Gulf War of 1991. China then instituted new strategic guidelines emphasizing the importance both of modern hi-tech conditions and of having officers educated in the new technologies necessary to fight under such conditions. This led to a further deepening of educational reforms and an even greater emphasis on officer education, reflecting a major rethink of the PLA's basic strategy.[37]

Further Development and Reform of PME, 1995-Present.

The "Two Transformations" announced in 1995 marked another major point in the development of Chinese PME. While the reforms in PME that have followed build on trends that had already started in the 1980s, they also represent a reevaluation of what kind of officer the PLA needs and what kind of PME it will need. The two transformations are: (1) From an army preparing to fight local wars under ordinary conditions to an army preparing to fight under modern high-tech conditions, and (2) From an army based on quantity to an army based on quality.

The 1991 Gulf War, the conflict in Kosovo, and the 1995-96 crisis in the Taiwan Strait all served to convince Chinese leaders that they had to reassess how they should prepare for future conflicts, and this has included reassessing how they should conduct PME and train more technologically proficient officers and men for the 21st century.[38] In addition, economic growth and change stemming from the economic reforms of the 1980s was increasingly having an impact on military modernization in terms of providing greater resources for military transformation and creating new security concerns, such as protecting trade.

In terms of PME, the Two Transformations mark the beginning of a new round of reforms that are moving the PLA away from past practices and toward a PME system that more closely resembles Western practice. In 1999, the PLA began a new round of reorganization and consolidation of military academies, closing some and merging others. Most of the reductions in the number of military educational facilities have taken place in the past 7 years, with the total number of academies now being just 63 institutions, roughly half the number that existed 25 years ago.[39]

In addition to restructuring and downsizing the academies, since 1988 the PLA has issued several new sets of regulations dealing with education and training. Among other things, they define the scope of military education, academic standards, and time required to reach certain qualifications, as well as the duties of school administrators and departments.[40] New regulations institutionalize a process of continuous officer education, requiring officers to periodically upgrade their education and military knowledge.[41] The new regulations more clearly tie promotion to education and professional skills than in the past. There is now greater emphasis on the quality of education in the military academies, and there are new guidelines for teaching excellence[42] and for the dismissal of unqualified instructors.[43] More recently, the PLA has begun to bring officers from combat units to act as instructors and has initiated programs to get instructors out to operating units to observe training exercises.[44] This is a significant change. For most of the last 50 years, educational instruction in the PLA was conducted by individuals who spent their entire careers in teaching.

There has also been considerable curricular reform at military academies. For example, the PLA has tried to make it easier for officers and NCOs on active duty to improve their knowledge by developing correspondence courses and by experimenting with distance learning.[45] The PLA has also tried to improve the classroom experience by promoting active learning and by encouraging debate, creativity, innovation, and spontaneity.[46] Another important innovation was the introduction of electronic equipment into the classroom, with a heavy emphasis on computers and electronic simulation. As James Mulvenon documents in his chapter, there has been a huge push to create an "informationalized" PLA in the military academies and in the field, which has accelerated as the PLA promotes the idea of modern warfare under informationalized conditions.

Another set of important changes in PME revolve around the turn to civilian education since 1999. Prior to that, education of officers and NCOs was a purely military affair, and officers did not attend civilian educational institutions. Since then, there has been a major effort to increase the number of PLA officers educated at civilian universities. This reflects both continuing problems in providing a quality education at military academies and the expansion and improvement of China's civilian education system over the past 3 decades. These efforts have centered on the following policies:

- Recruiting college graduates. The PLA has made a concerted effort to recruit college graduates into the officer corps. This includes changing regulations so that college graduates can enter the PLA directly without first having to go through 4 years at a military academy and establishing innovative "2+2" degree programs.
- Creating a national defense scholarship program to fund promising students in return for a period of military service.
- Creating a reserve officer training program similar to the U.S. Reserve Officer Training Corps (ROTC) program.
- Developing cooperative research and teaching arrangements with civilian universities and recruiting civilian university professors to teach at military institutions.
- Sending military personnel to civilian institutions for postgraduate work.

According to the *2006 Defense White Paper*, 112 civilian universities are engaged in educating national defense students for the PLA.[47] In turning to civilian universities, the PLA is also following a practice seen in many Western militaries, which recruit most of their officers from civilian universities.

A new round of reforms in training and education has begun following the U.S. invasion of Iraq in 2003. One of the catalysts for these latest changes appears to be the inability of NDU faculty to accurately predict how the U.S. invasion would progress.[48] New curriculum changes are being introduced at NDU and many of the service academies.[49] New teaching methods introduced include scenario simulation, case studies, "issue awareness," and teaching methods adopted from civilian master of business administration (MBA) courses.[50] Interestingly, one of the new courses is on how to talk to the foreign press.[51] This appears to reflect greater awareness that PLA officers, at least at the senior level, need greater exposure to foreign affairs and other economic and political issues.[52] In addition, starting in 2006, there has been a push to extend such education to lower level academies. For the first time, the mid-level command academies are beginning to experiment with multiservice training and education. The initial experiments are being conducted at the Shijiazhuang Army Command Academy, the Nanjing Army Command Academy, the Naval Command Academy, The Air Force Command Academy, and the Second Artillery Command Academy.[53] This a major step forward in promoting the idea of joint operations and bringing the level of training and education in joint operations down to officers below general rank. This move coincides with greater emphasis on practical experience in training and education and participation by faculty and students in military exercises. As the Chinese press describes these latest developments as experimental, it is very probable that further changes in education and training will become apparent in the next few years.

ANALYSIS AND DISCUSSION

As the historical overview above indicates, Chinese PME has undergone many changes in the past 80 years. This section offers some general observations about what this history means in terms of assessing the current state of PME in China.

Development of PME in China is Not Necessarily Linear.

There are a few constants in the development of Chinese PME, most notably the role of political work. The tradition of political work as an important component of the military can be traced back to Whampoa. The PLA has been a party-army since its inception. Political work is an integral part of the PLA, including its education system. More generally, however, the evolution of the PLA's education system has not been linear. PME as it currently exists in China is *not* the product of 50 or 80 years of steady evolution. Rather, PME in China today should be thought of as a product of many different trends.

Most obvious are the sharp breaks that have occurred in the PLA's history. There was a major transition in the early 1950s when the education system went from one geared to providing basic education to a largely infantry force engaged in guerrilla war to a highly structured PME system designed to educate and train a modern military force. The Cultural Revolution was also a sharp break from the educational system that came before it. The rejection of the Cultural Revolution and its extreme focus on revolutionary rectitude and disdain for professional education was another sharp break. The shift from a Soviet-style PME based exclusively on military academies to one which seeks to incorporate officers recruited from civilian universities was another major break.

But there are also other discontinuities. The PLA has veered several times between being open to foreign military ideas and influences and being isolationist in education. At Whampoa and into the early 1930s, there was great interest in Soviet military thought, and, to a lesser extent, the experiences of other armed forces. After the mid-1930s, the PLA increasingly based its education and training on its own experiences and needs. In the 1950s, the PLA was once again open to foreign military ideas and methods and looked to the Soviet Union as a model in military education. After 1958, the PLA was once again largely isolated from foreign military ideas and trends. Since the 1980s, the PLA has been increasingly interested in learning from foreign militaries and is perhaps more open to adopting ideas from other militaries than at any other time in its history. It pays close attention to developments in U.S., Russian, Japanese, and European armed forces, and incorporates that information into its educational system. The movement toward reliance on civilian universities is just one example.

The balance between professional and political education has always varied. As already noted, a role for political education is one of the few constants in PLA education. However, the degree of time spent on political education has varied widely from period to period. Before 1949, political education was just as important as learning the military art. In the 1950s, the portion of military education that was devoted to politics declined, then climbed again following the Anti-Dogmatism Campaign. During the Cultural Revolution, political work dominated what passed for an education system in the PLA. Since 1980, political work has once again declined, and greater emphasis has been placed on professional education. Just as the balance between professional and political education has varied, so has the role of education in promotion. In the Cultural Revolution, political qualifications were almost the sole criteria for promotion. Now there is much greater emphasis on professional education in promotions.

This is very important in assessing the current state of PME in China. Many of the features of PLA education and training being discussed at this conference are the products of, at best, only 20 to 25 years of development, and some are much more recent. For example, "jointness" in education and training in the PLA has only been around since the creation of NDU in 1985, and it is only in the last 2 to 3 years that there has been a real effort to introduce joint service training and education at the mid-levels of the PLA. In contrast, American PME is the product of more than 100 years of steady evolution. As Cynthia Watson has pointed out, PME in the United States has been joint in every sense of the word since 1946 and is still evolving. The PLA cannot hope to achieve in a few short years what has taken the United States decades, and it will need many more years of practice and experimentation to absorb these changes and derive the benefits of a more Western-style PME.[54]

PME in China Has always Been a Work in Progress.

Chinese PME has always been a work in progress. This does not mean that Chinese military and civilian leaders do not know what kind of military education system they want or how best to achieve it. At every identifiable period discussed in this chapter, there has been a clear vision of what kind of education officers should receive. What this does mean is that the vision of what kind of PME the PLA should have has gone through many revisions. In some respects, the history of PLA education can be thought of as a history of the PLA moving toward certain goals in education only to replace them with new goals before they have achieved the first set of goals. It is a history of change, experimentation, and frequent reassessment of what kind of soldiers the PLA wants and needs. In the revolutionary period, PLA cadres were part of both a military and a revolutionary force, but wartime prevented the PLA from fully developing the educational system that it wanted. In the 1950s, there was another set of goals, but the new educational system that was introduced was never fully developed before the 1960s saw a very different set of politics and policies introduced during the Cultural Revolution. Since the early 1980s, there has been a broad consensus on the need to build a professional PLA that can conduct modern combat operations. Yet, as the historical overview shows, there have been reassessments about what that means and what kind of education is needed for PLA officers and enlisted personnel. The PLA has been trying to play catch up for the past 25 years as it tries to learn from conflicts such as the Gulf War, Kosovo, and current operations in Iraq and Afghanistan.

Military Concerns Are Not the Only Driver in the Development of Chinese PME.

As in all militaries, defense issues are the most important driver of change in Chinese PME. In the 1930s, the armed struggles with the Guomindang and the Japanese obviously shaped the nature and content of education and training. The Korean War, the Cold War, and the Sino-Soviet split all had their impacts on Chinese views of military education. As already noted, foreign conflicts and the Taiwan Strait crises of 1995-96 have had a huge impact on the development of PME and help explain the timing of a number of changes noted above.

But defense issues are not the only driver of change in Chinese PME. At various times politics, economics, and social issues have also been important factors driving change. The nature of guerrilla war and the revolutionary goals of the CCP meant that political considerations were just as important as military concerns in shaping PLA education in the 1930s and 1940s. The ideology of the Maoist years, 1949-76, had a huge impact on all aspects of Chinese society, including the PLA. The Anti-Dogmatism campaign is a good example of this, and during the Cultural Revolution, it can be argued that ideological concerns trumped military concerns, at least with regards to education. In the 1980s, the political shift from a regime focused on building a new revolutionary society to one focused on economic modernization, and growth was a huge change in the political and economic environment for the PLA.

Economic and social factors have also been important drivers. For much of the early history of the PLA, China's low economic development impacted the quality of military education. As noted earlier in this chapter, part of PLA education was devoted to literacy and basic education from the 1930s well into the 1950s. Many PLA officers and enlisted personnel had little or no schooling, which hampered the development of PME. Low levels of economic development also meant limited resources available for military education.

China's rapid economic growth over the past 3 decades has changed all that. Economic growth means that there are considerably more resources available to fund PLA modernization, including training and education. It means that China now has a large, well-funded, and better quality civilian education system from which the PLA can recruit the officers and enlisted personnel it needs for warfare under "informationalized" conditions. It means that the PLA is now recruiting personnel whose social and economic backgrounds are often very different from those of previous generations. Perhaps most important, it means that China is a major economic force in the world with growing maritime, trade, energy security, and other interests abroad. The need to protect those interests and the well-being of Chinese citizens in other countries might very well become a driver for future developments in PME.

In other words, for the first 50 or so years, military and political considerations were the most important drivers in the development of PME in China. In the last 30 or so years, however, the most important drivers in PME have been military and economic factors.

CONCLUSION

In sum, the Chinese are taking a PME system that is the product of many different trends and historical experiences and moving it in a very different direction from those of the past as the PLA tries to adapt to what it sees as its educational needs for the early 21st century. It will take many years of further experimentation and reform to achieve their goals.

ENDNOTES - CHAPTER 2

1. *China's National Defense in 2006*, Beijing: State Council Information Office, December 2006.

2. Yuan Wei and Zhang Zhuo, chief eds., *Zhongguo junxiao fazhanshi* (*History of the development of China's military schools*), Beijing: Guofang daxue chubanshe, 2001, p. 289.

3. *Ibid.*, p. 291. It should also be noted that both Zhou Enlai and Ye Jianying were instructors at Whampoa.

4. *Ibid.*

5. *Ibid.*, pp. 287-89.

6. *Ibid.*, p. 275.

7. *Ibid.*, pp. 322-324.

8. For an excellent and very detailed history of this period on PME, see *Ibid.*, pp. 321-396.

9. *Ibid.* pp. 383-384.

10. Xiaobing Li, *A History of the Modern Chinese Army*, Lexington: University of Kentucky press, 2007, p. 67.

11. Yuan and Zhang, *Zhongguo junxiao*, p. 397.

12. *Ibid.*, p. 437.

13. *Ibid.*, pp. 434-436.

14. *Zhongguo junshi jiaoyu tongshi* (*A Comprehensive History of Chinese Military Education*), Shenyang, Liaoning chubanshe, Vol. 2, 1997, p. 957, hereafter *Jiaoyu tongshi*. See also Yuan and Zhang, *Zhongguo junxiao*, p. 654.

15. *Jiaoyu tongshi*, p. 957. The numbers varied from year to year as new academies were set up, old ones merged, and some closed down.

16. See Ellen Jones, *Red Army and Society: A Sociology of the Soviet Military*, Boston: Allen and Unwin, 1985, pp. 80-81.

17. PLA Service Branch History Series, *Haijun shi* (A History of the Navy), Beijing: Jiefang chubanshe, 1989, pp. 252-253.

18. Han Huaizhi and Tan Jingqiao, eds., *Dangdai Zhongguo jundui de junshi gongzuo (Contemporary China's military work)*, Beijing: Zhongguo shehui kexue chubanshe, 1989, Vol. 1, pp. 483-484.

19. Yuan and Zhang, pp. 692-698, 706-709.

20. *Dangdai junshi*, p. 485.

21. Yuan and Zhang, pp. 759-760.

22. *Ibid*.

23. Ellis Joffe, *The Chinese Army After Mao*, Cambridge: Harvard University Press, 1987, p. 122.

24. "A Great Military Reform: Roundup of Strategic Changes in our Army Building," *Jiefangjun Bao* in *Foreign Broadcast information Service (FBIS)-CHI*, December 18, 1998.

25. "PLA Officers, Soldiers Become Better Trained," *Xinhua*, in *FBIS-CHI*, September 29, 1994, p. 57.

26. *Dangdai junshi*, Vol. 1, p. 487; and *Jiaoyu tongshi*, p. 958.

27. Xue Lianxin and Zhang Zhenhua, eds., *Zhongguo junshi jiaoyu shi (A History of Chinese Military Education)*, Beijing: Guofang daxue chubanshe, 1991, p. 404.

28. *Ibid*. p. 1065.

29. Yuan and Zhang, pp. 839-845.

30. For a thorough discussion of all these changes, see Yuan and Zhang, pp. 803-848.

31. *Ibid.*, pp. 890-894.

32. *Ibid*. p. 895.

33. *China's Defense White Paper*, 2006.

34. Xue and Zhang, p. 403.

35. "China National Defense University: Cradle of Generals," *Kuang Chiao Chuang*, in *FBIS-CHI*, December 16, 1998.

36. NDU is active in exchanges with leading military academies in other countries, invites foreign military experts to present lectures to its students, and has a special military course for students from other countries.

37. Yuan and Zhang, p. 927.

38. See for example, "Hi-Tech Local wars' Basic Requirements for Army Building," *Zhongguo Junshi Kexue* no. 4, in *FBIS-CHI*, 20 November 1998.

39. *The China Defense White Paper, 2006*.

40. *Xinhua* release, in *FBIS-CHI*, February 28, 2000.

41. *Xinhua* release in *FBIS-CHI*, July 9, 1999.

42. See for example, "PLA Departmental Chiefs Express Appreciation To Military Academy Teachers," *Jiefangjun Bao* in *FBIS-CHI*, September 22, 2003; "Regulations on Teaching Work of Military Institutes Promulgated," *Jiefangjun Bao*, English internet version, *English.pladaily.com.cn*, April 9, 2004.

43. "Military Service Law of the People's Republic of China," *Xinhua* in *FBIS-CHI*, December 30, 1998.

44. "Report Details Changes in China's National Defense University," *Jiefangjun Bao*, November 10, 2006.

45. For example, at least six different naval academies offered correspondence courses in the 1980s, and between 1983 and 1987 some 3,400 naval personnel took part in correspondence course covering different subjects. See *Haijun shi*, Beijing: Jiefang chubanshe, 1989, p. 254. See also "PRC: PLA Promulgates Regulations on Correspondence Education at Military Academies," *Jiefangjun Bao* in *FBIS-CHI*, February 6, 2003. On distance learning,

see "PRC: PLA's First Online University Profiled," *Xinhua* release in *FBIS-CHI*, June 17, 2002.

46. "Major Reform of the Concept of Military Education: Guo Anhua Discusses Questions of Carrying Out Innovative Education," *Jiefangjun Bao* in *FBIS-CHI*, 1999.

47. *China Defense White Paper, 2006.*

48. "Report Details Changes in China's National Defense University," *Jiefangjun Bao*, November 10, 2006.

49. See, for example, "PLAAF Command Academy Undergoes Reform, Emphasizes 'Real Combat'," in *FBIS-CHI*, June 10, 2006.

50. "Report Details Changes in China's National Defense University," *Jiefangjun Bao*, November 10, 2006.

51. *Ibid.*

52. See "NDU's Research and Development Platform 'Immersion Style' Strategic Confrontation Exercise," *Xinhua*, December 1, 2006.

53. "PRC PLA Command Academies Conduct Joint Training to Nurture Command Talent," in *Jiefangjun Bao*, translated in *FBIS*, December 19, 2006.

54. The author would like to thank Cynthia Watson for these ideas, as well as the many insights she has provided over the past several years on PME in China and the United States.

CHAPTER 3

"TRUE IS FALSE, FALSE IS TRUE, VIRTUAL IS REALITY, REALITY IS VIRTUAL": TECHNOLOGY AND SIMULATION IN THE CHINESE MILITARY TRAINING REVOLUTION

James Mulvenon

INTRODUCTION

Simulations, virtual exercises, and other forms of technology-assisted training are mainstays for the modern military. Not only do these forms of training reduce costs and lower physical risk to military personnel, they also offer the opportunity to experiment with new operational concepts and bridge vast geographic and bureaucratic divides to improve operational performance. As the Chinese People's Liberation Army (PLA) rapidly modernizes, it has also embraced technology-assisted training, though perhaps more the efficiencies that it offers in a relatively resource-constrained environment. This chapter explores the role of technology in the development of PLA training, describing the range of "virtual" training systems and tools employed by the PLA, and then assessing the impacts of virtual training on overall force modernization. The author argues that the Chinese military has aggressively pursued technology-assisted training because of the efficiencies it offers to an institution operating in a relatively resource-constrained environment. On the one hand, PLA focus on simulation and virtual training may not provide as many external indicators of skill progress, but it may also reduce Beijing's confidence in the force's actual operational performance against a real opponent.

THE STRATEGIC CONTEXT FOR PLA TRAINING: WINNING LOCAL WARS UNDER INFORMATIZED CONDITIONS

To understand the role of technology in PLA training, it is first important to place PLA training within the larger context of Chinese military modernization. In recent years, the PLA has modified its core military guidance to reflect the goal of "winning local wars under informatized conditions."[1] But what is this mysterious and ambiguous term "informatization"? What does it mean in the PLA parlance? And what are the implications for training, especially technology-assisted training, that emphasizes the use of information technologies? Are they the same thing?

Confusing to nonspecialists, informatization was succinctly defined in an article published during the 2004 National People's Congress.[2] It described informatization as the "core of the revolution in military affairs (RMA) with Chinese characteristics," driven by the reality that the Chinese military, unlike the militaries of developed countries with mature mechanization, was attempting to carry out an RMA without having completed the mechanization phase. Advocates of informatization have concluded that "it is not necessary to completely follow the entire mechanization process of the developed countries and then carry out informatization." Instead, the military plans to "strengthen mechanization building" while at the same time attempting to "speed up the pace of informatization," following the "path of development by leaps and bounds [*kuayueshi fazhan*]." In this respect, the PLA is explicitly embracing the notion, first articulated by Gershenkron, that latecomers to modernization can take advantage of the experiences of earlier modernizers and thus skip certain stages of development. As one expert puts it, the PLA can "avoid the tortuous road followed by others and take maximum advantage of the strong points of a latecomer."

The critical factor enabling this leap ahead is the larger information technology revolution underway in China. China's status as the world's information technology workshop has facilitated the transfer of state-of-the-art information technologies, production capacity, and know-how to the mainland, much of which can be plugged in as commercial-off-shelf systems or modified to meet military requirements. An article by the Academy of Military Sciences doctrinal development unit argued this linkage explicitly: "At the same time, the information industry in our country is also developing rather rapidly, and this will certainly lay a good material foundation and provide great support for the informationization of our armed forces."[3]

The result is the "revamping the development of mechanized and semi-mechanized weapons by means of information technology," which is "a short-cut method of achieving our army's development by leaps and bounds."[4] Specifically, the PLA believes that the introduction of information technologies can "enhance the overall combat capability of existing weaponry by system integration."

As an example of American-style "informationization," consider the A-10 *Warthog*. The A-10 is a 35-year-old airframe, but the periodic introduction of advanced, black-box, line-replaceable units like new avionics packages can enable the *Warthog* to fight and win on the modern battlefield. For its part, the PLA retains a great deal of legacy equipment, in addition to its new modern systems, and relatively constrained funds for upgrading them. As one recent PLA article asserts, the "limited funds for the informationization of weapons and equipment" requires a prioritization of the "digital and informationized refitting of existing weapons and equipment."[5] By "replacing portions of hardware, developing and upgrading related software, and grafting on mature civilian technology," the PLA can "realize a rise in the informationized combat capabilities of old weapons and equipment."[6] To be clear, this is not the same as the RMA described by American strategists like Admiral Arthur K. Cebrowski or an even more futuristic, fully digitized military. Instead, the PLA is crafting a new path, using its relatively advanced command, control, communications, computers, intelligence surveillance, and reconnaissance (C4ISR) architecture as a force multiplier to network together its relatively primitive conventional forces in ways that can defeat a more technologically advanced adversary, like the United States.

INFORMATIZATION AND TRAINING

In the process of developing and interpreting the PLA's guidance on "winning local wars under informatized conditions," the military leadership has promulgated parallel sets of guidance on professional military education and operations training. Hu Jintao's first called for emphasis on military training in an April 2005 speech in the Jinan MR:

it is necessary to earnestly step up military training in close connection with the tasks that we shoulder . . . Strengthening military training is not only important practice in preparation for military struggle but is also an important way of ruling and managing the army. We must fully understand the importance of stepping up military training, truly regard it as the units' regular central task, and concentrate efforts to get a really good grasp of it. We must persist in proceeding from being hard and strict and the requirements of actual combat, uphold high standards and strict demands, and improve and innovate the content, ways, and means of training. We must imbue the entire training process with the cultivation of fighting spirit, carry forward our army's glorious tradition of daring to fight and being sure to win, and cultivate a heroic and stubborn combat style and iron discipline.[7]

The seminal moment was the June 2006 All-Army Training Work Conference, where Hu Jintao personally delivered instructions on implementing informatized training: "We must promote abundantly bringing science and technology into play in military training exercises, improve science and technology's contribution ratio in the increase of combat force, and improve the quality and effectiveness of military training."[8]

According to the official commentator article from the meeting, the PLA was directed to pursue a three-prong training strategy of "simulation, networking, and base-based training," with the goal of "promoting the transformation to military training under informationized and mechanized conditions, and improving troop operational capability under informationized conditions."[9] In the fall of 2006, this transformation of training reform was described as a "fundamental and directional strategic policy decision"[10] To underscore the importance of Hu's instructions, the senior military leadership has repeatedly and consistently echoed this guidance since the summer of 2006. In January 2007, Central Military Commission (CMC) Vice-Chairman Guo Boxiong was quoted as saying that the PLA must "actively push for the transformation from conducting military training under mechanized conditions toward conducting military training under informatized conditions."[11] More recently, Chief of the General Staff Liang Guanglie told a National People's Congress military delegates meeting that the military must "continually deepen reform of the content, methods, mechanisms, and measures of military training" and "actively promote the transformation from military training under mechanized conditions to military training under informatized conditions."[12]

Informatized Training in Historical Perspective.

Informatization marks a significant sea-change in training guidance, rather than a minor modification. Indeed, the accompanying commentary, while touting the new direction, also provides useful contrasts with previous periods of training guidance.[13] The 1950s were marked by "regularization [*zhengguihua*] training," while the 1960s are characterized as "great contests of arms" [*da bi wu*]. The slogan "three attacks and three defenses" [*san da san fang*] was the hallmark of the 1970s, while the 1980s witnessed a focus on "campaign tactical training reform." Finally, the 1990s consisted of integrated training, which has now been informatized in content.

Origins of Informatized Training.

With this history as backdrop, it is instructive to explore the explicit root origins of this transformation, as well as its main goals and methods. In terms of creation myth, PLA commentary and writings make clear that the origins of informatized training are inexplicably linked to the historical and strategic milieu in which they are being implemented:

> As a kind of important and special social practice activity, military training develops simultaneously with the progress of mankind's social and technological patterns, the evolution of war patterns, and the modernization construction of our Army; military training is closely related with national politics, economy, science, technology, and security. Promoting a transformation in military training is the strategic choice our Army has selected in order to adapt to the requirements of the times.[14]

To assess their current progression in history's sweep, Chinese military authors often draw from their Marxist historicism toolbag, arguing that the demands of the current era derive from a deterministic historical progression through the stages of the agricultural, industrial, and now information eras:

> As mankind's social development enters an information era from the agricultural and industrial era, three historical stages — using training to enhance the personal ability of troops as the mainstay, using training to enhance the ability of joined military operations as the mainstay, and using training to enhance the ability of combined military operations as the mainstay — have emerged in military training. In an information era, information technology, with microelectronic techniques, computers, artificial intelligence, telecommunications technology as its foundation, and its extensive application in the mili-

tary field, are creating a general trend of army building in various countries to achieve battlefield digitization, to make intelligent weapons, to achieve command automation, and to ensure accuracy. Colorful changes in military training of the world have fully proved that a transformation in military training is the inevitable outcome of information technology and its extensive application in the military field and is independent of man's will.[15]

Apart from the inexorable forces of Marxist history, a second set of roots of informatized training derives from the perceived deficiencies of current training guidance. A 2006 survey article in *Liberation Army Daily* offers some general insights:

> Judging from the actual condition of our Army's military training at the present stage, the principal contradictions we are facing in pushing forward the innovative development of military training are: the content of military training fails to meet the requirements of expanding the mission and tasks of troops; the entire level of military training fails to meet the requirements of preparations for a military struggle; the scientific and technological content of military training fails to meet the requirements of speeding up the transformation of the pattern of increasing combat capacity; the quality of personnel training fails to meet the requirements of army building and combat preparations; the condition for safeguarding training fails to meet the requirements to increase the needs of safeguarding training under an informatization condition.[16]

Given the strategic goal of "winning local wars under informatized conditions," these deficiencies, if left unfixed, seem to increase the possibility of mission failure to an unacceptable level.

Goals of Informatized Training.

As a generic goal, the PLA must "promote a transformation from mechanization-oriented military training to information-oriented military training," using "a scientific system for information-oriented military training." But this process is not pure science, and its application is "to meet the purpose of actual combat"[17] and "win an informatized war."[18] At the same time, informatized war involves one or more adversaries who themselves are informatized to varying degrees. PLA writings explicitly assert that informatized training must be geared to "defeating fighting opponents whose informatization degree is higher."[19] To counter such an adversary, informatized training "must comprehensively enhance military units' ability to gather intelligence, to transmit information, to control command, to move quickly, to carry out electronic countermeasures, to strike accurately, and to carry out all-round defense and comprehensive protection."[20] Indeed, the PLA must do all of these things faster than the more technologically-advanced adversary, getting inside his observation, orientation, decision, and action (OODA) loop and taking away the advantages of his superior firepower.

To achieve this goal, however, the PLA, like all militaries seeking to integrate increasingly advanced technology, confronts a difficult set of personnel problems. Despite some modest success in recruiting college graduates through its nascent reserve officer training program (ROTC) program and high-tech personnel through the development of an noncommissioned officer (NCO) corps and the expansion of technology-oriented militia and reserve units, the vast majority of Chinese military manpower are undereducated peasants from the rural areas with little acumen for modern military technology. While these soldiers can be trained to perform simple technical tasks, it is not realistic to expect them to operate complicated advanced systems without substantial training. In the same way that informatization is designed to overcome variation in the sophistication of equipment, it also helps smooth out these variations in personnel capacity by introducing systems with significant elements of "command automation" (*zhihui zidonghua*), an important Soviet-derived concept that assumes machines can be programmed to supplement weaknesses in human decisionmaking. While these artificial intelligence systems may reduce the negative effect of poor technical skills in the general force, it is arguable whether they are truly a substitute for well-trained personnel able to adapt to rapidly changing and sometimes unexpected operational situations in crisis and wartime, which is the philosophical core of American military culture.

Principles of Informatized Training.

From Chinese commentary and writings on the subject, there appear to be at least two core ideational principles at the heart of informatized training. The first principle is that technology is a deterministic feature of training. As a long, definitive survey article in *Liberation Army Daily* asserts, "technology not only decides tactics but also decides training."[21] The second principle is that training is fundamentally about people, not technology alone, though not in the same sense as Mao's dictum about man being a "spiritual atomic bomb":

Military training is in the final analysis training of people, and we must at all times assign first place to enhancing their quality. And in informatization conditions, war sets still higher demands on people's qualities that are different from those under mechanization conditions. In promoting the innovative development of military training in the new historical conditions, we must respect the status of officers and men as the main body and their innovative spirit, promote transformation of the knowledge and capability structure of officers and men, and make efforts to cultivate them into military personnel who meet the demands of adapting to partial war under informatization conditions.[22]

While training focuses on all personnel, special attention to paid to commanders and the use of informatized training to improve command through the application of technology, which falls under the general PLA rubric of "command automation" [*zhihui zidonghua*]:

To guarantee the central status of military training, it is necessary to give prominence to the command capability training for the command and staff organs. While organizing and guiding the training of the subordinate units, leaders and organs at and above the regiment levels should also make great enhancement to their own command capability training. Through holding simulation war games in the command posts and participating in tactical exercises, they should master the features of operation command under the condition of informatization, become familiar with the methods of sizing up the situation, making command decisions, and handling various complicated conditions.[23]

Evolutions of Informatized Training.

After Hu Jintao's first speech on training in April 2005, the PLA began with small steps. While "informatized conditions" were mentioned in the 2005 and 2006 directives, it was not characterized as the main theme. The "principle tasks" of the 2006 directives were to train with realistic combat scenarios, to raise the level of standardized [*zhengguihua*] military training, and to "actively and prudently" study integrated [*yitihua*] training. The 2005 main theme likewise emphasized integrated and standardized training.[24] In 2006, the General Staff Department (GSD) directives called for enhancing officers' and soldiers' knowledge of informatized technologies and their use of this "informatized knowledge" to solve problems. In addition, a GSD Military Training and Branch Department official said in an interview that the PLA wanted to focus on tri-service joint operations under informatized conditions.[25] The 2005 directives required the PLA to push towards integrated training on the basis of joint and combined arms training [*hetong xunlian*] under informatized conditions; "innovate" the leadership system, content, and methods of joint training under informatized conditions; and strengthen basic knowledge on informatized operations [*xinxihua zuozhan*]. The 2007 GSD Training Directive builds upon these evolutions, calling for the PLA to increase "research on military training under informatized conditions, develop training in a complex electromagnetic environment, focus on improving units' integrated joint operations capabilities under informatized conditions, and continue to explore integrated training [*yitihua xunlian*], which includes training that integrates the key factors of joint operations under informatized conditions."[26] An official from the PLA GSD Military Training and Service Arms Department outlined the progression:

Focusing military training on informatization will enable our armed forces to go from taking combat units and platforms as the center and laying particular emphasis on conducting internal single-service or single-branch combined training at successive levels to taking systems as the center and conducting lateral joint integrated training among several services and branches. Advanced information technology will replace industrial-age conventional technology as the primary technological force in guiding training.[27]

Categories of Informatized Training.

In its current form, the primary modalities for informatized training reform are eight-fold and include the following:

- Regional joint training;
- Networked, synchronized training;
- Simulation training;
- Distributed interactive training;
- Reality simulation training;
- Systems integration training;
- Fuzzy authorization training; and,
- Long-distance monitoring and control training.[28]

Regional joint training: This is a kind of joint training which our Army conducts in the present phase in which joint training mechanisms are still imperfect. This is an initial form of integrated training. Mainly it focuses on improving joint operations capabilities under informatized conditions, tapping and exploiting in full the multi-arm and service and civilian resources within a region. It draws on information network systems such as advanced "distributed interactive" training simulation systems, the "*Qudian*" system, the "joint tactical radio communication system," and the "online three-dimensional comprehensive support simulation system," for the conduct of coordinated training with the joined networks within a region. Different service arms and different units within a region revolve around the same intent, objectives, and line of thought, make effective "linkups," and simultaneously conduct a series of opposing-forces, real-war like training events involving online planning, decision making, and command, and integrated attacks. This reduces the mobilization of units, personnel, and equipment. It economizes, integrates, and exploits human, information, and equipment resources within a region. And it tempers "joint skills."

Networked, synchronized training: This is an entirely new form of training under informatized conditions, relying on computer networking and network technology. It mainly includes online education, online operations, online training exercises, OPFORs [opposing forces] operations, online troop training, long-distance learning, and online examinations. As an entirely new form of training, the military training information network can promptly provide officers and soldiers various training information resources and services, saving a lot of training time, and improving the quality and effectiveness of training. Some examples are: using interconnected electronic mailboxes, videoconferencing, and video technology to link up training participants and instructors for education and training; the use of advanced long-distance networked teaching and communications measures, creating the "21st century long-distance network classroom," enabling all field operations units and structures to obtain digital information by way of a networked joint training center; integrated use of various technologies, carrying out "long-distance study," providing soldiers the conditions for study and training at the times and places they need it, linking trainees with instructors, and ensuring that officers and soldiers learn more within a limited length of time.

Simulation training: This is the use of computers and simulation devices to imitate the performance of weapons and equipment, battlefield environments, and combat actions for the purpose of training. Mainly this includes the use of various kinds of simulation devices in simulation training of a technical nature, and the use of computer simulation systems for campaign and tactical simulation training. Using these training methods can not only greatly increase the content and iterations of training, accelerate the frequency of training, and enhance the effectiveness of training, it can also save financial and material resources, overcome arbitrariness in assessing training achievements, train both staffs and units, practice both command and jointness, practice both tactics and strategy, and greatly increase the effectiveness of training.

Distributed interactive training: This relies on computer network theory, it uses computer distributed interactive network technology and command automation systems, it connects units, personnel, and equipment scattered in different locations within a manmade electronic environment to form up a training arrangement coupled in time and space with simultaneous sharing of a combat environment. This is mainly used in opposing-forces command and control training for joint operations by multi-arm, multiservice information operations units. It is especially applicable in tactical and strategic training of commanders of various levels, and unit joint coordination exercises. With the development of computer network technology, new types of "distributed interactive simulation training systems" will more realistically reflect changes in war situations, forms of combat operations, operational methods, operational environments, and aspects of decision making and command and control relationships. This will allow better training exercises of new tactics under informatized conditions, and multiarm, multiservice, multicommand level, multitraining subject exercises conducted simultaneously in different locations.

Reality simulation training: This is the use of virtual reality technology to set up a combat operations simulation laboratory, transforming information into physical phenomena people can hear and see, creating war "environments" realistic to future warfare. This enables officers and soldiers in training to exercise training methods for information recognition, information processing, information transformation, etc., in a virtual combat operations environment. The goal is to make use of advanced information network technology and simulation measures, bring into full play the "pre-experience" role of military training, train as units will fight, check and prove the concept of combat operations theory, derive relevant data and conclusions, and serve unit informatization and the effort to make training realistic to actual war.

Systems integration training: This is a training method with the continual development of network information technology as a foundation, and with key operational factors and operational elements as the main targets of training, organically reorganizing and integrating network systems, achieving precise interaction among the various key factors within a system, so as to seek to bring the system's integrated functions into play. Systems integration training can help different operational entities share a battlefield situation, strengthen connections and communication between decision making structures and key combat operations elements, and achieve organic unity and a high degree of merging between decision making and execution. As systems confrontations gain a more prominent place in future warfare, and informatized opposing-forces training becomes more widespread, this training method will be used more frequently in the actual practice of military training. It will also become an extremely important way to generate combat power under informatized conditions.

Fuzzy authorization training: Because of the full use of information network technology in combat operations under informatized conditions, combat operations methods are becoming nonlinear. This is causing geo-value [*diyuan jiazhi*] to give way to objective value [*mubiao jiazhi*], random coordination is replacing planned coordination, and active matching [*zhudong pipei*] is replacing passive compliance. Tactical level units can carry out strategic or campaign level missions, and the ability of officers and soldiers to make decisions on their own and react flexibly is markedly stronger. This situation objectively demands corresponding training methods. The fuzzy authorization method is the use of the uncertain conditions and delegated authority method, and increasing the space for independent thinking by personnel in training. For example, strive for "four transformations" when organizing informatized campaign and tactical training; specifically, the transformation of combat missions from mainly specified missions [*guiding renwu*] to mainly planned missions [*guihua renwu*]; the transformation of command decision making from centralized decision making to mainly dispersed and ad hoc [*fensan, linji*] decision making; the transformation of combat actions from planned coordination to mainly random coordination; and the transformation of attack forces from prearranged dispositions to primarily last-minute, rapid reorganization. In this method, trainees no longer rely solely on orders to handle matters, they can make ad hoc decisions based on the continually changing situation. This strengthens their sense of active participation, and improves their ability to react flexibly in wartime.

Long-distance monitoring and control training: This is the use of digital cameras, optical fiber communication lines, multimedia, and other advanced technologies and monitoring and control equipment to construct a large-scale, base-focused, networked training exercise mechanism that integrates training, exercises, refereeing, and control. At appropriate times, images of the exercise situation are sent to a command and control center, achieving timely sharing of exercise information resources and real-time monitoring and control, coordination and direction, flexible monitoring and control, and examination and acceptance testing. This saves training time and resources, and it is effective in improving the quality and effectiveness of training. With the continual development of remote monitoring and control and networking technology, this sort of training method will be used more frequently in unit training exercises, and even in future combat operations.

The Dangers of Not Implementing Informatized Training.

Finally, Chinese authors address the dangers of *not* transforming training through informatization: "If we lag behind in this transformation, the gap between our military strength and that of developed countries will widen, thus increasing the potential threats in the field of military security in our country."[29] Given the larger demands of China's national security strategy in the 21st century, such an outcome is an unthinkable anathema to be avoided at all costs.

USE OF TECHNOLOGY IN PROFESSIONAL MILITARY EDUCATION

Chinese military writings are clear that informatized training must begin with informatization of professional military education. One author, reflecting a common view, argues that informatized training will only work by "integrating the power of departments, troops, colleges, and science research units" and unifying the theoretical and methodological content of training materials.[30] Indeed, informatization is judged to be the best hope for solving a core problem within the professional military education (PME) system, wherein "the weapons and equipment used for teaching in PLA academies and schools have in general been outmoded compared to that used in units," and "certain new types of weapons and equipment in particular have basically not been fielded to academies and schools for teaching purposes."[31] As a result, "the development of talented people urgently needed by many units is limited to book study and classroom work. Many students graduate without ever really seeing the weapons and equipment they will have to operate."[32] To solve this problem, PLA authors recommend introduction of robust simulation training into PME, and integrating the effort with simulation and actual training in units: "We should establish integrated training simulation systems. We should have troops, institutes, academies, and scientific units jointly pursue this goal."[33] As the following examples illustrate, some of this integration work between PME institutions and training units has begun to emerge.

Second Artillery Command Academy.

From the Chinese military press coverage, a "model" PME institution for the use of technology in education and training is the Second Artillery Command Academy. Articles on the Second Artillery describe its efforts to implement the "three transformations": base-focused training, networked training, and simulation training.[34] The school has created a battle lab for its students, known as the Combat Operations Simulation Training Center, focused on movement command, battlefield simulation, monitoring and assessment, training management, and "comprehensive support" [综合保障].[35] Within the lab, students can explore 10 specializations such as "strategic missile unit strategy, campaigns, tactics, command, training, engineering, communications, logistics, and equipment."[36] The facility consists of 43 laboratories with modern equipment and 80 sets of software for training purposes.[37] One system creates a "three-dimensional battlefield," consisting of a battlefield observation module, a scene simulator, and a scene database that reflecting all of the important elements of the battlefield, such as the sky and sea, geography and terrain, and personnel and equipment. It can verify and assess the battle plans of a missile base and missile brigade or regiment, and can quantify and examine the results of battle and training methods.[38] Using this platform, students can carry out all sorts of campaign and tactical operations on a small screen, they can conduct all sorts of complex offensive and defensive missile wars, verify and evaluate the operations plans of missile bases, brigade, and regiments, and do quantitative analysis of research results with tactics and training methods.[39] One article, written by a reporter attending a wargame in the battle lab, described a "missile battle" involving nearly 100 graduate students and their advisors. The simulation training command system incorporates the three levels of base, brigade, and battalion. Command Academy Commandant Li Tilin, on the scene observing the exercise, told reporters:

> Online confrontational training exercises have been made a mandatory course for advanced study by our graduate students. The goals are to give the students a clear understanding of their own capabilities and qualities, let them see how far short of the demands of the future battlefield they fall, heighten their sense of urgency, and promote the transformation of theoretical knowledge into capabilities and qualities.[40]

Army Aviation Academy.

The PLA's Army Aviation Academy operates a flight simulation training center.[41] The effect of the simulator has been to "greatly reduce the number of hours of flying training for flying commanders and significantly decrease training costs."[42] To integrate this simulator work into the operational training for army aviators, the simulation flying command training has been formally included in the Flying Training and Examination Outline for the Army Air Corps. The use of simulators has also helped students adapt to new helicopter models, providing more than 70 hours per year in all-weather simulation flying for each pilot and filling a major gap in the training for "highly risky and complex meteorological situations."[43]

Nanjing Army Command Academy and Shijiazhuang Army Command Academy.

The Nanjing Army Command Academy's Campaign Experiment Center has developed what it calls the "Army Combined Tactics Field Command Training Simulated Engagement System" [陸軍合同戰術野戰化指揮訓練模擬對抗系統], which provides "combined tactics simulation training" to the mid-ranking officers attending the school.[44] For its part, the Shijiazhuang Army Command Academy has developed an "exercise assessment system" based on the "demands of actual warfare."[45] Using the new design concept of "assessing combat effectiveness through quantified results" and employing computer technologies and mathematical models, information such as the messages, positions, and images collected by a movement monitoring system is automatically processed. Various types of data are created from this information, and it is compared with the standard data accumulated from each exercise, thus giving an "objective, accurate assessment of the troop exercise."

In 2006, the Air Force Command Academy established a campaign training center that included a training simulation system similar to the command system in a real war. The training simulator can also link up with operations simulation laboratories and the command systems of unit command posts of other arms and services. After the newly established campaign center went into operation, the academy initiated the construction of a "blue force" command post. The academy:

70

organized experts to conduct thorough research in the blue force's unit structure, combat equipment, tactics, and external relations [*wai bu guan xi*], and constructed models and a command system. It devoted effort to creating a corps of blue force commanders consisting mainly of graduate students, instructors, researchers, and experts invited in from elsewhere. With that as a foundation, the academy exerted all possible effort on making the blue force command post personnel more stable, and frequently organizing focused training which continually strengthens the blue force's big and powerful combat capabilities in the simulated training system. Prior to this exercise, one of the command personnel from the blue force command post said, "I daresay that the 'red force' will not get off cheaply at the hands of us."[46]

From January 4-18, 2007, the Air Force Command Academy arranged for 13 classes of graduating students to conduct an "online joint operations exercise."[47]

The Navy Submarine Academy reorganized itself to focus on three missions: command of submarine operations, the maritime environment of submarine operations, and submarine information systems and their application in combat operations. To better train for these missions, the academy built more than 10 equipment laboratories and 13 simulation laboratories, with the goal of "achieving simulation of equipment and realistic operations in training subjects."[48] Moreover, the Academy integrated its training with "actual submarine unit training in the field" by incorporating unit experts into exercises and linking with units via networks.[49]

USE OF TECHNOLOGY IN UNIT TRAINING

Technology, particularly simulation training centers and online exercises, now play an important role in informatized PLA training, helping to facilitate the new objective of integrated joint operations. The goal of these efforts is "a single network linking the three branches of the military and training the three branches of the military through a single network."[50] According to PLA sources, the use of distributed computer network systems to conduct long-range interactive training in remote locations is especially advantageous to improving joint combat command capability.[51] Specifically, networked training allows various arms and branches of the military, depending on the level and scope of training, to implement integrated training involving a common scenario without having to travel far from where they are stationed.

One of the primary impetuses for the development of simulation training centers and online exercises for integrated joint training was the problems arising from the prior lack of a joint combat exercise system. In its stead, the PLA first implemented a "regional coordination training mechanism that straddled the branches of the military and organizational systems to open up new territory for the development of campaign training."[52] This system suffered from weak linkages, including 'the lack of authority of temporary agencies, the lack of commands in consultative cooperation, and the lack of norms in random organizations."[53] An article in *Liberation Army Daily* insisted it was "imperative that the PLA expand the scope of regional coordination and uniformly coordinate regionally-organized exercises at a higher level, straddling the branches of the military and organizational system."[54] A nationwide system of networked training is touted as the primary mechanism for smoothing this regional cooperation and socializing different *xitongs* in the military system to adopt integrated joint warfare.

As a secondary benefit, this network would also permit uniform evaluation of progress toward integrated joint operations:

> We should establish integrated, real-time guidance and evaluation systems. The establishment of integrated information collection, long-range acoustic image transmission, supplemental decisionmaking systems, and the like would permit continuous monitoring of the campaign training process and situation. Real-time analysis and random guidance would provide support for the preparation, implementation, guidance, monitoring, analysis, evaluation, judging, and appraisal of integrated exercises. Thus, reform and perfection of the guidance evaluation system should be conducted on a larger scale and more rapidly.[55]

Finally, a simulation and exercise network would facilitate training for "real war":

> To construct a campaign training battlefield environment approximating real war, we should fully exploit simulation technology, virtual reality technology, artificial intelligence technology, and remote monitoring technology. We should establish training counterforces that exist in both form and spirit to provide realistic opponents in campaign exercises and to increase the specificity of campaign training. At the same time, we should establish a quantitative analysis and evaluation system for campaign training bases, scientifically evaluate campaign training results, explore comprehensive appraisal methods, and test joint combat capability.[56]

In concrete terms, units train for "real war" by first participating in integrated training in scattered locations to connect the information systems of various branches of the military. Based on mission tasks and combat missions, joint exercises involving real combat units and their logistics support are then conducted in an effort to form an integrated combat capability.[57]

Two important modalities for informatized training are simulation training centers and online exercises.

Simulation Training Centers.

Simulation training centers are an increasingly central component of PLA informatized training, appearing at every unit level and across the service branches. The press coverage of these centers is by no means uniform, and the following data points are offered as illustrative examples of the phenomena rather than a comprehensive analysis of the universe of training centers in the Chinese military.

- Second Artillery brigade: "In the past, due to the huge size and the high price of strategic missiles, it was impossible to use actual weapons and equipment in daily training. The weapons and equipment operating training had to be done by way of 'looking for a fine horse with the aid of its picture', and the tactical training usually had to be done by way of 'talking about strategies on paper', which limited the production and enhancement of the combat capability of the units. Now, this brigade has developed a complete set of simulated missile launching training equipment to enable it to conduct simulated training, effectively lift the unit's actual weapons and equipment training level, saved a lot of training resources, and brought profound changes to the field of training."[58]

- "A new kind of armored vehicle communications, navigation, and firing simulation training center for those at the division level and various regiments underneath it, working with scientific research institutes to develop more than 70 sets of training software and simulation operating systems, such as command and control emulation training software for a certain new kind of tank and integrated information systems simulation training software."[59]

- Flight testing simulation: "The Three-Year Construction Plan of the Flight Simulation Training System promulgated and put into effect in 2002 has now produced remarkable effect: The large flight simulation equipment have on the whole covered all types of combat planes; the development of the simulation training center for all kinds and types of planes has fit in with the needs of the flying schools, training bases and the combat forces, and the flight training of the Air Force has realized massive simulation. It is said that through the highly energetic development of the flight training equipment in the past 3 years, the Air Force currently possesses over 100 pieces of flight simulation training equipment of various types covering all types of planes. In addition, simulation training centers have been established respectively in the Aviation University, the flying schools, a number of training bases for flight test, the aviation combat forces with new-type planes and the aviation transportation units with new-type planes. The general view of the pilots is that simulation flight is of great help to getting to know the usage of the equipment in the cabin, to the mastering of the aviation skills and to the improvement of the ability to handle the special situation. The simulation training has stretched the space of the tactical training and boosted the great change from the skill-orientated training to the tactical-orientated training."[60] In one regiment, "any pilot making major errors during simulation trainings will be disqualified from actual flight training. After a long 'no fly' period, and after assurance of flight safety prior to starting new subjects, all pilots must first pass tests by a simulator to qualify to be able to participate in training."[61]

- "A tower flight controller training simulation system now has a three-dimensional image of the tower and the airspace over the airfield. It has flight dispatch patterns for different types of warplanes, day and night, in a thunderstorm, in a large aircraft group, etc. Thus, a breakthrough has been made in the Air Force's traditional training method for flight controllers, not only saving training resources, but improving the quality and effectiveness of training."[62]

- Nanjing armored regiment's simulated opposition force (OPFOR) training exercise center: "Reporters learned from the exercise directorate that in order to construct an information simulation environment, this regiment cooperated with several military academies and schools and scientific research institutes, and it researched and developed a field combat operations command automation system with a field command shelter as the main element, supported by computer technology. The regiment relied on campaign and tactical training systems and visualization systems to initially achieve a network which connects all levels vertically and all key factors horizontally, and which allows multifunctional OPFOR to play on line. This network provides the technical support for organizing online combat operations exercises."[63]

- A submarine damage escape training center — the only training site of its kind in the Navy, located at a submarine detachment of Nanhai Fleet. The center houses a "huge submarine with interconnected compartments in the same size as true submarine compartments. Participating crewmembers carry out leak stopping, fire extinguishing, and tube climbing training according to orders issued by the command in order to have a perfect mastery of operational techniques and mental quality."[64]

- Submarine simulations: "The creation of 'specialist chief petty officers' was like spring rain invigorating the detachment's efforts in training sailors in science and technology. The detachment brought into play these petty officers' role as 'seeds' and 'yeast,' inviting them to the submarine simulation training center to act as specialist instructors and guide specialist sailors undergoing in-port training."[65]

- At an armored division NBC training center, a certain type of chemical defense reconnaissance vehicle training simulator, with software including a "contamination check training simulation system" and a "vehicle mounted radiation reconnaissance training simulation system." The simulator can create unique tactical settings, complex and unusual enemy situations, and other information confrontation training content. It "shortened the chemical defense element's specialized training cycle, and improved the effectiveness of training."[66]

- A new generation of Second Artillery simulation training equipment for different types of guided missiles. The entire training hall permits conducting of guided missile firing drills, not only achieving complete simulation training but even increasing simulation training for management of breakdowns and unexpected circumstances.[67]
- Shenyang MR patrol boat battalion: "Because this area is located in a high and cold area, the Heilongjiang River freezes every winter. Ships have to be docked in port, making on-board training impossible for six months each year. In response to this, the battalion invested over RMB2 million to develop software — such as the ship and vessel navigation simulation system — and to build a ship and vessel simulation training center. Officers and soldiers of the battalion can conduct simulated full-drainage-area and all-item technological and tactical practice. This has not only eliminated difficulty in winter military training, but has also shortened the turnaround time for every practice session and has cut training expenses. . . . The simulation training system has allowed the battalion to start simulation training for new recruits as soon as they arrived at the battalion. The simulation training system allows the battalion to finish an 8-month training program within only 4 months and ensures that raw recruits can take part in patrol and duty performance in the same year they join the army."[68]
- Laser simulation equipment on tanks: "If a tank fitted with a laser OPFOR simulation system is attacked, the system will automatically shut

off the tank's electrical circuits and fuel supply, forcing the tank to withdraw from the battle. Every tank's operational status is displayed in real time on a large screen in a mobile exercise direction vehicle. Before the use of the laser OPFOR simulation system, the impossibility of tank confrontations using live ammunition often led tank units to charge and attack fiercely in a dense formation. Superficially, this looked great, but it fell far short of meeting the requirements of real war. The installation of the laser OPFOR simulation system introduced real-war requirements into unit training exercises."[69]

- "Dingxin military airport in Gansu Province has already become the shooting range of the whole PLA Air Force (PLAAF). In addition, China has built a simulation project of Taiwan Qingquangang Airport. This base is now the airport with the highest standard of comprehensive combat tactics training within the Air Force, and different types of new fighters, KJ2000 and KJ200 airborne warning and control system (AWACS)/airborne early warning and control (AEW&C) have constantly entered this base. In addition to Su27/Su30MKK fighters, at least five J7 fighters and J8II fighters were sighted at this airport, which gives some clues of the features of comprehensive tactic training and weapon firing tests at this base. It has also been noticed that Il76, Y8, and Y7 transport aircraft are fielded. Kanwa's analysis is that Y8 and Y7 could be the experimental air platforms for airborne radar systems, and are mainly used to test the performance of the newly developed airborne radars for combat aircraft. In terms of the assignment of combat missions, Dingxin and Yanliang Airports are both used as the testing bases. The latter is mainly used for the test flights of different types of combat aircrafts, while the former is for testing weapon systems."[70]

Online Training.

Online exercises are a critical component of informatized training, because they permit cross-training between different units and services across China's broad geographic expanse and facilitate experimentation with the joint campaign command system. In the latter case, "online training has now become an important platform for senior staff officers to improve their command capabilities."[71] The PLA's online exercises can be divided into two rough categories: (1) skills and coordination exercises and (2) online OPFOR exercises.

Online Skills and Coordination Training. Online training in the PLA has a number of purposes, one of which is to exercise command relationships, both vertically and horizontally. A good example is the following description of the use of online training in the Jinan MR:

> The MR's party committee actively raised 900,000 renminbi in funds to build an information network that could connect three levels — the MR, the regiment, and the battalion — and integrate combat and command with informatized training. Drawing support from modern simulation technology, the "group of people" practiced planning, command, and operational methods on the lifelike battlefield. At the same time, they brought the command and staff organs together to conduct online study of such essential elements of command as combat coordination, integrated support, and situation handling

so as to improve their informatized combat and command capabilities under various battlefield postures.[72]

Online training also precludes the need for the PLAAF to train in inclement weather, which could increase the rate of accidents and loss of valuable airplanes.

> In order to break through the restrictions of weather, in recent years, the Chengdu Air troops have developed more than 40 types of online training software that involves aviation troops, radar, and ground-to-air missile troop operations, greatly expanding online training . . . Not only can it imitate warplane, ground-to-air missile and radar operations, it can also carry out air to air fighting, air to ground fighting, electronic interference, and many other types of training . . . Online training does not suffer from the limitations of time, space, and the conditions of the outside world. It is not the same one thing for each soldier, but it can set up various types of nearly real battlefield environments, causing the pilots and commanders to achieve a sense of having personally experienced it . . . the pilots and commanders drill strategy, drill command, drill coordination, and drill combat methods in conditions very similar to actual combat. This year, the proportion of the troops belonging to the Chengdu Air Force doing online tactical training reached more than 80 percent.[73]

Online OPFOR Exercises. For the PLA, online OPFOR exercises "are simulated OPFOR training exercises supported by computer networks and simulation technology," blending "computer simulation technology with the advantages of network communications." The main challenges of online exercises are three-fold: (1) technical support, (2) network security and (3) scenario realism.

- Technical support: "The smooth implementation of online OPFOR exercises mainly depends on fast, unbroken network communications, hardware in good working order, and stable software. None of these three can be lacking. As soon as online OPFOR exercises begin, the difficulty of last minute adjustments is very high. Therefore, before OPFOR exercises begin, computer hardware, software, and network technical personnel and staff officers must be grouped into a technical support *fendui*. All equipment involved in the operation of the exercise must be rigorously checked and repeatedly inspected. Equipment requiring frequent support must be replaced on schedule. All software for simulation systems and staff operations systems used in the exercise must not only be correctly installed, but also go through practical online testing. During the implementation of OPFOR exercises, the technical support *fendui* should be intently aware of the working conditions and system operations conditions of all software and hardware equipment. Emergency solutions must be rapidly implemented to take care of equipment and systems that malfunction. When OPFOR exercises are completed, a technical support special report about the technical support situation during the exercises must be written to summarize and share good experiences and methods, and to analyze existing problems and the measures used to handle them."[74]

- Network security: "Online OPFOR exercises, which mainly rely on computer networks and distributed combat command training simulation systems to carry out corresponding combat tactics and methods of operations in

OPFOR exercises, are military training events that require a high level of security. Lack of precautions can easily cause network security exposures. Currently, in organizing online OPFOR exercises, especially long distance online confrontations, we mostly use the national defense network for data transmissions, or civilian communications networks when needed. The shared nature of information equipment, the use of non-dedicated transmission lines, the complexity of network viruses, and the variety of methods used by network 'hackers' require us to strengthen awareness of network security throughout the whole process of the exercise. First, we must use the wide area networks (WAN) when carrying out OPFOR exercises. Since the exercise data must be transmitted through national defense fiber optic cables or civilian communications networks, it requires the exercise unit to use encryption cards to encrypt data whenever using network transmission signals. Using computers with encryption cards to receive the encrypted signal, the receiving unit automatically starts decryption and ensures that the exercise contents are safely transmitted over the network. Second, we must integrate the application of network anti-virus and firewall technologies to strengthen network integrated implementation of total protection with the server as the center to ensure the anti-virus safety of the entire OPFOR exercise network. Third, we must stress the installation of hardware (and software) firewalls or system patches in all network terminals to prevent 'hacker' penetration and improve security for normal use of the networks by exercise units."[75]

- Scenario realism: "Online OPFOR exercises are a form of training method developed on the basis of computer combat simulations. They require both sides of the OPFOR exercise to strictly follow the 'agreed upon' technical and tactical stipulations and confrontational and military rules, to move closer to fair and realistic confrontation. Confrontations employing wishful thinking cannot be set up. In the past when 'Red and Blue' OPFOR exercises were organized by some units, the OPFOR exercise concept was 'the Red Forces always win and the Blue Forces always lose.' On one hand, it was a blow to training enthusiasm of the Blue Forces, and it decreased the quality of confrontation in OPFOR exercises. On the other hand, it decreased the level of difficulty for the Red Forces, and did not reach the goal of achieving intense fighting by both OPFORs. Therefore, when organizing online OPFOR exercises, the principle of 'fair conditions' must be followed. First, insure both sides of the confrontation have the same operations environment and battlefield environment. This mainly means that both sides of the confrontation should be as equivalent as possible in terms of personnel organization, technical support, battlefield equipment and operational environment. Second, we must ensure that the confrontation level and combat strength of both sides of the confrontation are relatively the same. This mainly means that there is not too big a difference between the two sides' number of participating troops, organization and equipment, assistance and support, and combat capability indices. Only in this way can both sides be truly confrontational and realistically oppose one another. Third, we must ensure that the contents of confrontations are as real as possible, which mainly means staying close to real battlefield requirements, using various complex situations and setups to draw both sides into contests on the 'battlefield,' and avoiding inflexible, formulaic, and rote confrontations to ensure realism and intensity, and to closely adhere to actual combat."[76]

As an illustrative example of the use of online exercises in the PLA, *Air Force News* in August 2006 carried a highly detailed description of a Chengdu MR Air Force exercise.[77] Centered in the headquarters Campaign Training Center, the exercise pitted a friendly "blue force" against an opposing "red force." The division-level exercise was designed to explore the integration of a "new type of airplane" with surface-to-air missile and radar units, along with anti-aircraft artillery, electronic countermeasures, and air defense units. Within the "command center" of the "red force," the online exercise displays provided "battlefield situation charts, diagrams of operational courses of action, various combat documents, and live images of command in real time." The commander of "red" was commanding units and platforms hundreds of miles away. These units confronted a "blue force" located elsewhere. On the screen in the Campaign Training Center, it could be seen that "groups of blue force aircraft had taken off from different airfields under cover from electronic jamming aircraft, with the intent of attacking red force command posts, airfields, radar sites, groups of air defense sites, and other important targets." In the Campaign Training Center, the exercise director explained to reporter that:

> this networked training platform operating with a new-generation command automation system integrated with the Military Region Air Force Training and Combat Readiness Information Network can not only set up a realistic battlefield environment, its advanced combat operations simulation system also allows up-to-date management, monitoring, control, and assessment of training, expanding networked training to every tactical and technological aspect.

It was possible, for instance, to

> click a mouse button and see in real time the training time, progress, and quality of every unit, every aviator, every training subject, and every sortie. On a training monitoring and control board are displayed accurate graphs and tables for each unit's "key elements" of training, training quality, effectiveness, and safety for a given period of time. In the command center, landing radar information, weather information, and each aviator's landing information is displayed in real time before the commander's eyes.[78]

All of the software was reportedly built upon "mathematical models for air-to-air, air-to-ground, and electromagnetic confrontations" that can "simulate the combat actions of warplanes, surface-to-air missiles, radar, and electronic jamming" as well as provide "a dynamic simulation of the whole course of an offensive and defensive battle between red and blue force service arms." At the end of the exercise, the networked system permits "all the participating units to watch in real time from different locations, learning from others' strong points and improving themselves."

Other online OPFOR exercises permit Chinese forces to operate in complex battlefield environments, simulating the tactics of the adversary, such as jamming and other electronic countermeasures. One Guangzhou MR missile brigade:

> . . . invested over 300,000 RMB to set up an information center and simulation teaching office, thus providing effective hardware support by which to improve the quality of teaching about electromagnetism . . . In simulation training, the brigade randomly inserts scenarios such as being under enemy reconnaissance or subjected to enemy jamming. This has improved the unit's operational capabilities in complex electromagnetic environments.[79]

The Future of Technology-Assisted Training.

Despite the progress described above, Chinese military writings often discuss the future improvements needed in technology-assisted training. One main concern is that the training is too stovepiped and must be better integrated across the force: "We must establish an integrated training information network system. The comprehensive integration of various communication networks, computer networks, and simulation network systems can effectively support long-range distributed campaign training."[80]

More than just connecting pipes, this integrated system should be able to share a wide range of training and operational-related data, including geospatial information:

> We should establish shared, integrated training technology platforms. The normalization of components, such as various databases, geographic information systems, general-purpose situation map-generating systems, and information sharing protocols, will provide standardiza-

tion and generalization services for various training system operations. In establishing these shared technology platforms, we should adhere to uniform database format standards and information transmission protocols; integrate software resources; and effectively fuse the functions of the various systems to achieve information sharing, functional complementation, and secure transmission.[81]

Higher bandwidth networked training, however, will require much more sophisticated network management, which must itself be regularly trained:

We should conduct training in information system networking. Campaign training supported by a network background generally comprises the three steps of the introduction of a scenario, information processing, and monitoring and evaluation. The training organizer uses the network to transmit the training conditions to the recipient by different methods. Using actual equipment or the support of a simulated integrated information environment, each entity taking part in training obtains the dynamic information required for training from a simulated battlefield environment and shared information platform. Each training information system rapidly analyzes and assesses the information that is obtained, generates decision proposals, and distributes the decision proposals to the training entities over the network. The network evaluation system monitors various combat elements in real time and evaluates the persons being trained and the combat systems in three areas: accuracy of information, rate of information flow, and system stability.[82]

With all of these elements working together, the authors assert that the PLA will be better able to achieve its future goal of "fully informatized training."

CONCLUSIONS AND IMPLICATIONS

This chapter has argued that the Chinese military is aggressively pursuing technology-assisted training, primarily because of the efficiencies it offers to an institution operating in a relatively resource-constrained environment. The use of simulations allows units to maintain and even raise skill levels while reducing wear and tear on equipment and possible physical risks to personnel. The use of online coordination exercises permits the PLA to exercise different units from different services across vast geographic divides, knitting together the elements of integrated joint operations described in the military's campaign literature. Finally, the use of online OPFOR exercises facilitates realistic training against high-tech adversaries, pushing PLA units to operate in a hostile environment with noncooperative targets. All of these activities offer the possibility of increasing the military's operational performance on a modern military battlefield.

The implications of the PLA's focus on technology-assisted training for the United States are more complicated, but can be divided into intelligence and operational categories. On the intelligence front, the PLA focus on simulation and virtual training may undermine our ability to collect against Chinese exercises and analyze the relative progress of the military in achieving training benchmarks, since the online exercises do not provide the same level of robust external indicators as field exercises. Often, the only external indicators of online or virtual training are newspaper or journal accounts describing the initiative, and these sources suffer from lack of detail, brevity, bias in favor of putting a positive spin on a new effort, and reluctance to discuss problems in detail.

Operationally, the use of simulation and online exercises creates the danger of strategic surprise in the level of Chinese capabilities or integration, though it is debatable whether the Chinese Communist leadership would be as risk-acceptant of a conflict with a high-tech power like the United States based solely on performance in simulations and online training. At the end of the day, the PLA needs to prove its combat power in the field against real adversaries, not electrons on a screen. Still, comfortable assumptions about lack of PLA capability to knit together elements of the joint warzone campaign plan or command structure, based on lack of evidence of physical exercising of the various moving parts from around the country, may prove to be overly optimistic. For this reason, greater study and scrutiny of PLA simulations, gaming and online exercises is warranted.

ENDNOTES - CHAPTER 3

1. *China's National Defense in 2006,* Beijing: State Council Information Office, December 2006.

2. The remainder of this paragraph is taken from Huang Guozhu, Cao Zhi, and Xu Zhuangzhi, "Speed Up the Revolution in Military Affairs with Chinese Characteristics: PLA Deputies Discuss National Defense and Armed Forces Modernization," *Xinhua,* March 12, 2004.

3. Operations Theory and Regulations Research Department of the Academy of Military Science, "Strive to Promote Historic Changes in Military Training," *Jiefangjun Bao,* July 11, 2006.

4 . Huang Guozhu, Cao Zhi, and Xu Zhuangzhi.

5 . Xu Hongsheng, "In Search of Road To Informationization of Mechanized Units," *Zhanyou Bao,* August 24, 2006.

6 . *Ibid.*

7. Wang Wenjie and Ding Haiming, "Hu Jintao Emphasizes When Inspecting a Group Army of Jinan Military Region and Meeting Cadres At and Above Divisional Level of Units Stationed at Weifang: Resolutely Carry out the Sacred Tasks Given Us by the Party and People in the New Century and New Phase," *Jiefangjun Bao,* April 15, 2005, p. 1.

8. Cao Zhi, "Hu Jintao Emphasizes Importance of Reform and Innovation in Promoting Development of Military Training," *Xinhua,* June 27, 2006.

9. *Ibid.*

10. Zhong Xun, "The Strategic Policy Decision for Invigorating Military Training and Strengthening the Army in the New Period of the New Century: On the Scientific Connotations and Epoch-Making Significance of Transforming Military Training," *Jiefangjun Bao,* November 28, 2006, p. 1.

11. Wang Shibin, "During His Meeting With Personnel Attending Special Training on Conducting Military Training Under Informatized Conditions, Guo Boxiong, Member of the Political Bureau of the CPC Central Committee and Vice Chairman of the Central Military Commission, Called for Taking the Scientific Development Concept as the Guide and Actively Pushing for Military Training Transformation," *Jiefangjun Bao,* January 18, 2007, p. 1.

12. Xin Shihong, "Delegate Liang Guanglie Speaks at Sub-Session of National People's Congress," *Jiefangjun Bao,* March 6, 2007, p. 1.

13. Xinhua contributing commentator, "The Inevitable Choice for the People's Army in Effectively Carrying out its Historic Mission: Written at the Close of the All-Army Military Training Conference," *Xinhua,* June 27, 2006.

14. Zhong Xun, "The Strategic Policy Decision for Invigorating Military Training," p. 1.

15. *Ibid.*

16. *Ibid.*

17. *Ibid.*

18. *Ibid.*

19. *Ibid.*

20. *Ibid.*

21. *Ibid.*

22. Xinhua contributing commentator, "The Inevitable Choice."

23. Commentator's article, "Conscientiously Guarantee the Central Status of Military Training: First on Launching a New Upsurge in Military Training," *Kongjun Bao,* July 15, 2006, p. 1.

24. *Jiefangjun Bao,* January 17, 2005, and January 18, 2006.

25. *Jiefangjun Bao,* 3 January 2006.

26. "PRC General Staff Department Issues New Year Military Training Directive," *Jiefangjun Bao,* January 12, 2007.

27. Guo Jia and Xu Zhuangzhi, "People's Liberation Army's Military Training Undergoes Historic Transformation With Focus on Informatization," *Xinhua,* February 23, 2007.

28. Pan Jinkuan, "Exploring Methods of Military Training Under Informatized Conditions," *Zhanyou Bao,* September 22, 2006.

29. Zhong Xun, "The Strategic Policy Decision for Invigorating Military Training," p. 1.

30. Zhong Xun, "Deepening Military Training Content Reform From a Scientific Approach," *Jiefangjun Bao,* January 9, 2007, p. 1.

31. *Ibid.*

32. Ma Dezu and Yang Chunyuan, "Joint Operations Exercise by Students Graduating from Air Force Command Academy," *Kongjun Bao,* March 10, 2007, p. 4.

33. Cao Shuxin, "Exploring Ways to Change Campaign Training Under Informatized Conditions," *Jiefangjun Bao,* December 26, 2006, p. 6.

34. Kang Fashun and He Tianjin, "Sidelights on the Second Artillery Military Training Conference," *Huojianbing Bao,* August 18, 2006, p. 2.

35. Wang Yongxiao, Cao Jienbing, and Tao Shelan, "Second Artillery Uses Science and Technology to Strengthen Forces: Rapid Missile Strike Capability Makes New Strides," *Zhongguo Xinwen She,* July 23, 2007.

36. *Ibid.*

37. Feng Chunmei, "Put the Scientific Development Concept in Command of Running Schools and Training Personnel: A Record of Implementing the Scientific Development Concept by the Command College of the Second Artillery Corps," *Renmin wang,* July 11, 2007.

38. Wang Yongxiao, Cao Jienbing, and Tao Shelan.

39. Wang Yongxiao, "Report from the Training Ground of China's Strategic Missile Force," *Jiefangjun Bao,* June 28, 2006, p. 3.

40. Yu Zengshuang and Liu Yidai, "Eyewitness Account of Command Academy Graduate Students' Online Confrontational Exercise," *Huojianbing Bao,* April 11, 2007, p. 2.

41. Tian Qiang and Zhou Jiawang, "Chinese Army Aviation Strengthens Coordinated Operation Command Capability," *Zhongguo Xinwen She*, July 3, 2007.

42. *Ibid.*

43. "ZXS Details Flight Training Facilities at PLA Army Aviation Flight and Command Simulation Training Center," *Zhongguo Xinwen She*, July 9, 2007.

44. Liu Yueshan, Luo Hongxiao, and Guo Jiaxue, "Quantifying Combat Effectiveness: The Pace of Troop Informatization Picks Up," *Wen Wei Po,* July 17, 2007.

45. *Ibid.*

46. Ma Dezu and Yang Chunyuan, p. 4.

47. *Ibid.*

48. Liu Jian, "Submarine Academy Emphasizes Teaching and Training Under Complex and Emergency Conditions," *Renmin Haijun,* 15 December 2006, p.1.

49. *Ibid.*

50. Cao Shuxin.

51. *Ibid.*

52. *Ibid.*

53. *Ibid.*

54. *Ibid.*

55. *Ibid.*

56. *Ibid.*

57. *Ibid.*

58. Li Xuanliang and Wu Dengfeng, "PLA Launched Vigorous Campaign To Promote Military Training; Overall Combat Capability in Informatized Defensive Operations Given New Boost," *Xinhua,* June 23, 2006.

59. Shao Min and Lu Ping, "Adjusting Content, Coming Up With Innovative Modes, and Constructing Platforms: A Certain Armored Division Uses Training on New Equipment To Transform Unit Training," *Renmin Qianxian,* July 17, 2007, p. 1.

60. Zhang Jinyu, "Flight Simulation Training Covers All Types of Combat Planes," *Jiefangjun Bao,* May 30, 2006.

61. Yu Lei and Hong Wenjun, "Flyer's Permit Now Needed for New Training: Chengdu Military Region Air Force Regiment Links Quality of Simulation Training with Qualification for Actual Flight Training," *Jiefangjun Bao,* July 30, 2007, p. 2.

62. Lu Feng, Lu Xi, and Wang Bin, "Watching Chengdu Military Region Air Force Conduct Online OPFORs Exercise to Research Carrying Out Missions Under Informatized Conditions, Part 1," *Kongjun Bao,* August 31, 2006, p. 1.

63. Yang Xiaoyong and Li Ping, "Armored Regiment's Command and Staff Conduct Online Exercise, a Battle Under Complex Electromagnetic Conditions," *Renmin Qianxian,* January 12, 2007, p. 1.

64. Li Gencheng, Peng Jiu, and Zhang Lei, "PRC Magazine Profiles PLA Navy SSF Submarine Damage Control Training," *Xiandai Junshi,* June 1-30, 2007, pp. 7-9.

65. Cao Jieyu and Li Yibao, "East Sea Fleet Submarine Detachment's 'Chief Petty Officer' Corps Swims Out of the 'Dragon King's Palace'," *Renmin Haijun,* May 1, 2006, p. 1.

66. Zhang Jianqi and Kui Zhang, "Unit Uses Simulation Devices to Improve the Quality of Training," *Qianwei Bao,* May 20, 2007, p. 2.

67. Gao Zhiwen and Pan Li, "Computer Simulation Operations Increasingly Realistic; Second Artillery New Simulators Improve Training Results," *Jiefanjun Bao,* May 4, 2007, p. 1.

68. Wang Bing and Zhou Jun, "The Warship and Vessel Simulation Training Center of a Patrol Boat Battalion Is Sweating over Military Training," *Jiefangjun Bao*, February 23, 2007, p. 1.

69. Bi Ren and Ding Haiming, "PLA Tanks in Intense Confrontation in Desert Exercise," *Zhongguo Quofang Bao*, September 19, 2006, p. 5.

70. Wu Xincheng, "Special Report: Prospect of PLA Air Force Development and Deployment," *Kanwa Defense Review*, January 1, 2007.

71. Lu Xi and Lu Feng, "A Set of Software Enlivens the Exercise: Eyewitness Account of the Confrontation Exercises by the Chengdu Military Region Air Force Units," *Jiefangjun Bao*, September 1, 2006, p. 1.

72. Sun Yipo, Zhuang Sujun, and Jiang Shuyi: "Sturdy and Improved Platform: Chronicle of 'A Group of People' at the Qingdao Garrison Command's Party Committee Improving Their Informatized Combat and Command Capabilities."

73. Hu Xiaoyu, "Flight Training No Longer 'Relies on the Sky,' the Subject Is No Longer 'One Size Fits All': Proportion of the Troops Belonging to the Chengdu Air Force Doing Online Tactical Training Reaches 80 Percent," *Jiefangjun Bao*, January 1, 2007.

74. Xia Junyou, "Scientifically Organize Realistic Online OPFOR Exercises," *Qianwei Bao*, 3 July 2006, p.1.

75. *Ibid.*

76. *Ibid.*

77. The description of this exercise and all quotes are taken from Lu Feng, Lu Xi, and Wang Bin, p. 1.

78. *Ibid.*

79. Chen Mei and Mu Lin, "Guangzhou Military Region Air Force Missile Brigade Steps Up Training in Simulated Complex Electromagnetic Environments," *Kongjun Bao*, March 13, 2007, p. 2.

80. Cao Shuxin.

81. *Ibid.*

82. *Ibid.*

SELECTED CHINESE MILITARY TRAINING BIBLIOGRAPHY

Hu Xiaofeng. *U.S. Military Training Simulation* [M]. Beijing: National Defense University Press, 2001.

Li Changsheng, Jiang Jingzhuo, Zeng Xianzhao, *et al. Research and Application of New Methods of Military Operations.* Beijing: Military Science Press, 2002.

Military Simulation Terminology Standards Research Topics Group. *Military Modeling and Simulation Common Use Terminology Compilation* [M]. Beijing: National Defense Industry Press, 2001.

Wang Keding. *Combat Simulation Theory And Methods* [M]. Changsha, University of National Defense Science and Technology, 1998.

Xu Xuewen and Wang Shouyun. *Modern Combat Simulation.* Beijing: Science Press, 2001.

Zhang Zuiliang, Li Changsheng, Zhao Wenzhi, *et al. Military Operations Research* [M]. Beijing: Military Science Press, 1992.

CHAPTER 4

PLA CONSCRIPT AND NONCOMMISSIONED OFFICER INDIVIDUAL TRAINING

Dennis J. Blasko[*]

Well, I try my best
To be just like I am
But everybody wants you
To be just like them . . .

— Bob Dylan, "Maggie's Farm," 1965

INTRODUCTION

Individual training for People's Liberation Army (PLA) conscripts and noncommissioned officers (NCOs) consists of common-task training and political indoctrination conducted after induction, as well as specialty training for specific jobs and skills for some, but not all, soldiers, sailors, and airmen. Responsibility for individual training is decentralized to units from independent regiment- and brigade/division-level up to Military Region (MR)-level. Induction and specialty training takes place in operational units and at a variety of training bases and schools throughout the country. The methods used incorporate many elements of modern technology and also rely to some extent on support from the civilian sector. The current individual training regimen has been influenced by many other aspects of the PLA modernization program and is a building block for overall force transformation.

---

* Special thanks go to Justin Liang, Ivan Szpakowski, and James A. Bellacqua for help in research and transplation.

One of the most visible elements of the PLA's modernization program has been the demobilization of 500,000 and 200,000 personnel since 1997. As a result, the overall number of conscripts has decreased while the numbers of NCOs have increased. NCOs now perform some duties formerly assigned to conscripts, such as squad leader, and they also are assuming other jobs that junior officers previously held, like company mess officer (similar to a U.S. company supply sergeant). Additionally, NCOs are assigned to technical posts responsible for care of equipment. The Chinese government has not divulged the exact number of conscripts and NCOs in the roughly 2.3 million-strong active duty PLA, but according to a July 2007 report, NCOs comprise half of the PLA's enlisted force.[1] In order of magnitude, conscripts and NCOs each number several hundreds of thousands of active duty personnel.

All conscripts serve for 2 years and perform the many lower skill tasks necessary for the functioning of any military force. To a large extent, the shortened conscription period is a probationary period to determine which recruits are suitable to become NCOs or, in considerably lesser numbers, to become officers.

As the PLA has become smaller, it has also become more technologically-sophisticated, requiring higher education and training standards for all personnel. The goal of the "Strategic Project for Talented People," initiated in August 2003, is to improve the quality of all personnel, but the project has a realistic timeframe for implementation throughout the remainder of this decade and all of the next.[2] The influx of new equipment into the force, particularly advanced electronics and communications equipment, and a new fighting doctrine introduced in 1999 affect the type and content of conscript and NCO training. Furthermore, fewer personnel with new equipment and doctrine have required changes in force structure as well as reform of the professional military education system. Each of these elements of PLA modernization has had an impact on the content and conduct of individual training.

DEFINITIONS

Individual training (*danbing xunlian*, 单兵训练) formally takes place during both induction (basic) training (*ruwu xunlian*, 入伍训练) and specialty training (*zhuanye xunlian*, 专业训练). General guidance is found in the Revised Military Service Regulations of 1999: "New recruits shall receive common basic education and training; specialist soldiers shall receive special technical training for 3 months or longer; and squad leaders shall receive training at training centers for 3 months or longer."[4] The PLA categorizes its overall training regimen into several levels consisting of:

- Common subject training (*gongtong kemu xunlian*, 共同科目训练);
- Specialty (or specialized) technical training (*zhuanye jishu xunlian*, 专业技术训练);
- Tactical training (*zhanshu xunlian*, 战术训练);
- Campaign training (*zhanyi xunlian*, 战役训练);
- Noncombat action training (*feizhanzheng xingdong xunlian*, 非战争行动训练, includes nontraditional security missions, such as anti-terrorism, disaster relief, internal security, peacekeeping, search and rescue, etc); and,
- Strategic problems research (*zhandou wenti yanjiu*, 战略问题研究).[3]

This formulation accurately recognizes that each level of training provides the foundation for the next higher level, with individual skills as the bedrock for all other training.

Common subject training occurs primarily during induction training, a period comparable to U.S. military basic training. Specialty technical training follows afterwards and can be compared to Military Occupational Specialty (MOS) training. Specialty technical training focuses on the theory and practice of the functioning, operation, maintenance, and repair of weapons and equipment.[5] Not all PLA conscripts receive specific specialty technical training, but it is a requirement for NCOs. Small units also conduct specialty technical training to ensure they have mastered the functional skills necessary to participate in larger operations. Tactical, campaign, nontraditional security, and strategic training are conducted by units and headquarters, all of which are dependent upon competent, properly trained individuals. After basic training, individuals improve and expand skills through personal study, training in garrison, and during unit field exercises. For example, a large proportion of what is referred to as "amphibious training" actually concentrates on individual skills like swimming and avoiding seasickness.

This chapter focuses only on common subject training and individual specialty technical training for conscripts and NCOs. In particular, it does *not* address the various types of unit training, especially unit training that takes place at the combined arms training bases (*hetong zhanshu xunlian jidi*, 合同战术训练基地) in each MR, amphibious training bases, or large "coordination zones" used for integrated joint training. The first section discusses the process of conscription and basic training and is followed by a brief examination of college students entering the PLA to become conscripts or NCOs. A discussion of the selection and training of NCOs follows. The next section of the chapter is devoted to the various bases in each service involved in specialty technical training for both conscripts and NCOs. The decentralized nature of individual training requires close attention by commanders and higher headquarters to assure that training quality is maintained and shortfalls corrected. The system described below is expected to continue to change as the PLA modernization program adapts to contemporary requirements.

CONSCRIPTION PROCESS

Around August or September of each year, elements of the General Staff Department (GSD) and General Political Department (GPD) consult with operational units to determine the number of conscripts needed for induction in the fall.[4] Conscription eligibility extends from ages 18 to 22 for males, with females to be inducted according to needs of the units. The minimum educational requirement is middle school graduation; students enrolled in full-time education programs may be deferred from conscription. Specific education requirements for induction and male/female and urban-rural ratios vary from year to year depending on social conditions and the needs of the PLA. According to *China's National Defense in 2004*, "Enlistment in peacetime usually takes place once a year," a statement that allows flexibility for additional conscription orders to be levied in times of emergency. Annual quota numbers include both PLA and People's

Armed Police (PAP) recruits and are estimated to amount to a total of around 500,000 personnel for both forces.[5]

The Central Military Commission (CMC) and State Council then jointly issue a "conscription order" to the MRs. Quotas are passed to Military Districts, which send specific requirements for numbers of conscripts to be inducted to the Military Subdistricts and local People's Armed Forces Departments (PAFD). Local PAFDs, which are manned by both active duty military and uniformed civilians working for the local governments, are responsible for enlisting the number of recruits necessary from their districts.[6] PAFD personnel also decide which new soldiers go into the PLA (Army, Navy, Air Force, or Second Artillery) or into the PAP. According to regulations, new recruits from a single district are sent at most to three separate division or brigade-level units. Some recruits may be assigned to units near their homes, but others are dispatched outside of their province so that every PLA and PAP unit is composed of soldiers from many parts of the country. Conscription expenses are shared between the official military budget and local government finances as "military service and conscription expenses."[7]

In 2007, the winter recruitment campaign was announced on September 7, with age limits focused between 18 and 20 for males, 18 and 19 for female high school graduates, and extending to 22 for men with higher education qualifications. An officer from the GSD said, "Higher standards will be imposed to new recruits so as to meet the challenges of the accelerated pace of Chinese military reform." Specifics standards were stated as "rural middle school graduates, urban junior college graduates, and vocational school graduates."[8] Thus, the goal is for urban male recruits to have at least a high school education (12 years), but preferably some junior college or technical training, and those from the countryside a middle school education (9 years). Preference is given to university students who seek to enlist voluntarily. The announcement recognized that higher educational standards were a goal that those who conduct conscription work should "try hard" (*jinliang*, 尽量) to attain; however, it also implies that meeting them will be difficult.

The PLA publicly recognized problems in bribery and quota manipulation during the 2007 fall conscription period. The GSD, GPD, and CMC's Discipline Inspection Commission issued a "Circular on Seriously and Earnestly Carrying Out the Work of Recruiting Soldiers Through Honest Means" that requires accountability and transparency in conscription work. Specifically, in an effort to combat bribery, no individual is allowed to have "the final say" on examining and approving new recruits. If recruits reach their training units and are found to have health or physical problems causing their discharge, then those who oversaw their conscription will be investigated. The circular also stipulated for military headquarters to set up mailboxes and telephone numbers for the public to report problems and voice complaints.[9] Besides unqualified personnel who have bribed their way *into* the military, others certainly have attempted to avoid conscription by feigning health problems or attempting to bribe government officials to keep them out. It is not known whether conscription quotas can officially be traded among PAFDs (so that one area's shortages can be made up from nearby locales with an abundance of volunteers), but the circular's requirement for transparency in quota numbers appears aimed to eliminate under-the-table deals brokered by PAFD personnel cooperating illegally among themselves.

Personnel who are selected or volunteer to serve as conscripts are notified around the beginning of November and undergo political evaluation and physical examinations, which now include tests for acquired immune deficiency syndrome (AIDS) and drug addiction. As of 2006, all recruits also receive psychological evaluations.[10] If recruits pass the screening process, in early December they are issued uniforms and bedding, and then travel to their assigned training units. Units receiving new soldiers establish reception committees to meet and escort the incoming recruits to their induction training locations. Considerable effort is expended to ensure the safety and comfort of recruits in this initial period, especially those assigned to remote or austere locations. For example, an adaptability base in Tibet was opened in 2006 so that new recruits can acclimate themselves during basic training before moving on to their duty stations at higher altitudes.[11]

CONSCRIPT TRAINING

Under the guidance of army-level headquarters, division and brigade-level units (as well as independent regiments) in each service establish temporary recruit basic training units, usually of regimental size, that operate out of "training centers" located in or near their garrison areas. (Many training centers are also used for other types of training after the new soldiers graduate from basic training.) Commanders and political officers are responsible for basic training to be conducted according to standards set by the GSD and supervise closely the activities of their subordinates. A training cadre of specially selected NCOs and junior officers is responsible for conducting instruction. Other members from the permanent unit assist the training cadre to provide logistic and administrative support to basic training. Recruits are organized into companies of about 100 personnel, further subdivided into platoons and squads.

Though much of the content of basic training is common throughout all PLA units, service and branch traditions and skills are emphasized as appropriate. Training begins around mid-December and lasts for up to 3 months until approximately February/March and/or around the Chinese New Year. Induction training is divided among military skill, political, and physical training.

During the induction training period, military skills training accounts for 24 training days, not to exceed 168 hours.[12] These numbers suggest a 7-hour training day (not including administrative time, such as equipment issue and meals, and physical training), which is divided between military and political training. According to regulations, induction training time is conducted at a ratio of 6:4 for military and political training.[13] (The percentage time spent in political training during basic training is higher than political training in operational units.) At this ratio, if military training accounts for a total of 24 days, then political training amounts to another 16 days. Thus, basic training lasts for about 40 training days, not including weekends and administration time, which takes it from mid-December to late February or early March.

Common subject military training includes basic knowledge and skills that all members of the PLA must master no matter what rank or service. Topics include military regulations (such as wearing of the uniform and military courtesies), marching and formation training, small arms operations and use, basic tactical movements (which likely vary among services), hygiene, first aid, etc. Political training includes subjects such as military discipline and law, ideology, and "the glorious traditions" of the PLA and specific unit histories. Physical training proceeds on a separate track throughout basic training and builds to a 5-kilometer run three times a week.[14] Daily training schedules vary classes among military, political, and physical training subjects.

Weekly training schedules are prepared at the training company level according to monthly guidance from regiment headquarters consistent with an overall plan from division or Army level. The *Staff Officer Guidebook on Peacetime Work* suggests:

> Training courses and times must be reasonably separated, and the training contents must be scientifically inserted and distributed in order to rationally arrange and thoroughly combine military training and political education, theoretical courses and operating courses, indoor courses and outdoor courses, and mental and physical training. One single course should not be taught for a long time, and one topic should not be dragged on till the end of the training.[15]

During basic training, conscripts are called "new soldiers" (*xinbing*, 新兵) and do not wear insignia of rank or cap insignia. No information on the "washout rate," or percentage of new soldiers who do not complete basic training, was uncovered during research. Upon completion of basic training, recruits pin on their rank (private second class) and insignia and take the "Soldier's Oath" pledging their allegiance to the Communist Party, the people, and the Army.

New soldiers are then integrated into operational units or may attend specialty training on a temporary duty basis. However, some "new soldiers" may be authorized to move through basic training faster than others.

COLLEGE STUDENTS ENTERING THE PLA

Since the turn of the century, the PLA has tried to attract more college educated people into its ranks, not only as officers but also as NCOs and conscripts. So far, the number of college students entering the military as privates is relatively small. According to a 2006 *Xinhua* report, "more than 10,000" college students have entered the Army in the 5 years this policy has been in effect.[16] Nonetheless, this trend appears to be on the rise, as 2,850 undergraduates from 73 institutions of higher learning in Beijing alone were reported to have volunteered for the Army in 2006.[17] In early 2007, the political commissar of the Shenyang Military Region Air Force Equipment Training Base stated that "university graduates account for 10 percent of new recruits" and that, overall, "the Air Force aircraft maintenance support department has recruited more than 500 university graduates." In previous years, college graduates made up less than one percent of new recruits in this high-technology specialty.[18]

Many of these students enter the military as undergraduates, serve for 2 years, and return to college after demobilization, often with their tuition paid by the PLA. In addition to patriotic reasons, students volunteer to join the Army as a break from their normal routine to "broaden their horizons," to develop discipline, and to help better determine their long-term interests (i.e., "to help find themselves").

Some college students enter the PLA as soldiers after graduation because of difficulties in finding civilian jobs. Prior to their enlistment, while in college, most students undergo some military training. If they paid attention at school and demonstrate proficiency in required tasks, recruits from colleges can skip parts of basic training. They then are able to move on to new subjects quicker than other recruits.[19] Because of their educational background, many college students are assigned to the more technical branches in the PLA Air Force or Second Artillery.

Graduates of institutions of higher learning are also sought out to enter the PLA directly as NCOs with the incentives of higher pay and not having to spend 2 years as privates. Many of these graduates have finished 2- and 3-year courses in civilian schools (respectively known as *zhongzhuan* (中专) "secondary technical degree," which is a high school equivalency degree in China, and *dazhuan* (大专) "senior technical degree," roughly equivalent to a vocational or associate's degree offered by a community college in the United States),[20] and are assigned as technical NCOs responsible for equipment repair and maintenance. Before entering units, they undergo a special basic training program to ensure they have the proper military skills to function in a unit.

The PLA considers personnel with 2- and 3-year secondary and senior technical degrees different from those with undergraduate college degrees. In early September 2007, *PLA Daily* reported that 30 NCOs, who had "already received full-time junior college education," were enrolled for the first time at the Second Artillery Qingzhou NCO School for a 2-year undergraduate program in missile testing and control. This pilot program is intended to allow NCOs to go "from junior college education to regular college education" in order "to accelerate cultivation of new type high-quality NCOs."[21]

Like the number of college students volunteering to become privates, the overall number of directly-recruited graduates from various types of institutions of higher learning who become NCOs appears to be small compared to the total number of NCOs in the force. NCOs with civilian college background account for perhaps only a few thousand among the hundreds of thousands of NCOs in the PLA. A *Xinhua* report from October 2004 stated "in 2003, the PLA recruited 630 NCOs directly from localities for the first time, and in 2004, it would recruit 1,064 NCOs—including 300 female NCOs—directly from localities."[24] In a later report, the same Shenyang Military Region Air Force Equipment Training Base that trains undergrads who volunteer to be privates was said to also provide initial training to college graduates who have joined to become NCOs. As of late 2005, this base had trained "over 150 college educated NCOs recruited directly from civilian life."[25] Such reporting strongly suggests that directly-recruited college graduate NCOs remain a small minority of the NCO corps.

NCO SELECTION AND TRAINING

The vast majority of NCOs are selected from conscripts who volunteer to extend their duty near the end of their second year of conscripted service.[26] An NCO candidate must submit a formal, written application and be recommended by his grassroots unit. NCO candidates are evaluated by the unit party branch and approved by regimental or brigade headquarters. According to regulations, NCO candidates "must have received training at a military training institution at or above the regimental level, or in a military academy or school. Priority shall be given to technological personnel who have received training at a military academy or school, a PLA general department, or a military training institution run by a major unit."[27] However, due to the 2-year conscription period, it appears that some of that training may occur after a candidate has been selected to become an NCO.

In order to raise the technical standards of the NCO corps and to achieve compatibility with civilian technical standards (as set by the Ministry of Labor and Social Security), after 2008 "a condition for selection as a noncommissioned officer will be that all types and all levels of NCO have received a relevant certificate of professional qualification."[28] Obtaining a professional skills qualification certificate will also assist soldiers in finding jobs after they separate from active service. The PLA has exerted considerable effort in training NCOs to this standard and according to *Xinhua*, since 1999, more than 300,000 NCOs have obtained professional certificates, increasing at a rate of 30,000 annually.[29] Moreover, NCOs are encouraged to concentrate in one profession but attain more than one skill, as captured by the slogan, "One Proficiency, Multiple Skills" (*yi zhuan duo neng*, 专多能). Accordingly, many NCOs may earn more than one professional certificate.

NCOs receive their requisite professional training by a variety of means: attendance at an NCO school or at an NCO course at an officer academy; at a training base run by a regiment or higher level organization; through off-site, remote distance education courses connected to PLA academies or civilian institutes of higher learning; or through on-the-job training within units. The clear preference is for formal attendance at an academy, university, or school for 2 or more years, but the reality of numbers of NCOs to be trained requires many to attend shorter periods of instruction at training bases. Duty performance, completion of educational programs (in residence or through correspondence), attaining professional certificates, awards, and achievements are all considered in deciding which NCOs are promoted to higher ranks.

Enlisted applicants seeking to attend PLA educational institutes are required to take nationwide college entrance exams. NCOs who have received the "PLA Outstanding Noncommissioned Officer Award First and Second Class" need not take the exam. NCOs who received "PLA Outstanding Noncommissioned Officer Award Third Class" receive 30 extra points on their score. In 2007, 35 PLA professional education institutions were programmed to admit 16,000 enlisted personnel as NCO cadets for 2- and 3-year courses of study, slightly above the 15,000 input for 2006. In 2006, that number was broken down as follows: about 6,000 personnel were enrolled in senior technical degree courses, with 60 percent of students from second-year conscripts and 40 percent as NCOs; of the 9,000 enrolled in secondary technical degree courses, 65 percent of students were second-year conscripts and 35 percent NCOs. While overall input numbers may be known, no statistics were found that revealed attrition or graduation rates for NCO students and schools.

Of the 35 PLA institutions that educate NCOs, six are NCO schools (*shiguan xuexiao*, 士官学校) and 29 are officer academies with NCO departments. The six NCO schools are divided among three in the Army and one each in the Navy, Air Force, and Second Artillery:

- Beijing Mechanics NCO School (*Beijing jixie shiguan xuexiao*, 北京机械士官学校)

- Wuhan Ordnance NCO School (*Wuhan junxie shiguan xuexiao*, 武汉军械士官学校)
- Xuanhua Communications NCO School (*Xuanhua tongxin shiguan xuexiao*, 宣化通信士官学校)
- Navy Bengbu NCO School (*Haijun Bengbu shiguan xuexiao*, 海军蚌埠士官学校)
- Air Force Dalian Communications NCO School (*Kongjun Dalian tongxin shiguan xuexiao*, 空军大连通信士官学校)
- Second Artillery Qingzhou NCO School (*Di er pao Qingzhou shiguan xuexiao*, 第二炮青州士官学校)

Space and the amount of data available preclude detailed descriptions of each NCO school, but, in general, every school offers a number of 2- and 3-year programs with core curriculum common to colleges anywhere in China, such as Chinese language, foreign languages (especially English), mathematics, physics, physical education, political education, etc. Specialties are appropriate for the type of school. For example, the Xuanhua Communications NCO School offers mobile communications, satellite communications, optical-fiber communications, and shortwave communications, while the Navy NCO School has 24 specialties in nine categories including chemical defense, communications, navigation, logistics, machinery, mechanical and electrical, and weapons.[30] Instructors have more educational and practical experience than in previous years, and many now go down to units to observe exercises. Schools incorporate into their curriculum classes on many of the new weapons and equipment that are being introduced into the force, so students can become familiar with them before arriving at their units. The use of many types of weapons and equipment simulators is widespread. Large sums of money have been spent to upgrade instructional equipment and facilities with computers, electronics, and internet access.

The number of students in the 2- and 3-year programs varies among schools, but probably averages several hundred per year, with one article reporting over 800 graduates from the Second Artillery NCO School in 2004. While in NCO schools, students do not use their previous military ranks; rather they are called "NCO cadets" (*shiguan xueyuan*, 士官学员) and wear cadet rank insignia (similar to officer cadets).

In reaction to complaints from units that many NCOs were unable to function in their jobs after graduation from professional military schools, for several years now practical work has been stressed in addition to theoretical studies. For example, in 2001 the Xuanhua Communications NCO School began a "2+1" program in which students attend 2 years in school and then spend another year in the field for practical training. In 2002, the Second Artillery NCO School restructured its curriculum to increase the amount of practical instruction and tactical training to consist of half of all courses by decreasing the total amount of course work by 20 percent.[31]

Along with technical and degree-producing programs, NCO schools also provide shorter-term rotational, specialty training sessions usually lasting from 1 to 3 months. Schools also have established working relationships with civilian universities and have set up long-distance learning courses for continuing education for troops in units. Short-term specialty classes are available online for soldiers in units, and recently full 2- and 3-year technical courses for online study have been created.[32]

Most of the 29 officer academies with NCO departments or classes (*shiguan ban*, 士官班) have been identified in the Chinese media. (See Appendix.) NCO cadet enrollment appears to be generally in the low hundreds (200 to less than 500 personnel) per academy per year. Not unexpectedly, officer academies have a large role in educating NCOs to perform functions formerly assigned to officers, such as mess officers, nurses, club managers (a duty under the supervision of the GPD), vehicle unit commanders, small boat commanders, PAFD management personnel, technicians, and, in the Navy, electronic countermeasures, land-based radar, sonar technology, and signals communication.[33]

The number of NCOs enrolled in PLA institutions for formal training does not meet the educational requirements for the entire NCO corps. Therefore, the PLA has turned to civilian universities and enterprises for help. Two examples out of Lanzhou MR probably are indicative of civil-military link-ups in other MRs. In the first instance, "five regular colleges, six research institutes and 15 production and maintenance and repair enterprises" in the region will:

- train 300 equipment "technical backbones" each year;
- accept 100 "equipment technical backbones" to factories and institutes to work with technical experts and learn from them each year; and,
- enroll 150 "information and equipment technical backbones" to receive intensified training in colleges.[34]

The "technical backbones" are mostly likely NCOs and perhaps some officers. This training probably will result in attendees obtaining professional skills qualification certificates in most cases and perhaps technical degrees in some cases. In another program, the civilian August 1st College of the China Central Radio and TV University (located in Beijing and under the supervision of the Ministry of Education) established 15 tutoring stations for remote education and vocational qualification training programs for 3,300 NCOs from a group army in the region.[35] The August 1st College also has a program for the Navy in which "any naval vessel with satellite digital receiving antenna and Inter Video Card can receive TV courses." The college offers courses in "580-odd specialties in 10 major disciplines, such as science, engineering, agriculture, medicine, literature and laws, hence an 'air university' at sea." Reportedly "nearly 1,000 sailors on some 100 surface vessels" are taking advantage of this program.[36] No details have been released about how the civilian educational programs that support the military are funded.

Even with civilian assistance, many NCOs likely do not yet have the opportunity to attend college to obtain a degree or obtain a professional certificate. Instead, much NCO individual specialty training takes place during short courses at the many military training bases that perform a number of functions in support of the PLA education and training system.

SPECIALTY TECHNICAL TRAINING

Individuals (conscripts, NCOs, and officers) and units receive specialty technical training which varies according to the service and types of units within each service. Methods to conduct specialty technical training include classroom lecture and study, individual practice, use of simulators, and team/crew work. Training is often "progressive," starting with simple basic tasks and building to larger, more complex operations moving from individual tasks to the integration of many individual functions within a unit as part of a combined arms team.

Specialty technical training may be conducted in units through on-the-job training, in formal schools and academies, and at a number of training bases (*xunlian jidi*, 训练基地) operated by units at and above regimental level and by individual services. Policies appear to vary among the services for which personnel get what type of specialty technical training. For example, according to *China's Navy 2007*, "now that conscripts serve for only 2 years, the PLA Navy (PLAN) elected to abolish technical training *for the majority of its conscripts*, starting with those who arrived in late 2002."[37] (Emphasis added.) On the other hand, it appears that many conscripts in the ground force still undergo specialty technical training at large training bases for varying lengths of time.

All units, no matter what type or service, require certain specialties to perform their military missions whatever they might be. For example, all units require clerks, cooks, wheeled vehicle drivers, mechanics, and communicators. Accordingly, the number of bases where these specialties are taught is large, and they are found in all parts of the country. On the other hand, there are fewer locations where the skills needed for airborne, amphibious, or ballistic missile operations are taught. Some specific skills necessary for functions within certain specialized units will be taught within the units themselves. Some low density skills for one service (such as the requirement for tank drivers in the PLAN marines) may be taught by training units in other services.

Each service operates a number of different types of training bases. In addition to specialty technical training for individuals, these bases may also be used for induction training, some small unit training, training competitions, and national defense student or reserve and militia training. The Army has the largest number of training bases for specialty technical training, with each MR having an assortment of large bases under MR control plus additional bases under group army or lower-level management.

In the ground force, the three main types of specialty technical training bases are Tank Crew Training Bases (*tanke cheng yuan xunlian jidi*, 坦克乘员训练基地), Comprehensive Training Bases (*zonghe xunlian jidi*, 综合训练基地), and Service Arms Training Bases (*bingzhong xunlian jidi*, 兵种训练基地).[38] Two unidentified training bases have also been noted in the PLA media, along with a Beijing MR NCO Communications Training Base (*Beijing junqu tongxin shiguan xunlian jidi*, 北京军区 通信士官训练基地), for a total of 14 various MR-level training bases for individual specialties (See Table 1).[39]

Initially, tank crew training bases (or regiments) were found in several, not all, MRs; new bases under MR supervision have been added as the PLA's educational and training requirements have changed. Analysis of Chinese media reports about individual bases indicates that, despite their names, these training bases provide instruction in multiple specialties and functions. Each training base has a number of subordinate training groups (*xunlian dadui*, 训练大队) or educational units (*jiao dao dui*, 教导队) staffed by both officers and NCOs responsible for instruction in a particular field.

Military Region	Tank Crew Training Base	Comprehensive Training Base	Service Arms Training Base	Unidentified Base/ New Speciality
Shenyang	Dalian, Liaonig	Dalian, Liaoning		
Beijing	Changzhi, Shanxi			
Lanzhou	Unknown			Unknown
Jinan	Unknown	Jinan, Shandong		
Nanjing	Zhenjiang, Jiangsu		Zhenjiang, Jiangsu	Zhangzhou, Fugian
Gaungzhou		Guilin, Guangxi	Guilin, Guangxi	
Chengdu			Sichuan	

**Table 1. Military Region-Level Ground Force
Training Bases
(With Locations When Known).**

As might be expected, class sizes, composition of students, frequency, and duration (some classes can last for an entire year) vary according to the different courses offered. The Beijing MR Tank Crew Training Base has been the subject of more reports than most training bases (and is likely to be the oldest Army specialty training base). The base trains soldiers from ground force armored and mechanized infantry units in the skills needed to become armored vehicle commanders, gunners, drivers, and mechanics. Some of its students also come from the marine armored force and the small armored vehicle contingent in the Air Force's airborne army. Courses offered include network communications, ballistics computers, navigation, laser recognition, and thermal imaging.[40] In 30 years of operation, this training base has trained over 66,000 personnel. In recent years, the base has greatly increased the use of simulators, allowing training time to be reduced by one-third.[41] The Chengdu MR does not have a Tank Crew Training Base, but its Service Arms Training Base is reported to have trained over 12,000 technical backbones in armored and engineer specialties in recent years. Guangzhou MR also lacks a Tank Crew Training Base, and its Service Arms Training Base is also reported to train armored personnel — in this case 40 reservists in a 1-month course.[42]

The PLA leadership has taken advantage of the downsizing of the professional military education system and the requirement for fewer officers to graduate from 4-year military academies to form new training bases. In particular, the former Guilin Army Academy was merged with a communications training group in February 2005 to form the Guangzhou MR Comprehensive Training Base.[43] Later in 2005, the former Army academies at Dalian and Jinan were closed, and new comprehensive training bases opened in their place.[44] More recently, in a slightly different development, the former PLA Physical Education Academy in Guangzhou has been transformed into the Comprehensive Military Physical Stamina Training Base subordinate to the GSD (*zongcan jun ti zonghe xunlian jidi*, 参军体综合训练基地). Over and above its training function, the base has established eight subordinate research centers with the mission "to optimize the physical stamina training of the frontline PLA troops."[45] The change in mission for these academies enabled their infrastructure and much of their faculty to be shifted to meet the contemporary needs of the service. Note that the Guangzhou Physical Stamina Training Base is different from the 14 MR-level training bases because of its relationship to the GSD and the presence of its research centers within its structure.

Numerous training bases run by group armies accommodate the large numbers of vehicle drivers, communications specialists, mechanics, and logistics personnel necessary to man units as they are "mechanized and informationalized" as part of the Revolution in Military Affairs with Chinese Characteristics. These lower level training bases also appear to play a significant part in providing the required squad leader courses to conscripts and NCOs.

Training bases in general seek to maximize efficiency and shorten the time students spend in specialty training. A good illustration is found at a drivers training group in the Beijing MR where a pilot "5-1>5" program for 756 drivers reduced instruction from 5 months to 4 months. Reportedly, better results were achieved by using simulation systems and decreasing theoretical teaching while increasing practice driving time.[46]

With fewer personnel, but often a greater need for technical specialists than the Army, the other services have correspondingly fewer specialty training bases. Moreover, many specialty training bases apparently are often used for new recruit training, too. *China's Navy 2007* identifies five technical training bases:

- The North Sea Fleet Training Base, located on Liugong Island (刘公岛) off the Shandong Peninsula near Weihai;
- The East Sea Fleet Training Base, located in Wusong (吴松), part of Shanghai Municipality;
- The South Sea Fleet Training Base, located near Dongguan (东莞), Guangdong Province;
- A Logistics Training Base; and,
- A Naval Aviation Training Base.[47]

The South Sea Fleet Training Base, also known as the Humen Shajiao Training Base (*Haijun Nanhai jiandui mou bu Humen Shajiao xunlian jidi*, 海军南海舰队某部虎门 沙角训练基地), is reported to train about 4,000 conscripts annually who spend half a year at the base in induction and specialty training before they are assigned to operational units. Since 2000, when complaints were received about the quality of the base's graduates, 41 out-of-date subjects were dropped and 17 new courses added, such as guided missile attack and aircraft warning radar operations. Instructor proficiency on new weapons has increased, and the base's teaching infrastructure improved.[48] The base also dispatches groups of instructors to ships in the fleet to provide on-site training to NCOs on various specialty subjects as requested by the units themselves.[49] Little detailed information is available about the other naval training bases, but the recent developments at the South Sea Fleet Training Base are consistent with PLA-wide training trends and are likely replicated to some degree at the other naval training bases.

As anomalies in their parent services, the marines in the Navy and the airborne army in the Air Force both run their own specialty training bases, which appear to be collocated with or near the garrisons of their parent operational units. Due to the size of these forces, the scale of their specialty training bases is about the same as a group army training base. As mentioned earlier, both marine and airborne forces take advantage of army specialty training for their armored troops. After basic training, conscripts move directly into specialized training appropriate for their unit. For example, by early March 2007, new airborne soldiers, who entered service in December 2006, were reported making their first parachute jump as part of an operational unit.[54]

With a few exceptions, other than location data for the large Air Force and Second Artillery specialty training bases, research uncovered little detailed information about their operations, though most appear to conduct both basic and specialty training. In addition to these bases, smaller training bases and units have been established, especially in the Air Force for driver and communications training. The 2006 *Directory of PRC Military Personalities* identifies the following Air Force training bases:

- Air Force Radar Training Base,
- Air Force Training Base, Beijing,
- Beijing MR Air Force Airman Training Base, Langyashan, Hebei,
- Beijing MR Air Force Air Armament Technical Corps Training Base (*Bei kong mou zhuangbei jishu bing xunlian jidi*, 北空某装备技术兵训练基地),
- Guangzhou MR Air Force Equipment Training Base, Liuzhou, Guangxi,
- Jinan MR Air Force Training Base, Xuzhou, Jiangsu,
- Lanzhou MR Air Force Airman Training Base, and
- Shenyang MR Air Force Equipment Training Base (*Sheng kong mou zhuangbei xunlian jidi*, 沈空某装备训练基地), Gongzhuling, Jilin.[55]

And the following two Second Artillery training bases:

- Testing and Training Team, Base 53 and
- Training Base, Baishan, Jilin.[56]

Even with the extensive array of specialty training

bases in the PLA, an unknown percentage of personnel probably receive a lot of specialist training in operational units through self study, correspondence courses (including online programs), and on-the-job training where junior people learn while working under the tutelage of more experienced personnel.

The system of individual training will continue to evolve as the mix of conscripts, NCOs, and officers changes; new equipment enters the field; and the force structure is modified. From an outside perspective, the question of whether the 2-year conscription period has proved to be effective still has not been answered completely. Does 2 years allow enough time for conscripts to be trained so that they can perform something other than relatively simple, labor-intensive tasks when they are finally assigned to units?

CONCLUSIONS AND MORE QUESTIONS

In researching this chapter, no single Chinese source outlined the totality of the training system for conscripts and NCOs. Many definitions and reports were confusing, contradictory, or incomplete. Therefore, the system presented above is a best guess approximation based on numerous snapshots from various angles and sources — a situation not unfamiliar to much PLA analysis. As more data become available, perhaps additional insights will be garnered. Until then, a few conclusions and questions are offered.

The PLA is challenged to attract new recruits with mental and physical skills appropriate for its modernized force structure. As seen above, some young Chinese volunteer for service, but others still must be conscripted to serve. No statistics, however, were uncovered during research indicating the percentage of volunteers versus involuntary conscripts. While there appears to be some enthusiasm for military service among Chinese youth, that spirit is certainly not universal. At this time, it is not possible to say how much of the PLA is composed of true volunteers and how much is still a conscript army.

The Chinese military is attempting to make itself more attractive to high school and technical school graduates and college students. Recent pay increases and competition for civilian employment may make joining the PLA attractive to some students who might have looked elsewhere in previous years. But the number of college students entering the enlisted force is still only a small percentage of the entire force and likely to stay that way for many years.

The PLA therefore must look within itself to educate and train the majority of its conscripts and NCOs in the fields necessary to operate a modern military. The emphasis on obtaining professional certificates helps standardize and evaluate levels of technical training, but an over-emphasis on producing professional certificates may lead to the temptation to "teach the test" and inhibit innovation among students and faculty—just at the time the PLA is trying to promote greater innovation in its soldiers.

Some of more educated recruits, especially those from cities, are likely to be less physically fit and disciplined than necessary for a military career. *China Youth News* reported that "not a few" new recruits at a Shenyang training unit had difficulty carrying their equipment the 500 to 1,500 meters to their quarters, causing the cadre to complain about their physical fitness.[57] A *PLA Daily* article noted that some of more educated, older city youth also "refuse to obey orders of senior cadres because they feel superior in terms of age, seniority, and experience," while the less educated recruits "find it more difficult to grasp political education classes when compared to their counterparts who have received better education and have knowledge of national defense."[58] The article went on to describe a company commander who expressed concern that such "individual differences" have the potential to trigger conflict among new soldiers. Such problems are not unique to China but present PLA leaders with different challenges than they faced a generation ago.

An important consequence of the PLA's training system that has not been seen addressed in the PLA literature is the impact of new recruit and individual specialty training on unit manning and readiness levels. While a portion of a unit's officers and NCOs are training recruits from December to March, they are not available for other training in the unit (just as the unit itself is missing half of its conscripts!). Yet some unit training, especially winter field training, is reported to take place during these months. Do units go to the field at partial strength during this period, say with two instead of three regiments in a division present for training? Likewise, personnel in specialty training courses away from their home unit also are not available for unit training. How do units compensate for the functions these soldiers are supposed to perform in their absence?

Seven years after cutting the conscription period to 2 years and increasing the percentage of NCOs, the PLA is still trying to find the most effective means of training the individuals so they best can be integrated into their units. New facilities and infrastructure, electronics, and simulators help, but they all cost money. New advanced weapons and equipment also cost more to maintain and operate than the weapons of the past. Even if the PLA were to undergo future reductions in personnel levels, as standards for training and education rise, the cost of preparing the force for its deterrent, nontraditional security, and warfighting missions can be expected to continue to increase throughout the decades-long execution period of the "Strategic Project for Talented People."

APPENDIX

PLA OFFICER ACADEMIES IDENTIFIED WITH NONCOMMISSIONED OFFICER DEPARTMENTS OR CLASSES

Chongqing Communications Academy

Jinan Army Academy (specializing in training mess noncommissioned officers (NCOs), with period of instruction decreased from 3 to 2 years)

Shijiazhuang Army Academy

Xian Army Academy (training communications NCOs)

Artillery Academy (Nanjing Branch)

Art Academy (specializing in training club managers — similar courses for club managers are also conducted at the Dalian and Beijing NCO schools)

Logistics Engineering Academy

Military Economics Academy (Xiangfan Branch, specializing in training mess NCOs and cooks)

Army Zhenjiang Boat Academy

Fourth Military Medical University

Bethune Military Medical College

Armament Command and Technology Academy

Armored Force Technical Academy

Dalian Navy Vessel Academy

Naval Engineering University

Naval Service Arms Command Academy

Navy Submarine Academy

Navy Logistics Academy

Naval Aviation Engineering Academy[59]

ENDNOTES - CHAPTER 4

1. "Sergeants With Modern Professional Skills Take on Bigger Role in Chinese Army," *Xinhua*, July 15, 2007, *news.xinhuanet.com/english/2007-07/15/content_6378065.htm*. A rough guess would put the total number of conscripts and NCOs in the PLA between 1.2 million and 1.6 million. The ratio of conscripts to NCO to officers/uniformed civilians will vary from service to service and among the various types of units in each service, with higher technology units generally having a larger percentage of NCOs and officers than lower tech units.

2. For a description of the "Strategic Project for Talented People," see *China's National Defense in 2004*.

3. "New Revised Military Service Regulations," *Beijing Xinhua Domestic Service* (in Chinese), July 11, 1999, in Open Source Center (OSC) OW2807113499.

4. Zhang Yongyi, ed., James A. Bellacqua, trans., *The Science of PLA Navy Military Training*, Beijing: Academy of Military Science (AMS) Press, 2006, pp. 240-252.

5. The definition and discussion of specialty technical training is based on definitions found in *PLA Military Dictionary* (*Zhongguo Renmin Jiefangjun junyu* [中国人民解放军军语]), Beijing: Academy of Military Science (AMS) Press, 1997, p. 176; and *Soldiers Practical Dictionary* (*Shiguan shiyong cidian* [士兵实用辞典]), James A. Bellacqua, trans., Beijing: Academy of Military Science (AMS) Press, May 2005, p. 115.

6. Conscription procedures are extracted from "PRC: Full Text of Conscription Work Regulations for Military," *Central People's Government of the People's Republic of China*, September 1, 2005, in OSC CPP20061013325003; Dennis J. Blasko, *The Chinese Army Today: Tradition and Transformation for the 21st Century*, London: Routledge, 2006, pp. 49-52; and Office of Naval Intelligence, *China's Navy 2007*, pp. 74-80. For an excellent discussion of current problems regarding conscription, see Sijin Cheng, "The Challenge of Conscription in an Era of Social Change," in David M. Finkelstein and Kristen Gunness, eds., *Civil-Military Relations in Today's China Swimming in a New Sea*, Armonk, NY: M. E. Sharpe, 2007, pp. 235-254.

7. The number of conscripts inducted each year is my own estimate based on the publicly announced size of the PLA and PAP. This number is likely to change as the PLA force structure is modified. My guess is only a ballpark figure and may be off by 100,000 conscripts either way.

8. See *China's National Defense in 2006* for the most complete Chinese-source description of the duties and composition of local PAFDs.

9. "PRC: Full Text of Conscription Work Regulations for Military," Article 45. A significant percentage of these costs are captured in the salaries for the grassroots PAFD personnel, which are paid by local governments.

10. "PLA Starts Winter Recruitment Introducing Psychological Tests for First Time," *Xinhua* (Internet Version), September 7, 2007, in OSC CPP20070907968165; and "Quan guo zheng bing gongzuo dianshi dianhua huiyi zhaokai anpai bushu 2007 nian dongji zheng bing gongzuo" ("全国征兵工作电视电话会议召开安排部署 2007 年冬季征兵 工作, National Conscription Work Teleconference Begins, Prepares 2007 Winter Conscription Work"), *PLA Daily*, September 7, 2007, *www.chinamil.com.cn/site1/zbxl/2007-09/07/content_942419.htm*.

11. "PLA Circular Addresses Misdeeds in Military Recruitment, Seeks Public Oversight," *Jiefangjun Bao* (Internet Version), November 8, 2007, in OSC CPP20071109710007; and "China's PLA prevents illegal recruitment and ineligible recruits," in *PLA Daily*, November 12, 2007, *english.chinamil.com.cn/site2/news-channels/2007-11/12/content_1014968.htm*.

12. "Newly Enrolled Serviceperson's Educational Level and Physical Quality Rise Significantly," *Jiefangjun Bao* (Internet Version), December 19, 2006, in OSC CPP20061223702059; and "Psychological test first introduced in military academy enrollment," in *PLA Daily*, May 28, 2007, *english.chinamil.com.cn/site2/news-channels/2007-05/28/content_828850.htm*. The PLA had experimented with psychological evaluations for several years prior to formal widespread implementation.

13. "Summary: PLA's Highest Altitude Recruit Transit Base Built in Lhasa," *Jiefangjun Bao* (in Chinese), December 9, 2006, p. 1, in OSC CPP20061212715027; and "China: PLA Establishes New Adaptability Training Base in Tibet," *Xinhua Domestic Service* (Internet Version), November 13, 2006, in OSC CPP20061113702003.

14. *Soldiers Practical Dictionary*, p. 9.

15. "Zhongguo Renmin Jiefangjun sixiang zhengzhi jiaoyu dagang (shixing)" [中国人民解放军思想政治 教育大纲（试行）] ("PLA Ideological and Political Education Program"), *Jiefangjun Bao* (Internet Version), January 23, 2007, *www.chinamil.com.cn/ site1/xwpdxw/2007-01/23/content_713726.htm*.

16. CCTV, "'Focus' Program on Red Army Division Under Jinan Military Region," *CCTV WWW-Text* (in Chinese), July 16, 2007, in OSC CPP20070717038003.

17. Excerpt of "PLA Guidebook on Political Officers' Peacetime Work," *Canmou Junguan Pinshi Gongzuo* (in Chinese), April 1, 2002, pp. 1-174, in OSC CPP20060309320001.

18. "China Daily Article Says Increasing Number of College Students Joining Military," *China Daily* (in English), November 30, 2006, in OSC CPP20061130053019.

19. "3,000 undergraduates in Beijing sign up for the Army," in *PLA Daily Online*, November 14, 2006. Beijing is known, however, for its large concentration of colleges and universities, so this number is an aberration compared to other provincial-level governments.

20. "Over 500 College Grads Enrolled in Jet Fighter Ground Maintenance Training," *Jiefangjun Bao* (Internet Version), January 8, 2007, in OSC CPP20070109715012; and "Summary: University Graduates Support Military Aircraft Maintenance," *Jiefangjun Bao* (in Chinese), January 7, 2007, p. 1, in OSC CPP20070108715025.

21. "College Grads Proved Quick Learners in Training of PLA Second Artillery Corps," *Jiefangjun Bao* (Internet Version), January 13, 2007, in OSC CPP20070113716002; and "Over 500

College Grads Enrolled in Jet Fighter Ground Maintenance Training," *Jiefangjun Bao* (Internet Version), January 8, 2007, in OSC CPP20070109715012.

22. Office of Naval Intelligence, *China's Navy 2007*, p. 65.

23. "PLA's first undergraduate course for NCOs opens in Qingzhou ," *PLA Daily Online*, September 5, 2007, *english.chinamil. com.cn/site2/news-channels/2007-09/05/content_940720.htm*.

24. This Xinhua report is found in "Highlights: PRC Military's Domestic, International Affairs, 8 Aug – 28 Oct 04," *China – FBIS Report* (in Chinese), October 28, 2004, OSC, trans. Other reports suggest that experimentation with direct recruiting of college graduates to become NCOs started in 2001 or 2002.

25. "Non-commissioned Officers Assigned Important Tasks at Shenyang MR Air Base," *Jiefangjun Bao*, December 26, 2005, p. 1, in OSC CPP20051226502014.

26. NCO selection procedures and requirements are found in "PLA Regulations for Managing Noncommissioned Officers," *Jiefangjun Bao* (in Chinese), May 23, 2001, p. 2, in OSC CPP20010523000055.

27. *Ibid.*

28. "Selection Criteria for PLA Noncommissioned Officers to be Tightened Beyond 2008," *Jiefangjun Bao* (in Chinese), July 22, 2006, p. 1, in OSC CPP20060722708018.

29. "Sergeants With Modern Professional Skills Take on Bigger Role in Chinese Army."

30. "Summary: PLA Academies, Schools Admit Award-Winning Noncommissioned Officers," *Jiefangjun Bao* (in Chinese), June 6, 2007, p. 1, in OSC CPP20070612711005; and "Quan jun qiuji shiguan xueyuan zhao kao 6 yue jinxing yuji zhaosheng 15000 ren" (全军秋季士官学员招考6月进行 预计招生15000人) ("Army NCO autumn trainees recruited in June; 15,000 expected to enroll"), *PLA Daily*, March 30, 2006, *www.pladaily.com.cn/site1/ images/2006-03/30/jfjb01b330b.PDF*. In 2006, another 5,000 enlisted

personnel were selected to attend PLA officer academies, see "Enrollment of cadets from among soldiers wraps up," *PLA Daily*, August 3, 2006, *english.chinamil.com.cn/site2/news-channels/2006-08/03/content_544859.htm*.

31. Office of Naval Intelligence, *China's Navy 2007*, p. 83-4.

32. "Di er pao bing Qingzhou shiguan xuexiao shenhua jiaoxue gaige peiyang rencai" (第二炮兵青州士官 学校深化教学改革培养人才) ("Second Artillery Qingzhou NCO School Deepens Educational Reform and Training Personnel"), *Xinhua* (Internet Version), November 8, 2004, *news.xinhuanet.com/mil/2004-11/08/content_2191277.htm*.

33. "Zhongguo jundui kaishi shishi shiguan daxue zhuanke "2+1" peixun moshi 中国军队开始实施士官 大学专科"2+1"培训模式" ("Chinese Units Begin Implementation of NCO University Specialized '2+1' Training Model"), *Chinanews.com*, July 10, 2003, *www.chinanews.com/n/2003-07-10/26/322835.html*.

34. "China: One NCO Academy of PLA 2nd Artillery Carries Out Teaching Reform," *Jiefangjun Bao* (in Chinese), August 26, 2002, p. 8, in OSC CPP20020826000046.

35. "Summary: Armed Forces Schools Nationwide Admit 16,000 Soldiers As Cadets," *Jiefangjun Bao* (in Chinese), July 22, 2007, p. 1, in OSC CPP20070801711003.

36. "Wo jun shiguan zhidu gaige jinru shizhixing jieduan" (我军士官制度改革进入实质性阶段) ("PLA NCO System Reform Enters Substantive Phase"), *People's Daily*, March 27, 2004, *www.people.com.cn/GB/paper464/11645/1049681.html*; and Office of Naval Intelligence, *China's Navy 2007*, p. 84. Since officer academies already had courses in these fields, switching to NCOs as students should not be a difficult transition.

37. "Army-Civilian Technical Personnel Training Cooperation Network Starts Operation in Lanzhou MAC," *Jiefangjun Bao* (Internet Version), August 27, 2007, in OSC CPP20070827702002.

38. "Group Army of Lanzhou MAC Builds Up Remote Education Platform for NCOs," *Jiefangjun Bao* (Internet Version), March 15, 2007, in OSC CPP20070316715002.

39. "August 1 College Transmits Teaching Resources by Way of 'Blue Network Project,'" *Jiefangjun Bao* (Internet Version) September 4, 2007, in OSC CPP20070904702011.

40. Office of Naval Intelligence, *China's Navy 2007*, p. 79. Nonetheless, as will be illustrated later in the discussion about the South Sea Fleet Training Base, a number of Navy conscripts still undergo some degree of specialty training.

41. These bases are included in the *Directory of PRC Military Personalities*, October 2006. Chinese sources usually use the following format when referring to these bases: name of Military Region; *mou* (某 "a certain"); and type of training base, such as *Beijing junqu tanke cheng yuan xunlian jidi* (北京军区某坦克乘员训练基地), *Shenyang junqu mou zonghe xunlian jidi* (沈阳军区某综合训练基地), or *Chengdu junqu mou bingzhong xunlian jidi* (成都军区某兵种训练基地). Sometimes the city name may be used instead of the Military Region and in some cases the *mou* (某) is not present.

42. Although bases in other regions train communications NCOs, no other specific NCO communications training base has been noted. The number of headquarters in Beijing probably necessitates a unique communications school near the capital.

43. "6.6 wan yu ming xin xing zhuang jia bing huoyue san jun budui" (6.6万余名新型装甲兵活跃 三军部队) ("More Than 66,000 New Armored Personnel Invigorate Tri-Service Unit"), *PLA Daily*, April 27, 2006, *www.chinamil.com.cn/site1/xwpdxw/2006-04/27/content_464711.htm*.

44. "Zhongguo lujun tanke cheng yuan mo ni fangzhen xunlian jidi jie mi" (中国陆军坦克乘员模拟仿真 训练基地揭秘) ("Chinese Army Tank Crew Simulation Training Base Unlocks Secrets"), *Sina News*, January 20, 2006, *mil.news.sina.com.cn/p/2006-01-20/0730345679.html*.

45. "'Suoding' di yi zhanchang'" (锁定'第一战场) ("Lock in 'The First Battle'"), *PLA Pictorial* 4A, 2007, *www.plapic.com/txt/200704a/20070405-2a.htm*.

46. "Guangzhou junqu 'Y' zifang zhen juan qi 'suo jia xuanfeng'" (广州军区'Y'字方阵卷起'铁甲旋风') ("Guangzhou Military Region 'Y' Formation Creates an 'Armored Whirlwind'"), in *PLA Daily*, October 2, 2006, *military.people.com.cn/GB/1076/52980/4883987. html*. Here, "'Y' Formation" refers to a PLA reserve unit.

47. "Guangzhou junqu zonghe xunlian jidi chengli Guilin lu yuan wancheng shiming" (广州军区综合训练 基地成立 桂林陆院 完成使命) ("Guangzhou Military Region Comprehensive Training Base Established, Guilin Army Academy Mission Accomplished"), *Xinhua*, February 4, 2005, *www.gx.xinhuanet.com/dtzx/2005-02/04/ content_3689013.htm*.

48. Compare the *Directory of PRC Military Personalities*, October 2004, p.279, with the *Directory of PRC Military Personalities*, October 2005, p. 266.

49. "Summary: PLA Military Physical Stamina Training Base Pursues Training Research," *Jiefangjun Bao*, August 6, 2007, p. 1, in OSC CPP20070817711005.

50. "PLA Driver Training Reformed to Maximize Practical Lessons, Troops Taught," *Jiefangjun Bao* (Internet Version), July 19, 2006, in OSC CPP20060720720001.

51. Office of Naval Intelligence, *China's Navy 2007*, pp. 79-80.

52. "Nanhai jiandui mou xunlian jidi chuang xin rencai peiyang moshi jishi" (南海舰队某训练基地创新人才培养模式纪事) ("Chronicle of a South Sea Fleet Training Base Blazing New Trails in Personnel Training"), in *PLA Daily Online*, November 28, 2006, *www.chinamil.com.cn/site1/xwpdxw/2006-11/28/content_659663.htm*.

53. "Summary: PLA Navy Training Base Train Crew Members Aboard Warships," *Jiefangjun Bao* (in Chinese), May 11, 2007, p. 2, in OSC CPP20070514711004.

54. "Parachute blossoming in the sky," *PLA Daily*, March 14, 2007, *english.chinamil.com.cn/site2/news-channels/2007-03/14/ content_762758.htm*.

55. *Directory of PRC Military Personalities*, October 2006, pp. 53-66. Note the *Directory* does not specifically identify the Shenyang

MR Air Force Training Base as an equipment training base; however, there are multiple references to it as such in the Chinese media.

56. *Ibid.*, pp. 74, 77. Some of the Air Force or Second Artillery training bases included in these lists may be used for unit training, not individual training.

57. "Jiefangjun xin bing tizhi cha shi zhan yanlian guanjian shike diao lianzi" (解放军新兵体质差实战演练 关键时刻掉链子) ("PLA Recruits' Physical Ability Not Up to Actual Combat Training, Drop the Ball at a Critical Juncture"), *China Youth News*, April 30, 2007, *mil.qianlong.com/4919/2007/04/30/198@3818790. htm.*

58. "Summary: JFJB: Shenyang Air Force Training Base New Recruit Management Challenges," *Jiefangjun Bao* (in Chinese), March 1, 2007, p. 3, in OSC CPP20070302715031.

59. The six PLA Navy academies with NCO programs are found at Office of Naval Intelligence, *China's Navy 2007*, p. 83.

CHAPTER 5

BUILDING THE FIGHTING STRENGTH: PLA OFFICER ACCESSION, EDUCATION, TRAINING, AND UTILIZATION

John F. Corbett, Jr.
Edward C. O'Dowd,
David D. Chen

INTRODUCTION

The Chinese People's Liberation Army (PLA) recognizes that the human leadership element is a critical part of its ongoing modernization process. As then Chairman of the Central Military Commission (CMC) Jiang Zemin stated in a 2003 speech commemorating the 50th anniversary of the National University of Defense Technology:

> The key to strengthening national defense and military modernization is fostering and bringing up a large batch of high quality, new-model, talented military personnel, and vigorously increasing the ability to make innovations in science and technology. We must grasp these two aspects as the primary responsibility of military academies, properly grasp the development trends of modern technology and the development patterns of military education, diligently have the military academies succeed in becoming the cradles for developing high quality, talented military personnel — the foundations of new high technology and military theory innovation.[1]

To this end, the PLA has invested in a series of programs to build a military officers (cadre) corps more capable and more highly educated than the officers of today's PLA. To do this, the PLA has reformed its accession, education, training, and officer utilization policies in recent years. It has been consolidating and closing down military academies, while simultaneously expanding the role of civilian universities in the process of PLA officer accession.[2] Within the framework laid out by PLA leadership, there has developed a state of open experimentation, by academies and the armed services, for developing multiple paths of accession into the PLA officer corps. This chapter will examine the PLA's officer accession programs in an effort to understand the PLA's officer accession objectives, the sources and process for recruiting new officers, the entry-level officer education structure, and the contents of its training programs. The chapter will also identify changes in policies associated with new officer accession.

OFFICER ACCESSION AND SOURCES OF PROSPECTIVE OFFICERS

Prior to 1978, most PLA cadre had little formal or military education. Many senior officers were of the age where guerrilla warfare experience was the greatest part of their military education. Intermediate grade officers had either little education beyond lower-middle (junior high) school, or were of the generation of the Cultural Revolution whose studies had been interrupted.[3] However, since 1978, the PLA has made revolutionary changes in its officer education programs, a revolution predicated on establishing modern educational requirements for PLA officers in contrast to the earlier, largely ideological-based standards. During the course of two decades of consolidating and improving the quality of military schools, carrying out force reductions of 1,700,000 personnel—a large portion of whom were officers—and establishing new educational requirements for promotion, the PLA has made great progress in reforming the officer education system.[4]

However, the PLA leadership has recognized the continuing, if not growing, need for technically proficient and academically credentialed officers. The PLA leadership also has recognized that the capacity of the military academies—the traditional source of new officers for the PLA—to produce qualified leaders is limited. This has led the PLA to experiment with innovative methods of exploiting civilian institutions of higher learning and recruiting civilian graduates into the PLA officer corps. Combined with the military academies, the civilian university-educated military cadre offer fresh infusions of intellectual rigor and technical proficiency intended to improve a still-educationally deficient military force.[5]

Today, there are two major sources of new officers for the PLA: those who graduate from the PLA military academy system, the traditional way; and those who enter the officer corps directly from civilian universities, either as direct appointments recruited for a certain specialty and needs of the PLA, or as graduates who participated in the "National Defense Student" (*guofang sheng*, 国防生) Program. Current policies on recruiting from civilian universities are authorized under the "Decision on Establishing a Military Cadre Training System Relying on General High Level Education" issued by the State Council and the Central Military Commission (CMC) on June 23, 2000.[6] A General Political Department (GPD) official pointed out the inadequacy of the military school system as the sole source of new officers in meeting

PLA modernization requirements and, thus, the need to recruit from civilian universities:

> Solely relying on cultivation by military academies already cannot satisfy the requirements for high quality talent among the troops. We must search out new avenues, and widen the pathways for cultivation. Fully utilizing the talent resources and knowledge superiority of general high-level institutions to cultivate military cadres is the necessary choice for accelerating our army's high quality cadre corps development.[7]

Previously, a third source of new officers was via the traditional method of promoting enlisted personnel "up from the ranks" directly into the officers corps without a college education.[8] It is difficult to determine numbers of new officers from this channel but, given the emphasis on college degrees for officers, it is likely to be approaching or at nil. In fact, some press reporting asserts that this method has not been in practice since 2001.[9] The current system is set up to select candidates for the military academies from among younger enlisted personnel.

NUMBERS OF NEW OFFICERS

The PLA does not provide precise numbers, but estimates based on available reporting suggest that approximately half of new PLA officers now come from PLA academies and half from civilian universities. The PLA reported that in 2006, 30 PLA academies and 20 People's Armed Police (PAP) academies enrolled over 10,000 senior middle (high) school graduates.[10] In addition, in 2006, approximately 5,000 PLA enlisted personnel, including 200 females, passed standardized entrance examinations and were enrolled in PLA academies.[11] At the same time, "over 11,000 National Defense Students graduating from senior middle schools" were enrolled in "112 ordinary universities and colleges" under contract with the PLA.[12] In addition, there are an unknown number of civilian graduates who join the PLA without having gone through the National Defense Student Program. Current numbers are not available but there are some past examples. For example, the PLA Air Force newspaper, *Kongjun Bao*, reported in 2002 that 2,079 college graduates entered the Air Force directly.[13] *Jiefangjun Bao* in 2000 reported, "Since the 14th CPC National [Party] Congress, the PLA has recruited 36,577 regular college graduates, of them 2,740 or 7.5 percent are graduates of postgraduate schools and 30,101 or 82.3 percent are graduates of undergraduate schools."[14] Over this period of 13 years, nearly 3,000 college graduates per year entered the PLA directly from civilian universities. The trend is on the rise as the PLA works to meet the increasing technological needs of all the PLA services and branches. Barring disproportionate attrition, a majority, perhaps as many as 60 percent, of the cohort of incoming officers likely will have graduated from civilian institutions by 2010.[15] Based on these generalized estimates, the PLA is capable of producing approximately 29,000 new officers annually, entering the PLA to support a force of about 2.3 million personnel.[16]

30 PLA and 20 PAP Universities	10,000 high school graduates enrolled 5,000 PLA enlisted personnel enrolled
National Defense Student Program	11,000 high school graduated enrolled
Civilian University Recruits	3,000 per year since 1990
Total Estimate	29,000 new officer candidates per year

Table 1. Numbers of New Officer Candidates Per Year.

Clearly the PLA has made a vigorous effort to improve the academic preparation of its rising officer corps. As already pointed out, the practice of sending serving enlisted personnel through the military academies in order to become officers has all but displaced the traditional PLA method of "promoting officers directly from the ranks."[17] In 1980, less than 10 percent of all PLA officers had a technical college degree. By 1998, most PLA officers had a degree from a technical college, and the trend towards increased tertiary education continues today.[18] Unlike the current group of senior PLA leaders, who generally only graduated from training courses, the PLA leaders of the future will have baccalaureate degrees from the military academies or 4-year civilian universities through the National Defense Student Program.

Military Academies.

PLA-run military schools, universities, and academies are the primary educational institutions for training new officers although the role of civilian universities is increasing. As recently as 2003, there were 95 PLA schools, with more than half providing entry-level officer training.[19] As part of the reform process seeking to reduce excess capacity and eliminate redundant programs, a number of schools have been closed, consolidated, or turned over to civilian authorities. The PLA now has 67 military educational institutions split between institutions that confer academic credentials and schools that conduct pre-assignment training. The first group refers to those schools providing undergraduate education for pre-commission officers and graduate education for officers, while "pre-assignment training" refers to the professional military education and training conducted for officers and noncommissioned officers (NCOs) at entry, intermediate, and advanced-level schools in preparation for upcoming assignments throughout the course of their careers.

According to the 2004 and 2006 White Papers entitled *China's National Defense*, the PLA is shifting the emphasis of the military education system towards pre-assignment training, "as the main form."[20] The shift of resources to emphasize pre-assignment training associated with ongoing professional development of officers to prepare for their next higher level of responsibility explains, in part, the necessity of tapping the civilian university education system to supplement military academies "as the primary source for new" officers. This shift has coincided with the increase in state-backed programs geared to investing in and developing the civilian education system, as well as with the massive growth in market demand for higher education.

The military academies that train new officers continue to draw their students from the ranks of military officers (without degrees), active duty servicemen—mainly enlisted personnel, and students from civilian middle schools, high schools, and colleges.[21] The entrance process for the PLA's military academies begins with a battery of tests that enable the selection officers to sort the applicants. Applicants must undergo a political review, physical examinations, and entrance tests.[22] In 2006, the enlisted entrance examination in Lanzhou Military Region (MR) consisted of six subjects: language (150 points), mathematics (150 points), English (100 points), politics (80 points), physics (60 points), and chemistry (60 points).[23]

The political review includes basic elements such as checking the applicant's criminal record and school disciplinary record. The applicant cannot be "politically and ideologically backward," and cannot have "express[ed] discontent with the party's current policies."[24] Not only does the applicant have to pass political muster, his "family members and close relatives" must also have clean political and personal records.[25]

The physical exam covers external and internal medical examinations. Additionally, there are ear, nose, and throat; ophthalmology; oral; gynecology; and psychological tests.

The psychological battery includes a general aptitude test to evaluate the candidate's written and mathematical abilities, as well as other tests. The second part of the psychological evaluation involves passing a Chinese equivalent of the Myers-Briggs Type Indicator (MBTI) personality test. If the scores are too strongly skewed towards certain personality types, he or she must undergo "discussions" about the makeup of their character.[26]

Enlisted personnel must pass military and literacy tests. Those candidates who do not pass the examinations on the first try must be retested. When the applicants have successfully passed all the tests, they are admitted to student status and sworn into the PLA.[27]

The political department of the military academy is responsible for organizing the admission procedures for the incoming students. The administrative affairs department of the academy has the responsibility for the admissions process. The General Political Department (GPD) and the General Staff Department (GSD) promulgate the rules and regulations for the accession procedures. These two departments also establish an overall training plan for the academies and approve courses and readings in the curriculum.[28]

Civilian Universities.

National Defense Student Program. The PLA has launched an educational renaissance for its officer corps in an effort to bring capable and talented young people into the service. Since the year 2000, the PLA has enrolled nearly 60,000 students in its National Defense Student Program.[29] The National Defense Student Program functions as a "PLA-style Reserve Officer Training Corps (ROTC)."[30] Currently, the National Defense Student Program has 40,000 students enrolled, and about 11,000 National Defense Students were to have been added from the ranks of the senior middle schools in 2007.[31] As of 2007, there are 116 participating universities, 70 of which are designated in China's "Project 211" initiative—a program to develop world class academic institutions specializing in science and technology disciplines including national defense and information systems.[32]

The entrance process for the National Defense Student Program at a civilian university is similar to the process for applicants at the military academies. Students seeking to enroll as National Defense Students must have an additional academic evaluation, a political evaluation, and a physical examination. Also, there is a recheck of the candidate's qualifications and suitability before being admitted to the National Defense Student group on campus. The selection process can be quite competitive. For example, in 2005, there were 1,300 applicants for positions in the group at the Xi'an Electronics University, but only 254

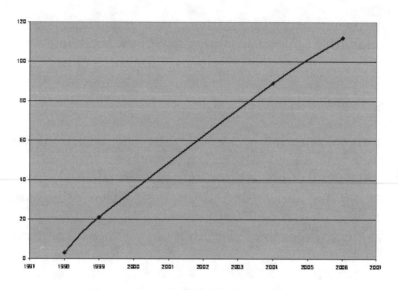

Table 2. Universities in the National Defense Student Program.

were chosen to enter the program.[33] More recently, 200 students competed for slots in the National Defense Student Program at East China Jiaotong University in 2006; the program accepted 20 freshmen.[34]

The organization that runs the program is the university's Selection and Training Office (STO) (*xuanba peixun gongzuo bangongshi*, 选拔培训工作办公室).[35] A few experienced military cadres led by a senior military representative staff the STO. In the case of the Xi 'an Electronics Science and Technology University, the senior military representative has been identified as a colonel with 28 years of service. This officer has been assigned to Xi 'an Electronics for 5 years. Presumably, other schools have equally experienced officers as military representatives and directors of the program.[36]

The Ministry of Education, Ministry of Personnel, and four PLA general departments issued the "National Defense Student Education Management Regulations" in May 2007, indicating high-level bureaucratic oversight of the program.[37] Although the GSD and GPD are sometimes mentioned in relation with the program, whether and how other staff organs may be involved is not entirely clear. For the PLA education system in general, the GSD and GPD share in establishing the standards and the procedures, as well as planning for military training and education. The particular agencies involved are most likely the GSD Military Training and Service Arms Department, along with the GPD Cadre Department. Presumably, other general departments make contributions as required.[38] The Selection and Training Offices at the various civilian universities appear to be associated with specific departments and services. For example, the program at Xi 'an Electronics and Technology University, "provided the Air Force with 294 National Defense Students" from 2001 to 2006,[39] and the program at Tsinghua University, which is under "contract with the General Political Department of the PLA for cultivating National Defense Students and has so far enrolled a total of 871 students in 8 years."[40] These examples demonstrate it is reasonable to infer that the sponsoring organizations of the offices are specific armed services. Local governments also play a role in supporting the activities of Selection and Training Offices. A combination of interests is clearly invested in the National Defense Student program and other civilian university recruitment programs, which, given the grassroots nature of program implementation, reflects a distinct level of self-restraint in terms of micromanagement from central authorities.[41]

At the lower level, military training and service arms department branch offices and the political departments of the military regions and military districts have supervisory responsibilities for university recruitment programs within their jurisdictions. The relevant departments of the services play a similar role in the supervising of the schools, students, and military representatives. Military academies near the National Defense Student-contracted schools also play a role by providing training facilities and training teams.[42]

The MRs also play a role early in the process of identifying students for the National Defense Student Program in what could be called a "fast-track" into participating local civilian universities. Before the applicants have been tested and accepted into the corps of National Defense Students, many have graduated from high schools that have been identified as "National Defense Student supply bases."[43] These schools have been assessed by cadre from the MR and the provincial military district and selected to serve in this capacity. In Chengdu MR, for example, 100 high schools have been so designated out of 300 eligible schools in the MR. In April 2007, there were 2,000 graduates from the "student supply bases" attending six civilian universities in Chengdu MR.[44]

Direct Recruitment Process. The traditional method for the PLA to recruit civilian college students and graduates into the PLA officer corps has been for the units to go directly to the civilian universities to recruit. In this chapter, this is referred to as the "direct recruitment process" for selecting college/ university graduates for the PLA. There probably is a centralized program where the various elements of the PLA—general departments, services, and MRs— justify their requirements and are allocated a quota of graduates. In the past, this recruitment may have been part of the standard career "assignment process" for new graduates wherein graduates from civilian universities were assigned jobs in accordance with national requirements, not individual choice. In recent years, with the growth of the competitive economic sector and liberalization of government controls over job assignments, the process has become more truly a "recruitment" activity. While comprehensive numbers are not readily available, there are anecdotal examples showing direct recruiting continues and is increasing. For example, the Air Force expanded recruiting requirements for college graduates into its pilot training programs to allow liberal arts graduates to compete for slots. In the past, only science and engineering students could enter the ranks of pilots.[45] In 2003, the Air Force identified 50 civilian colleges in which it planned to recruit college graduates — in accordance with Air Force requirements.[46]

The various services of the PLA, however, all face the same challenge of attracting the best talent in a growing domestic economy that offers lucrative alternatives to military service. This is leading the PLA to adopt some innovative recruiting approaches. The National Defense Student Program is one of the best known examples; however, other experimental recruiting programs have been initiated in recent years.

The Air Force has attempted to address its problem of qualified pilots by recruiting students early in their college careers. Beginning in 2006, the Air Force began "recruiting pilots from sophomores majoring in science or engineering disciplines in 160 universities and colleges" under a program called the "2+2 model," where students work toward a bachelor's degree after

2 years in a civilian college and 2 years at an Air Force flight academy.[47] The "2+2" model follows a 1999 decision by the Air Force Recruitment Department to evaluate the feasibility of recruiting students in their "third or fourth year of their undergraduate studies," the success of which encouraged the recruitment office to extend the program to sophomores.

In 2003, the commandant of the Nanjing MR Nanchang Army Academy, in a *Junshi Xueshu* article, suggested another example of an experimental recruitment and education program. In his "4+1" program of junior officer training, graduates of 4-year undergraduate schools attend 1 year of military command academy training before receiving their commissions.[48] A former military attaché in Beijing reported that the "4+1" is now a nationwide program.[49]

In the Guangzhou MR, Shenzhen University is focusing on the parallel challenge of recruiting NCOs by conducting an experimental program where students voluntarily interrupt their studies for 2 years to serve as enlisted personnel in local military units.[50] Students who volunteer benefit from preferential policies, such as tuition waivers, scholarships upon their return, and job placement assistance. Of the 96 students who had participated in the program and completed their 2-year assignment, 59 returned to school, suggesting some of those who did not, may have found careers as NCOs in the PLA.[51] These programs are separate, but complement the National Defense Student Program, indicating that the various services, MRs, and even individual units and schools are experimenting with ways to attract, educate, and commission high quality officers as well as NCOs.

Experimental programs have not been limited to the direct recruiting process. At Nanchang Aeronautical

University, the National Defense Student Program's Selection and Training Office and the university administration have gone so far as to create a "Navy Park," a "Navy College" for National Defense Students, and incorporated military courses into the general curriculum to better accommodate them.[52]

The PLA is not alone in its recruiting efforts. Civilian accession programs have benefited from local support and preferential policies by local governments and schools. For example, in 2001, Shanghai colleges and universities, including Tongji University, launched a "Recruiting On-Campus Student Soldier Experiment" (*Zhengji zaixiao daxuesheng bingyuan shidian*), which involved the Shanghai municipal government establishing regulations granting preferential treatment for soldiers leaving active duty and returning to their schools within 1 year.[53] These policies help attract students by assuring them that after leaving active duty they will receive support in completing their educations and finding civilian employment.

NEW OFFICER ENTRY SPECIALTIES AND THE DEMANDS OF A MODERNIZING FORCE

Students entering the PLA officer corps are accessed against requirements in specific military professional specialties (*zhuanye*, 专业) before they enter the school. To achieve this, the military region newspapers advertise the specialties and the number of applicants sought to fulfill the military region's "plan" (*jihua*, 计划). This type of recruiting clearly applies to enlisted soldiers, and it is likely that a similar quota system is used for recruiting high-school candidates into the PLA officer training schools.

The May 15, 2007, edition of the Nanjing MR newspaper advertised the career fields and quotas that were being sought for the next training year. According to the announcement, the command entry fields or command tracks needed the following number of recruits from the PLA's enlisted force to meet entry-level officer requirements.[54]

Infantry	55	15.6%
Reconnaissance	19	5.4%
Artillery	69	19.6%
Armor	71	20.2%
Engineering	35	10.1%
Anti-chemical	9	2.6%
Communications	39	11.1%
Automotive	38	10.8%
Total	351	99.8%

Table 3. Nanjing Military Region Officer Requirements.

In addition, the announcement called for 92 male applicants for technical and service schools and 16 female applicants for similar schools. Therefore, it appears there was a total of 459 school slots available for aspiring officers applying from the PLA's enlisted ranks in the Nanjing MR in 2007.[55] The academic programs for these students included communications engineering, electronics engineering, political work, and arts. Almost all of the advertised programs (92 percent) are 4-year programs. Only six are 3-year programs. It is worth noting that some of these Nanjing students will attend schools (e.g., Chongqing Communications Academy or the Xi 'an Communications Academy) that are not in the Nanjing MR. In fact, a comparison of the Nanjing quota announcement and a similar announcement by the Jinan MR reveals that the two MRs will send their students to the same 26 schools (see Appendix B). Also, not all of the graduates of these programs will be considered officers; the quotas include provisions for officers (*junguan*, 军官), cadre (*ganbu*, 干部), and a very small number of administrators (*zhuliyuan*, 助理员). It appears that combat and combat support functions are assigned to officers while some combat service support functions have been assigned to cadres and administrators.

On August 3, 2007, the Nanjing MR newspaper announced the slate of selectees for the schools, indicating that the entire selection process took only about 90 days.[56] It is likely that this process or one similar to it is used in determining quotas and requirements in the other MRs and services, as well as for recruiting civilian high school students into the PLA's academies and universities.

It is not clear if a similar process has been created for National Defense Students. In the early days of the National Defense Student Program, students who had graduated from college were sent to military schools for a year of basic military training. During this training period, the new "junior commanding officer" attended classes on the history of the PLA, political affairs, and common military subjects such as army rules and regulations, military topography, the use of small arms, and related topics. After the successful completion of an exam, the students are awarded the rank of first lieutenant, the grade of a deputy company commander, and an assignment as a platoon leader or equivalent position.[57] There is no indication that, at least in the late 1990s, there was additional technical, career-field specific education.

Today's system appears to be slightly different, in that PLA units, particularly technical units, have cultivated contacts with "military practice bases" that emphasize the technical skills the unit needs in its junior officers. Students study their academic subjects during the year and join the unit for periods of "learning by watching" during the summer. In July 2007, leaders of Unit 96151 of the Second Artillery met with the senior faculty of Hefei University of Technology to coordinate summer training. According to their plan, the National Defense Students from the university have joined the unit for political training, basic military skills, and physical fitness training. The unit also gave the students time to learn through observation.[58]

Academic Programs.

Academic work for the officer aspirants in the military academies varies widely. Since each new student attends an academy that focuses its courses on a certain military occupational specialty, the programs can be very different. While some officers may be recruited from civilian universities, many are selected directly from among enlisted personnel during their initial tour of duty. The PLA school system is, thus, built around a core of officer accession-level military academies that must provide a combination of civilian education and professional skill training. On paper, the military 4-year education programs appear similar to 4-year civilian university educational programs; however, the level of quality remains problematic. Most of the military academies are professional training schools with the addition of some undergraduate university level programs. Based on the entry level of the student, the academies provide 3- or 4-year programs. Reforms underway are aiming to eventually produce a quality of education comparable to that available at a civilian university.

The following paragraphs provide snapshots of the academic programs for new officers as of 2003 at two entry-level military academies—one for combat arms and one for logistics. Several additional examples are in Appendix C. One should assume that, although omitted from the descriptions below, there also is a core political education and military history curriculum at each academy. Also, since the education reform effort aspires to provide an education comparable in quality with a civilian university, there should be an increased portion of classes that would be found in a civilian university program.

Xi 'an Army Academy (*Xi 'an lujun xueyuan*, 西安陆军学院).[59] Xi 'an Army Academy is the primary basic level command academy for training army basic level military command officers in Lanzhou MR. It has a combined training field, tactical drill field, light arms firing range, Yan'an teaching base (*Yanan jiaoxue jidi*, 延安教学基地), experiment center, electronic teaching center, library, military gymnasium, swimming pool, academic assembly hall, teaching building, and auditorium. Currently, there are university bachelor-level, senior technical degree (*daxue zhuan ke*, 大学专科), secondary technical degree (*zhongdeng zhuanke*, 中等专科), high school student training, and basic level officer rotational training classes.

The primary specializations at the Xi 'an Army Academy include infantry command (*bubing zhihui*, 步兵指挥), light artillery troop command (*qingbian paobing zhihui*, 轻便炮兵指挥), small-unit tactical command (*fendui zhanshu zhihui*, 分队战术指挥), grass-roots political work (*jiceng zhengzhi gongzuo*, 基层政治工作), grassroots logistics management (*jiceng houqin guanli*, 基层后勤管理), key training for military command (*zhongdian peiyang junshi zhihui*, 重点培养军事指挥), political work (*zhengzhi gongzuo*, 政治工作), and troop logistics management (*jundui houqin guanli*, 军队后勤管理). The primary curriculum consists of: basic mechanized technology (*jixie jishu jichu*, 机械技术基础), electronic technology command (*dianzi jishu zhihui*, 电子技术指挥), military thought (*junshi sixiang*, 军事思想), military strategy (*junshi moulüe*, 军事谋略), military history (军事历史), operational command (*zuozhan zhihuixue*, 作战指挥学), military planning (*junshi yunchouxue*, 军事运筹学), military geography (*junshi dixingxue*, 军事地形学), foreign military studies (*waijun yanjiu*, 外军研究), infantry weapons and equipment (*bubing wuqi zhuangbei*, 步兵武器装备), applied shooting (*yingyong sheji*, 应用设计), military services knowledge (*junbingzhong zhishi*, 军兵种知识), infantry small-unit tactics (*bubing fendui zhanshu*, 步兵分队战术), troop grass-roots unit management (*jundui jiceng guanli*, 军队基层管理), troop grassroots unit political work (*jundui jiceng zhengzhi gongzuo*, 军队基层政治工作), backbone cadres study armed forces command (*jundui zhihuixue*, 军队指挥学), army tactics (*lujun zhanshuxue*, 陆军战术学), and troop management (*jundui guanlixue*, 军队管理学). Practical study coursework includes the following: computer applications laboratory study (*jisuanji yingyong shixi*, 计算机应用实习), unit fieldwork (*budui shixi*, 部队实习), tactical concepts demonstration (*zhanshu xiangding zuoye*, 战术想定作业), live-fire shooting (*shidan sheji*, 实弹射击), combined field training (*zonghe yanlian*, 综合

演练), and graduation thesis (*biye lunwen*, 毕业论文), etc.

Military Transportation Academy (Junshi jiaotong xueyuan, 军事交通学院).[60] The Military Transportation Academy in Tianjin is the only PLA Engineering Academy providing college-level education and training for military communications and transportation managers and commanders. The academy was established in 1973 as the PLA Transportation Technology School (*Yunshu jishu xuexiao*, 运输技术学校) and renamed the Military Transportation Academy in 1999. It has trained over 220,000 students.

There are 3- and 4-year programs that include military transport (*junshi jiaotong*, 军事交通), military vehicle engineering (*junyongqiche gongcheng*, 军用 汽工程), vehicle utilization engineering (*cheliang yunyong gongcheng*, 车辆 运用工程), vehicle unit command (*qiche fenduizhihui*, 汽车分队指挥), machining technology (*jixie jiagong gongyi*, 机械加工工艺), depot mechanization (*cangku jixiehua*, 仓库机械化), automotive repair engineering (*qiche weixiu gongcheng*, 汽车维修工), and diesel vehicle utilization (*chaiyouche yunyong*, 柴油车运用). This school offers undergraduate-level education and lower-level specialty certifications. It does not appear to offer any graduate-level education programs.

Training Results.

Although the military training of rising officers has not been extensively discussed in the Chinese press, it appears that the training is basic, but ample, to provide a base for further career field training or on-the-job training. Some parts of the PLA have gone beyond this basic approach. In 2006, the Beijing MR hosted

30 graduate engineering students from its training coordination zone (*xiezuoqu*, 协作区) at a live "force on force" brigade-level training exercise. This exercise gave the students first-hand exposure to combined arms tactics techniques and procedures. Although these graduate students had engineering majors at the university and are likely to be assigned to technical posts, the experience of this type of exercise and the ability to study it at close range is likely to improve the quality of these cadres' performance in their future training assignments.

MIXED RECEPTION OF THE NEW OFFICERS IN THE PLA

While a comprehensive survey of college applicants is not available, the characterization in press reports of why these students chose to join the PLA and how these officer candidates are faring is, at best, mixed. Many students join through these new recruitment programs for reasons of national duty, family tradition, or, as one student put it, the desire to "discipline myself through military training." The monetary compensation, while significant, appears to be a marginal factor rather than a primary one for most students, although the assurance of finding employment after leaving active service is an economic benefit that also plays an important role in the decision to join. Some students who were not accepted directly into a military academy have found the civilian recruitment programs to be a convenient alternate path into a military career. Some have found that taking an alternate path is actually more amenable to one's choice of lifestyle: "This kind of enrollment satisfied me with its more soft physical training and more colorful campus life," says one National Defense

Student.[61] The PLA, however, may be cracking down on what has been exploited as a back-door entrance to a military career. In 2006, Lanzhou MR "revoked the status of 35 National Defense Student graduates who did not meet standards" after a region-wide reexamination of program graduates. These 35 were assessed to be either lacking in dedication to the military or were below standards physically.

The new candidates entering from PLA accession programs have not been without their problems. The academic and military integration of the accession program appears to have been successfully managed, but, in some places problems appear with the individual candidates. *Huojianbing Bao*, the newspaper of the Second Artillery, recently discussed some problems the Second Artillery has encountered with National Defense Students from Northwest Industrial University, Hefei University of Technology, and Harbin University of Science and Technology. The new recruits are criticized for the following reasons:

- They are not physically strong.
- They find it difficult to communicate with fellow soldiers.
- They do not find it easy to accept criticism.
- They are not sufficiently interested in politics.
- They do not have a strong sense of group solidarity and the willingness to sacrifice for the group.[62]

On the other hand, *Renmin Qianxian*, the Nanjing MR newspaper, held an open online chat with three young college-educated officers to discuss the challenges they faced and their experiences serving in their respective units. Their reflections included the following points:

- They learn faster, particularly in technology-related subjects.
- They are better creative thinkers.
- They are more concerned with working efficiently.
- They chafe at arbitrary regulations and orders.
- They found it difficult to communicate with their fellow soldiers at first.[63]

Physical fitness likely can be quickly remedied when the students enter active duty, but the other flaws may require different approaches to political training. Only time will tell if this new generation will be responsive.

Additionally, it is paradoxical that the PLA requires engineering degrees for many combat specialties (e.g., infantry unit leader) when other armies accept liberal arts degrees.[64] A small unit combat leader is not likely to be called upon to apply an understanding of advanced electrical engineering mathematics or physics concepts in his day-to-day job. Given the inherent over-qualification of these officers and the lack of opportunity to exercise their academic skills, it is possible that the PLA may suffer turbulence in its junior leadership ranks as young officers seek to leave the PLA for lucrative work in their primary areas of interest or seek to avoid service in the combat arms in favor of service in technical and supporting arms.

CONCLUSION

The development of various paths of officer candidate recruitment in the PLA has coincided with significant social and policy shifts in the PRC and the PLA. Many forces within and beyond the control of the PLA are behind the observed changes in the officer accession system. The PLA's modernization effort has created high demand for qualified officers, in both leadership and technical acumen. The search for qualified officers is occurring against the backdrop of a strong domestic economy, creating more lucrative job opportunities for new graduates, against which the PLA is hard-pressed to effectively compete. This has led the PLA to explore new ways and methods in which officers are accessed, including tapping the civilian education system.

The growing economy has spurred the demand for higher education in general, and in turn, the development of more and better-funded civilian universities. In combination with state-sponsored initiatives such as "Project 211," the national educational system is turning out more technologically savvy graduates than ever before. Simultaneously, the PLA has been engaged in a drive to consolidate and reduce the number of military academies, and, of those remaining, to shift emphasis to pre-assignment rather than academic training. Given the PLA's human capital requirements needed for modernization, the constraints of the military academies' to produce qualified graduates, and the growth of the civilian education system, it is a natural choice for PLA planners to expand officer recruitment to include civilian colleges and universities. The PLA has done so through various programs, with the National Defense Student Program serving as a key example, but also with various local and service-specific initiatives.

The PLA as an institution faces serious personnel challenges in the future. As the ranks of college-educated officers increase, they will slowly but steadily change the character of the PLA. The frustrations encountered by those first few cohorts of National Defense Students represent a fundamental culture clash between a military institution with origins as a peasant army and the more educated youth of modern China. The motivations for college-educated recruits to join the PLA also are changing; traditional values such as patriotism, national duty, and family tradition are still strong, but are being challenged by pragmatic concerns such as avoiding tough post-graduation job searches and the desire for financial security. This poses a near-term challenge for the PLA to attract people with the right skill sets into the PLA and the long-term challenge of retaining them. As demonstrated by the various programs the PLA has undertaken in recent years, the military is able to open new sources of recruits and to recruit earlier in students' educational careers. Challenges in incorporating these new recruits into the officer corps raise doubts that the long-term retention of talented individuals, so badly needed for the PLA's modernization drive, can be achieved.

APPENDIX A

A TENTATIVE LIST OF PLA ENTRY-LEVEL OCCUPATIONAL SPECIALTIES (80)

Air Force (12)
Pilot (fighter, bomber, transport)
Navigator
Air Force Staff Officer
Air Force Anti-aircraft Officer
Air Force Small Unit Political Officer
Air Force Boat Unit Officer
Aviation Technical Officer
Aviation Technical Unit Commander
Aeronautical Engineer
Aeronautical Engineering Technician and Manager
Aviation Maintenance Technician, Flight Mechanic, Airborne and Space Technician
Air Force Logistics Command, Staff, and Technical Officer

Ground Force (7)
Artillery Officer
Ground Force Line Officer
Ground Anti-aircraft Officer
Armored Technical Officer
Armored Commander
Tactical Anti-tank Officer
Air Defense Officer

Navy (13)
Surface Ship Commanding Officer
Surface Ship Political Officer
Oceanographer
Naval Aviation Pilot

Naval Aviation Navigator
Naval Aviation Staff Officer
Naval Anti-aircraft Officer
Submarine Officer
Submarine Staff Officer
Naval Engineering Technical Officer
Naval Engineering Commander
Naval Aeronautical Engineering Technical Officer
Naval Logistics Command and Staff Technical Officer

Combat Support (28)
Military Doctor and Nurse
Engineering Unit and Installation Engineering Officer
Command Automation Specialist
Field Engineering Specialist
Military Meteorologist
Motor Vehicle Transportation Officer
Motor Vehicle Transportation Staff Officer
Artillery Engineering Technical Officer
Ground Force and Air Force Boat Unit Officer
Landline Communications Officer
Landline Communications Staff Officer
Engineering Commander
Military Communications Specialist
Base Construction Engineer
Engineering Technician
Logistics Engineering Technical Officer
Agricultural Production Officer
Veterinarian
Economic Management Officer
Transportation Engineering Technical Officer and Commander
Armored Force Management Officer
Chemical Defense Commander
Ordnance Commander and Technical Officer

Electronic Counter-measures Officer
Miscellaneous Repair Officer
Surveying and Cartographic Technician and Manager
Engineering Technical Officer and Commander
Doctor, Nurse, Medical Researcher, and Pharmacist's
Technician

Political Officers (6)
Engineering Unit and Installation Engineering Political
Officer
Political Officer (PLA generalist)
Legal Officer
Political Theory Instructor
Unit Political Instructor
Propaganda Officer

Foreign Affairs (1)
Foreign Affairs Officer

Physical Fitness (1)
Physical Fitness Training Officer

Research Officers (6)
Science and Technology (S&T) Research Manager
S&T Commander
S&T Technical Officer
S&T Researcher
Electronics Technicians for Research Institutes
Electronics Researchers for Research Institutes

Technical Intelligence Officers (3)
Cryptology Leader
Cryptology Technician
Technical Reconnaissance Specialist

Second Artillery (1)
Second Artillery Engineering Technical Officer

People's Armed Police (PAP) (2)
PAP Special Operations Unit Commander
PAP Medical Personnel Officer

APPENDIX B

ENTRY SPECIALTIES ADVERTISED BY NANJING MILITARY REGION FOR 2007[70]

111101   Political Studies / Basic Infantry Commanding Officer [71]

111102   Engineering Management/Basic Infantry Commanding Officer

111103   Information Engineering/Basic Infantry Commanding Officer

111104   Command Automation Engineering/ Basic Infantry Commanding Officer

111105   Mechanical Engineering and Automation Engineering/ Infantry Platoon Leader

111106   Mathematical Sciences and Technology/ Basic Infantry Commanding Officer

111107   Engineering Management/ Basic Infantry Commanding Officer

111201   Reconnaissance and Special Operations Force Command/Reconnaissance and Special Operations Force (SOF) Command Platoon Leader

111301   Mechanical Engineering and Automation/ Basic Artillery Commanding Officer

111302   Military Meteorology/ Basic Artillery Commanding Officer

111303   Mechanical Engineering and Automation/ Basic Artillery Commanding Officer

111304   Weapons Engineering/ Basic Artillery Commanding Officer

111305   Firepower Command and Control Engineering/ Basic Artillery Commanding Officer

111306	Engineering Management/ Basic Artillery Commanding Officer
111307	Mechanical Engineering and Automation/ Basic Artillery Commanding Officer
111308	Engineering Management/ Basic Artillery Commanding Officer
111401	Firepower Command and Control Engineering/ Basic Anti-aircraft Commanding Officer
111402	Engineering Management/ Basic Anti-aircraft Commanding Officer
111501	Tank Unit Command /Amphibious Tank Platoon Leader
111502	Mechanical Engineering and Automation/ Basic Armor Commanding Officer
111503	Mechanical Engineering and Automation / Basic Armor Commanding Officer
111504	Weapons Engineering/ Basic Armor Commanding Officer
111506	Engineering Management/ Basic Armor Commanding Officer
111507	Engineering Management/ Basic Armor Commanding Officer
111508	Armor Troop Command/ Amphibious Tank-Infantry Platoon Leader
111509	Armor Troop Command/Basic Tank-Infantry Reconnaissance Platoon Leader
111601	Engineering Troop Command/ Pontoon Bridge Platoon Leader
111602	Landmine and Explosives Engineering/ Basic Engineering Troop Commanding Officer
111603	Roadway, Bridge and Harbor Facilities Engineering/ Engineering Troop Platoon Leader

111604	National Defense Shelters and Engineering/ Engineering Troop Platoon Leader
111605	Landmine and Explosives Engineering/ Engineering Troop Platoon Leader
111701	Anti-chemical Warfare Unit Command/ Anti-chemical, Flamethrower, Smoke Platoon Leader
111801	Communications Engineering/ Basic Communications Commanding Officer
111803	Communications Engineering/ Basic Communications Commanding Officer
111805	Command Automation Engineering/ Communications Platoon Leader
111806	Communications Command/ Combined Communications Systems Platoon Leader
111808	Communications Command/ Communications Support Platoon Leader
111809	Communications Command/ Communications Systems Platoon Leader
111810	Communications Command/Secret Communications System Platoon Leader
111812	Communications Command/ Integrated Joint Command and Mobile Communications Platoon Leader
111901	Automotive Command/ Automotive Platoon Leader
121902	Automotive Command/ Automotive Platoon Leader
112001	Classified Equipment Engineering/ Confidential Cadre
122002	Confidential Commander/Confidential Staff Officer
122003	Electronic/Radio Reconnaissance/ Reconnaissance Support Cadre

112004	Electric Engineering and Power Generation Engineering/Communications and Power Source Platoon Leader
112006	Electronic Countermeasures Command and Engineering/ Electronic Countermeasures Command Support Cadre
112007	Aviation Weapons Systems and Propulsion Engineering/Anti-aircraft Mechanical Engineering Cadre
112008	Weapons Engineering/ Anti-aircraft Ordnance Engineering Cadre
112009	Journalism/ Journalism Cadre
112010	Petroleum Transportation Engineering/ Petroleum Pipeline Platoon Leader
112011	Engineering Management/Warehouse Management Cadre
112012	Engineering Management/ Barracks Management Cadre
112013	Engineering Management/ Petroleum Management Cadre
112014	Supply Service Command/Administrative Assistant
112016	Equipment Security Command/ Truck Maintenance Platoon Leader
112018	Equipment Security Command/ Small Craft Maintenance Platoon Leader
112019	Small Craft Power Engineering/ Small Craft Power Generation Leader
112020	Small Craft and Seagoing Engineering/ Small Craft Support Cadre
112021	Clinician (Naval Hospital)/ Naval Hospital Division Cadre
112023	Clinician (Air Force Hospital)/Aviation Unit Hospital Division Cadre
122024	Automotive Equipment Utilization

	Engineer / Equipment Repair Commanding Cadre
122025	Automotive Equipment Maintenance Engineering/ Equipment Repair Support Platoon Leader
112026	Surface Navigation and Aviation Management/ Aviation Management Cadre
112027	Remote Sensor Science and Support/ Aviation Reconnaissance Support Cadre
112040	Movie and Television Dramatist/ Cultural Cadre
112041	Actor/ Cultural Cadre
112042	Painter/ Fine Arts Work Cadre
211802	Communications Engineering/Basic Communications Commanding Officer
211804	Communications Engineering/Basic Communications Commanding Officer
211807	Communications Command/ Combined Communications System Platoon Leader
211811	Communications Command/ Cryptography Platoon Leader
222005	Intelligent Telephone/ Telephone Communications Platoon Leader
212015	Military Finance Management/ Assistant Finance Official
212022	Nursing/ Clinic Nursing Division Officer

The following 26 schools provided this training.

National Science and Technology University
Information Engineering University
Science and Engineering University
Ordnance Engineering University
International Relations Academy

National Science and Technology University
Artillery Academy
Bengbu Tank Academy
Armored Forces Engineering Academy
Shijiazhuang Mechanized Infantry Academy
Anti-Chemical Command Engineering Academy
Communications Command Academy
Chongqing Communications Academy
Xi'an Communications Academy
Military Communications (Transportation) Academy
Automotive Management Academy
Electronics Engineering Academy
Army Anti-aircraft Force Academy
Nanjing Political Academy
Logistics Engineering Academy
Military Economics Academy
The Second Military Medical University
The Fourth Military Medical University
Armored Force Technology Academy
Air Force Engineering University
The Art Academy

Source: Nanjing MR Newspaper, *Renmin Qianxian*, May 15, 2007, p. 2; and Jinan MR Newspaper, *Qianwei Bao*, June 29, 2007, p. 3.

APPENDIX C

EXAMPLES OF ENTRY-LEVEL ACADEMY PROGRAMS

Bengbu Tank Academy (*Bengbu tanke xueyuan,* 蚌埠坦克学院)[72]

The academy is primarily responsible for command and basic combined arms training. Additionally, all army tank battalion commanders and instructor training is conducted at this school. Currently, there are armored troop command, armored firepower application and command automation engineering, information engineering and command, armored technology logistics command, and other fields of study. There are also basic cultural courses, mandated by the Ministry of Education, set up for all engineering and science academies taught at this school. The primary curriculum also offers military strategy, digital model construction, and other basic and specialized basic courses. The academy recruits from the entire civilian and military population for four levels of training referring to masters' graduate students, university undergraduate, university professional training, and middle-grade professional training.

Logistics Engineering Academy (*Houqin gongcheng xueyuan,* 后勤工程学院)[73]

The Logistics Engineering Academy is a 4-year institution that also offers graduate education in a number of fields. Located in Chongqing, Sichuan Province, it was established in 1961. In 1969, it was renamed the Logistics Advanced Specialty School and then, in 1975, once again renamed the Logistics Engineering Academy.

The Logistics Engineering Academy trains and educates logistics engineering technology cadre for the entire Chinese People's Liberation Army, with five levels of education and training programs: doctorate (*boshi*, 博士), masters' degree (*shuoshi*, 硕士), baccalaureate (*benke*, 本科), advanced specialty (*dazhuan*, 大专), and polytechnic (*zhongzhuan*, 中转). The academy provides training in over 30 specialty areas and masters' degree programs in 15 subject areas. It offers doctorate degrees and post-graduate training in three fields — rock and earth engineering (*yantu gongcheng*, 岩土 工程); applied chemistry (*yingyong huaxue*, 应用 化学); and oil, natural gas storage, and transport engineering (*shiyou tianranqi chuyun gongcheng*, 石油天然气 储云工程).

Four-year baccalaureate programs include barracks architecture (*yingfang jianzhuxue*, 营房 建筑学), barracks supply and organization engineering (*yingfang jigou gongcheng*, 营房 机构 工程), underground engineering (*dixia gongcheng*, 地下工程), electrical power systems and other automation (*dianli xitong jiqi zidonghua*, 电力系统及其自动化), petroleum storage and transport automation (*youliao chuyun zidonghua*, 油料 储运 自动化), command automation (*zhihui zidonghua*, 指挥自动化), petroleum storage and transport engineering (*youliao chuyun gongcheng*, 油料储运自动化), petroleum chemistry (*youliao huaxue*, 油料化学), and depot automation (*cangku zidonghua*, 仓库自动化). In addition, there are at least nine additional 2- and 3-year programs of instruction in related logistics engineering fields.

Military Economics Academy (*Junshi jingji xueyuan*, 军事经济学院)[74]

The Military Economics Academy is a specialty school that trains military economics managers. The academy traces its origins back to 1946, when it began as the Northeast Democratic United Army Supply School in Heilongjiang Province. In 1949, the school moved to Hunan Province before settling into its present location in Wuhan. From 1949 to 1986, it went through numerous reorganizations, including closure from 1969 to 1977 during the Cultural Revolution. As it developed its academic focus over the years it finally was reopened as the Military Economics Academy in 1986.

The programs of instruction include military unit finance (*jundui caiwu*, 军队财务), military auditing (*jundui shenji*, 军队审计), capital construction finance (*jijian caiwu*, 基建 财务), quartermaster management (*junxu guanli*, 军需管理), military supply management (*jundui wuzi guanli*, 军队物资管理), quartermaster management for mess/quartermaster officers (*junxu guanli-siwuzhang*, 军需 管理 -司务张), and logistics unit command (*houqin fendui zhihui*, 后勤分队指挥). These programs have 2-, 3-, and 4-year curriculums: certification for polytechnic level (2-year programs), specialty level (3-year programs), and baccalaureate level (4-year programs) for junior officers who will serve in logistics units and staffs, as well as in research institutes and on school faculties.

The Military Economics Academy is distinguished from many of the other tier one schools in that it offers advanced degrees. At the graduate level, there is a national defense economics doctorate program, as well as seven master's-level programs in subjects such as public finance (*caizhengxue*, 财政学), national economics (*guomin jingjixue*, 国民经济学), and management science and engineering (*guanli kexue gongcheng*, 管理科学工程).

Guilin Air Force Academy (*Guilin kongjun xueyuan*, 桂林空军学院)[75]

The Guilin Air Force Academy is the primary command academy for the training of lower- and mid-level commanders, various technical officers for Air Force anti-aircraft artillery units, Air Force guard units (*jingwei fendui*, 警卫分队), lower-level airborne unit command officers (since 1999), Air Force unit staff officers, and Air Force political officers.

The Academy has comprehensive research and training facilities. Research centers include engineering mechanics, modern physics, mathematical circuitry, microwave technology, and other laboratories. The computer center has 450 microprocessors while the educational technology center has shooting, recording, editing, broadcasting, etc., capabilities, and has installed a closed-circuit television system. The library features a computer search system of the National Defense Science and Engineering Committee information network, 200,000 books, and more than 500 various journals. In addition, the academy has a physical training field (gym), natatorium, and small-arms firing range, modern specialty education and command training simulation rooms, and close to 600 individual information nodes on the campus network. The academy offers majors in anti-aircraft artillery mid-level command, basic level political work, staff work, air defense troop anti-aircraft artillery command, firepower control engineering, command-to-command protocol (*zhihui yi zhihui*, 指挥仪指挥), radar command, airborne troop command, ground force command, and guard command.

Naval Dalian Ship Academy (*Haijun Dalian jianting xueyuan*, 海军大连舰艇学院)[76]

Naval Dalian Ship Academy is a command academy that trains naval ship technology command officers, political officers, and ocean survey engineering technical officers (*haiyang cehui gongcheng jishu junguan*, 海洋测绘工程技术军官). There are eight specialty departments: the politics department, maritime navigation department, naval guns weapons department, ocean-going weapons department (*shuizhong wuqi xi*, 水中武器系), missile department, command control department, ocean surveying department, and foreign training department. In addition, the academy has one basic department (*jichu bu*, 基础部), one seaborne fieldwork center (*haishang shixi zhongxin*, 海上实习中心), one student brigade, 53 classrooms, 10 experiment centers, and two large-scale long-voyage training ships. Primary majors include ship command (bachelor's), anti-chemical troop command (bachelor's), survey engineering (bachelor's), cartographic and geographic information systems (bachelor's). As one of the PLA's key focal development academies (*zhongdian jianshe yuanxiao*, 重点建设院校), this school bears the mission for training naval ship technical command officers, naval political officers, and ocean survey engineering officers.

Second Artillery Engineering Academy (*Di'er paobing gongcheng xueyuan*, 第二炮兵工程学院)[77]

The Second Artillery Engineering Academy is a specialty technical academy for training various engineering technicians. It is one of the nation's highest-level key academies, and is one of the military's key focal point development construction academies.

In 1986, the academy was designated as a master's degree granting institution, in 1993, was designated as a Ph.D.-granting institution. Currently in the engineering, military, and law course series, there are 14 master's degree programs and two Ph.D. focal points (*boshi dian*, 博士点). In 1996, the two Ph.D.-granting courses of study—navigation, guidance, and control, and weapons launch theory and technology—were designated as all-PLA key courses of study. The firepower, weapons automation, and munitions engineering course laboratory also was designated as an all-army key laboratory. Another unique program is in the control science and engineering course series where there is a post-doctorate mobile program (*boshi hou liudong zhan*, 博士后流动站). The academy currently has four academic departments, 12 master's specialties, 19 bachelor's majors, 10 advanced specialty (*dazhuan*, 大专) majors, and one secondary technical (*zhongzhuan*, 中专) major, all geared toward area high-school graduates and excellent enlisted soldiers possessing high school graduate level certificates.

ENDNOTES - CHAPTER 5

1. Jiang Zemin, September 1, 2003, at the 50th anniversary of the founding of the National University of Defense Technology. Translated by authors.

2. Today the PLA uses the terms: academy (*xueyuan*, 学院), university (*daxue*, 大学), and school (*xuexiao*, 学校) to describe the PLA military education institutions. Academy and university, for the most part, apply to officer education institutions and schools apply to NCO educational institutions.

3. Lonnie D. Henley, "Officer Education in the Chinese PLA," *Problems of Communism*, Vol. 36, May-June, 1987, pp. 70-71.

4. For a comprehensive overview of the PLA professional military education system, see James Bellacqua *et al.*, *Professional Military Education in the Chinese People's Liberation Army: An Institutional Overview*, Alexandria, VA: The CNA Corporation, July 2005, Vol. I and II.

5. See Kristen A. Gunness, "Educating the Officer Corps" in David M. Finkelstein and Kristen Gunness, eds., *Civil-Military Relations in Today's China: Swimming in a New Sea*, New York: M. E. Sharp, 2007, pp. 192-195. This section on "PLA Officer Recruitment" provides background to the officer accession topic including historical details since the 1980s on the practice of recruiting students from civilian universities into the officer corps. For additional details, see Dennis Blasko, *The Chinese Army Today*, New York: Routledge, 2006, pp. 58-61.

6. "PRC Military Official on Cadre Recruitment," *Xinhua Domestic Service*, June 23, 2000, in *Foreign Broadcast Information Service* (FBIS)-CPP20000623000046.

7. *Ibid.*

8. *The Chinese Army Today*, p. 58.

9. "Interview with PLA Officer on Recruitment," *Zhongguo Qingnian Bao*, Internet Version, November 3, 2006, in OSC-CPP20061120325001.

10. "JFJB: Military Schools Plan to Enroll 10,000-Plus Civil Students," *Jiefangjun Bao*, May 16, 2007, in OSC-CPP20070517715003.

11. "Enrollment of Cadets From Among Soldiers Wraps Up," *Jiefangjun Bao*, August 3, 2006.

12. "JFJB: Military Schools Plan to Enroll 10,000-Plus Civil Students," *Jiefangjun Bao*, May 16, 2007, in OSC-CPP20070517715003.

13. *Kongjun Bao*, August 13, 2002, p. 1.

14. Zheng Gan and Tang Pingyue, "The Only Way To Train New-Type Qualified Military Personnel," *Jiefangjun Bao*, June 27, 2000, p. 1, in FBIS CPP20000628000043.

15. "General Political Department: National Defense Students to Comprise 60 percent of PLA Officer Recruits by 2010," *Xinhua*, May 8, 2007.

16. For comparison, the U.S. Army commissioned approximately 5,500 officers in 2006 to support an active duty force of about 550,000; the PLA figures are roughly in proportion to U.S. figures.

17. "Reform of Military Academies Discussed," *Zhongguo Junshi Kexue*, August 20, 1999, pp. 97-102, in OSC FTS19991023000273.

18. *Ibid.* This is reflected in the shift on emphasis towards getting a bachelor's degree instead of a technical degree.

19. Jin Peng and Huang Ming, eds., *Overview of Chinese Military Academies* (*Zhongguo junshi yuanxiao tonglan*), 8th Book, Beijing: AMS Publishing, 2003. This source identifies the 95 schools, provides a brief history, and describes the level of training and course content. *Professional Military Education*, Vol II, Appendix F, provides detailed information on these schools. Also, see *Professional Military Education*, Vol. I, p. 14, for a chronology of the changing numbers of PLA schools since the 1950s.

20. "China's National Defense in 2006," *Information Office of the State Council of the People's Republic of China*, Beijing: December 2006, p. 17. See also *China's National Defense in 2004*, Beijing: Information Office of the State Council of the People's Republic of China, December 2004, p. 9.

21. "PLA Regulations on PLA Academy Education," Article 43, *Chinese Laws and Regulations website*, March 1, 2000, in OSC CPP20061120325006.

22. *Ibid.*, Article 44.

23. "Grasp Policy Regulations, Properly Perform Enrollment Work" *("Bawo zhengce guiding zuo hao zhaosheng gongzuo")*, *Renmin Jundui*, May 13, 2006, p. 2.

24. "PLA Air Force Recruits Sophomores at Civilian Colleges as Pilot Cadets," *Zhongguo Kongjun*, January 1, 2006, in OSC CPP20060217325001.

25. *Ibid.*

26. The particular personality types that the PLA screens for further examination are ENFP, INTJ, ISTP. See "PLA Schools Student Physical Examination Standards" *("Zhongguo Renmin Jiefangjun yuanxiao zhaoshou xueyuan tige jiancha biaozhun")*, May 24, 2006, available from *www.guofangsheng.com/n2131c5.aspx*, excerpts translated by Ivan Szpakowski.

27. *PLA Regulations*, Article 44.

28. *Ibid.*, Articles 28 and 56.

29. "Selecting the Green Matrix, Allowing Youth's Dreams to Take Flight" *("Xuanze lushe fangzhen fangfei qingchun mengxiang")*, *Jiefangjun Bao*, June 14, 2007, p. 9, available from *www.chinamil.com.cn/site1/zbx1/2007-06/14/content_845994.htm*, accessed July 29, 2007, translated excerpts by Ivan Szpakowski. Note: The literal translation of the Chinese title is given, but an alternate translation is "Choosing the Army Life, Allowing Youth's Dreams to Take Flight," since *"lushe fangzhen"* may be an idiomatic reference to the army.

30. Roy Kamphausen, "ROTC with Chinese Characteristics: Training the PLA in Civilian Universities," *Jamestown Foundation China Brief*, Vol. 7, Issue 6, March 21, 2007. This article reviews in detail the development of the National Defense Student program.

31. "National Defense Students Train at Xi'an Electronics University," *Shaanxi Ribao*, June 29, 2006, in OSC CPP20060818145012.

32. "Selecting the Green Matrix." The Chinese government's "Project 211" (211, 工程) is a RMB36.5 billion (~US$4.9 billion), multiyear program encompassing 106 select institutions with the aim of developing them into world class "21st century universities." Project 211 goals specifically target science and technology disciplines, including national defense and information systems. See *www.eol.cn/article/20050701/3142376.shtml*.

33. "National Defense Students Train at Xi'an Electronics University," *Shaanxi Ribao*, June 29, 2006, in OSC CPP20060818145012.

34. "200 Undergraduates Compete for the Quota of 20 National Defense Students," *Jiefangjun Bao*, June 16, 2006, in OSC CPP20060616702002.

35. A number of sources translate this office as Selection and Cultivation Office, which does not fit the function.

36. "National Defense Students Train at Xi'an Electronics University," *Shaanxi Ribao*, June 29, 2006, in OSC CPP20060818145012.

37. "PRC Military, Civilian Authorities Jointly Issue Military Student Rules," *Jiefangjun Bao*, May 23, 2007, in OSC CPP20070528711008.

38. The four general departments of the PLA and the Ministry of Education and Ministry of Personnel participated in drawing up the rules for the program. However, the real leadership is likely to come from the General Staff Department and the General

184

Political Department due to the nature of their responsibilities for selecting, assessing, educating, training, and assigning individuals within the PLA. See "Summary: PRC Military, Civilian Authorities Jointly Issue Military Student Rules," *Jiefangjun Bao*, May 23, 2007, in OSC CPP20070528711008.

39. "National Defense Students Train at Xi'an Electronics University," *Shaanxi Ribao*, June 29, 2006, in OSC CPP20060818145012.

40. "Tsinghua University admits 129 national defense students," *Jiefangjun Bao*, English edition, September 6, 2007, available at *English.chinamil.com.cn/site2/news-channels/2007-09/06/content_942286.*

41. The four general departments of the PLA and the Ministry of Education and Ministry of Personnel participated in drawing up the rules for the program. The General Staff Department and the General Political Department, in general, have the responsibility for selecting, assessing, educating, training, and assigning individuals within the PLA. See "Summary: PRC Military, Civilian Authorities Jointly Issue Military Student Rules," *Jiefangjun Bao*, May 23, 2007, in OSC CPP20070528711008, and *Professional Military Education in the Chinese People's Liberation Army: An Institutional Overview*, Vol. 1, Project Asia, CNA Corporation, July 2005, pp. 33-37.

42. See "100th National Defense Student Supply Base in Southwest Theater Unveiled," *Jiefangjun Bao*, April 29, 2006, in OSC CPP 20070430715002, for some of Chengdu MR's activities. See "200 Undergraduates Compete for the Quota of 20 National Defense Students," *Jiefangjun Bao* (Internet Version), June 16, 2006, in OSC CPP20060616702002, for some of Nanjing's work on the program. "PRC 2nd Artillery Visit by 'National Defense Student' College Administrators," *Huojianbing Bao*, December 12, 2006, p. 1, in OSC CPP20070217478003, recounts an exchange between three universities and the Second Artillery.

43. It should be noted that in China's education system what are called junior high and high schools in the West are collectively known as middle schools, or *zhongxue* (中学), divided into junior-middle (junior high), or *chuzhong* (初中), and senior-middle (high school), or *gaozhong* (高中).

44. "JFJB: '100th National Defense Student Supply Base in Southwest Theater Unveiled'," *Jiefangjun Bao*, April 29, 2007, in OSC CPP20070430715002. The online *Jiefangjun Bao* translation uses "middle" school, but the context suggests it the article refers to "high" schools.

45. "PLA Air Force to Modify Selection Criteria for Pilot Cadet Recruits in 2006," *Xinhua Domestic Service*, January 20, 2006, in OSC CPP200612006603.

46. "For the First Time the Military Will Select and Train Graduate Age Students From Local Colleges as Double Track Flight Cadets," available from *Pladaily.com, www.chinamil.com.cn/item/flying/content/1601.htm*.

47. "PLA Air Force Recruits Sophomores at Civilian Colleges as Pilot Cadets," *Zhongguo Kongjun*, January 1, 2006, in OSC CPP20060217325001; and "PLA Air Force To Modify Selection Criteria for Pilot Cadet Recruits in 2006," *Xinhua Domestic Service*, January 20, 2006, in OSC CPP20060120066003.

48. Chen Dongxiang, "An initial exploration into military occupation education at junior command specialty academies" *("Chuji zhihui zhuanye yuanxiao junshi zhiye jiaoyu chutan"), Junshi Xueshu*, No. 8, 2003, pp. 53-54.

49. Comment by Colonel Frank Miller, former U.S. military attaché in Beijing, September 29, 2007.

50. "China Daily Article Says Increasing Number of College Students Joining Military," *China Daily*, November 30, 2006, in OSC CPP20061130053019.

51. *Ibid.*

52. "PLA Navy explores new mode for fostering national defense students," *Jiefangjun Bao*, September 6, 2007, available from *english.chinamil.com.cn/site2/news-channels/2007-09/06/content_942273.htm*.

53. "Shanghai City 64 Colleges and Universities Constitute the Cradle of University Student Soldiers" ("*Shanghai shi 64 suo guoxiao chengwei daxuesheng shibing de yuolan*"), Renmin Qianxian, June 6, 2007, p. 1.

54. See Appendix A for a tentative list of entry specialties.

55. See Appendix B for a list of the entry specialties advertised by the Nanjing MR for 2007. The command track is one of five PLA career tracks; the others are staff officer, political, logistics, and equipment/technical.

56. "Military Region 2007 Fall Semester Armed Forces Academies Recruitment of Soldier-Students Plan" ("*Junqu 2007 nian qiuji jundui yuanxiao zhaoshou shibing xueyuan jihua*"), Renmin Qianxian, May 15, 2007, p. 2, translated by authors. A similar list of 371 slots appeared in the Jinan MR newspaper, *Qianwei Bao*, June 29, 2007, p. 3.

57. "2007 Military Region Fall Season Armed Forces Academies Recruit Soldier-Students Personnel Enrollment Roster" ("*2007 nian junqu qiuji jundui yuanxiao zhaoshou shibing xueyuan luqu renyuan mingdan*"), Renmin Qianxian, August 3, 2007, p. 2, translated by authors.

58. "PLA to Recruit more College Graduates as Junior Officers," *Xinhua*, December 1, 1997, in OSC OW1312010097.

59. "PRC: 2nd Artillery Unveils 1st Military Practice Base for Nat'l [sic] Defense Students," *Huojianbing Bao*, July 14, 2007, in OSC CPP20070827436004.

60. Jin Peng and Huang Ming, eds., *Overview of Chinese Military Academies* (*Zhongguo junshi yuanxiao tonglan*), 8th Book, Beijing: AMS Publishing, 2003, p. 58.

61. *Zhongguo Junshi Yuanxiao Tonglan*, pp. 210-212.

62. "Beijing MR Hosts First University Student Observers at Group Army Drill," *Zhanyou Bao*, September 26, 2006, in OSC CPP20061024318008.

63. "China Daily Article Says Increasing Number of College Students Joining Military," *China Daily*, November 30, 2006, in OSC CPP20061130053019.

64. See Frank Miller, "Changing the Landscape of Civil-Military Relations in China: The PLA Responds to Recruiting and Retention Challenges," *Shaping China's Security Environment: The Role of the People's Liberation Army*, Carlisle, PA: Strategic Studies Institute, October 2006, p. 24, for a summary of interviews with 10 National Defense Students.

65. "China: PLA Enlarges Enrollment of Military Recruits in Civilian Universities," *Xinhua*, May 7, 2004, in OSC CPP20040507000119.

66. "35 University Graduates Have Had Their National Defense Student Status Revoked" *("35 ming daxue biyesheng bei quxiao guofangsheng zige")*, *Renmin Jundui*, May 13, 2006, p. 1.

67. "PRC 2nd Artillery Visit by 'National Defense Student' College Administrators," *Huojianbing Bao*, December 12, 2006, in OSC CPP20070217478003.

68. "Taking the Military Path" *("Cong jun zhi lu")*, *Renmin Qianxian*, May 15, 2007, p. 3.

69. The role of engineering degrees in PLA and PRC leadership positions is a topic ripe for further inquiry, with such examples as Jiang Zemin, Hu Jintao, Wen Jiabao, and Cao Gangchuan as leaders with educations in some type of engineering.

70. "Military Region 2007 Fall Semester Military Academy Recruits Soldier-Student Plan" *("Junqu 2007 nian qiuji jundui yuanxiao zhaoshou shibing xueyuan jihua")*, *Renmin Qianxian*, May 15, 2007, p. 2.

71. Billets identified as "commanding officer" probably indicate that individuals are being recruited for careers as leaders of units in their various fields. Other officers may be assigned a series of staff positions after their initial service with troops.

72. *Zhongguo Junshi Yuanxiao Tonglan*, pp. 170-171.

73. *Ibid.*, pp. 197-201.

74. *Ibid.*, pp. 206-209.

75. *Ibid.*, p. 81.

76. *Ibid.*, p. 75.

77. *Ibid.*, p. 161.

CHAPTER 6

REFORMING THE OFFICER CORPS: KEEPING THE COLLEGE GRADS IN, THE PEASANTS OUT, AND THE INCOMPETENT DOWN

Kristen Gunness and Fred Vellucci

INTRODUCTION

The Chinese People's Liberation Army (PLA) is in its third decade of focused and sustained modernization and reform. Beginning in earnest in the mid-1980s, the PLA has rededicated itself to becoming a more professional force in a corporate and institutional sense and a more capable force in an operational (warfighting) sense. Above and beyond the new weapons systems, technologies, and operational capabilities the PLA aspires to field or accrue, a fundamental imperative that undergirds nearly all of the PLA's aspirations is the requirement to produce and train a "new PLA officer" with the requisite education and technological savvy to fight the "new type of war" that Chinese strategists believe they will face in the future.

To reach this goal, the PLA is rethinking its personnel system, and is giving considerable attention to making the institutional and regulatory adjustments that will allow it to attract and retain the better educated officers and noncommissioned officers (NCOs) it requires. In particular, the PLA is focused on improving how it recruits, educates, promotes, and retains its officers and NCOs.

This chapter discusses personnel management for officers and NCOs in the PLA. It provides background on why the PLA needed to implement changes to its officer and NCO personnel management structure, discusses the major areas of change in officer and NCO management, and presents the key organizations and tasks of the officer and NCO management structure.

DRIVERS OF CHANGE FOR PLA OFFICER PERSONNEL MANAGEMENT: THE "TWO TRANSFORMATIONS" AND THE NEED FOR A "NEW TYPE" OFFICER

In 1995 Jiang Zemin announced the "Two Transformations" (*liangge zhuanbian*, 两个转变) in an effort to provide broad operational guidance for the overall implementation of the "Strategic Guidelines."[1] "The "Two Transformations" called for the PLA to undergo a metamorphosis "From an army preparing to fight local wars under ordinary conditions, to an army preparing to fight and win local wars under modern high-tech conditions," and "from an army based on quantity to an army based on quality."

According to one PLA writer, enabling the "Two Transformations" became "the vision driving the PLA's restructuring, training, weapons acquisition, as well as war planning."[2] Its influence on personnel reform was similarly broad: the "Two Transformations" implied the need to transform from a personnel-intensive military to a more scientifically and technologically capable force.

REBUILDING THE FORCE: THE "NEW-TYPE" OFFICER

Implementing the "Two Transformations" required the PLA to both recruit and retain a better educated and more technologically capable officer, as well as to raise the quality of its existing officers. In particular, the

PLA assessed that the "new type" of officer it required to fight the high-tech wars of the future would possess scientific and technical knowledge—meaning that officers should be familiar with modern technology and have the ability to obtain, assess, and use information from various sources—political awareness, versatility, creativity, and efficiency.[3] The PLA also assessed that officers should have both operational and managerial experience, as officers with such diverse experience are likely to have a high degree of military professionalism, a well-developed ability to think strategically, and the competence to lead troops.[4] In sum, the PLA now seeks officers who have science and technology know-how; can work as team players; and are prepared to think about, understand, and adapt to the changing nature of modern warfare.

The PLA has also sought to address the need for more skilled personnel, and to compensate for shortcomings on the conscript side of the enlisted force, by improving the quality of its NCOs. This has meant that the PLA has expanded educational and training opportunities for NCOs to improve their educational and technical skill levels. In many cases, junior NCOs have assumed the duties that normally would have been performed by third- and fourth-year conscripts. In addition, NCOs are now undertaking additional positions previously performed by junior officers.[5]

The PLA appears cognizant of the challenges it faces in recruiting and retaining the best and brightest for its officer corps. The rise of China's economy has led to abundant competition from the private sector for the type of well-educated college graduates the military would like to have as officers. At the same time, the rural poor still see the PLA as a means for personal advancement. The ranks of the military are being filled, but the challenge lies in filling them with the people the PLA desires.[6]

KEY AREAS OF REFORM IN PLA PERSONNEL MANAGEMENT

The PLA has instituted numerous reforms in order to build the force it feels it needs to fight and win the high-tech, local wars of the future. In general, reforms have focused on three areas:

- Downsizing the force to rid the military of "dead weight," particularly in the officer corps;
- Recruiting, developing, and retaining educated military professionals in the officer corps; and,
- Developing a more skilled NCO corps. This has been a two-step approach involving a reallocation of resources: decreased investment in training conscripts, and increased investment in training NCOs.

In order to implement the changes listed above, the PLA revised and promulgated new regulations. The most significant of these regulations with regard to officer personnel management was the revision to the *Active-Duty Officer's Law of the People's Republic of China* (*zhonghua renmin gongheguo xianyi junguan fa*, 中华人民共和国现役军官) issued in December 2000, and the subsequent issuance of *Regulations on the Appointment and Dismissal of Officers in Active Service.*

Downsizing the Force.

In keeping with the move away from an "army based on quantity" and in an effort to rebuild the officer corps with "new-type" officers, the PLA has undergone three mass demobilizations since 1985, when it announced a 1,000,000-man reduction. This was followed by a 500,000-man reduction in 1997, followed by an announcement of another 200,000-man reduction in 2003, which was implemented over a period of 3 years. As of completion in 2005, the number of PLA personnel had shrunk by almost 1.7 million since 1985.[7]

In addition to mass demobilizations, the PLA also instituted mandatory retirement ages for officers. Officers are required to be promoted to the next level or leave the PLA. The *Active-Duty Officers Law* lays out the minimum service period requirements before an officer is eligible to retire, as well as a maximum retirement age for each grade.[8]

Recruiting, Developing, and Retaining Educated Military Professionals.

Improving Officer Recruitment. The PLA's increasing need for highly educated officers in the science and technology fields has led to improvements in its officer recruitment process. The largest change has been the establishment of formal channels with civilian universities that enable the PLA to select from a larger, more diverse pool of candidates for its officer corps.[9] To date, the PLA has:

- Developed a more formal, widespread officer recruitment program at civilian universities across the country, seeking both undergraduates and individuals completing masters and doctoral programs.
- Established on-campus officer recruitment offices at civilian institutions of higher education.
- Created a national defense scholarship program to recruit young, potential PLA officers before they begin their college studies.[10]

It appears as though the success of the PLA's recruitment and retention of top civilian university graduates is mixed. One can find articles in PLA newspapers, such as one recently published by *Zhongguo Xinwen She*, China's official overseas news service, touting the increased numbers of commanders with Ph.D. and masters' degrees in the Second Artillery force. According to the article, the Second Artillery now has enough technologically qualified people to be considered "modernized."[11] However, the PLA has been facing increased competition for top university graduates from China's private sector, and this is likely to become more of a challenge as the economy continues to grow and the highly educated graduates the PLA seeks to recruit look to more lucrative options.[12]

Finally, the PLA also appears to recognize that it needs to raise the age ceiling for joining the military if it is to be able to recruit from the largest possible pool of civilian college graduates. Reportedly, the *Military Service Law* is being revised and the maximum age for joining the PLA will be raised from 22 to 24 years of age.[13] The implications of the PLA raising the age ceiling are twofold: Many college graduates are facing increased difficulty finding employment after graduation, and raising the age ceiling allows them to consider the PLA as an option, which could take some pressure off of China's job market. It also helps the PLA by expanding the pool of college graduates who can join the military.

Increased Training Opportunities for Officers: Professional Military Education as a Promotion Requirement. The Active Duty Officer's Law stipulates that all officer candidates must undergo professional military education (PME) training prior to accession into the PLA officer corps, and prior to promotion to the next

196

level. In the past, officers slotted for command were required to undergo training prior to assignment at only three command levels: company, regimental, and corps.[14] The revised law requires training prior to command at every level: platoon, company, battalion, regiment, division, corps, and military region (MR).[15]

While the decision to make training a requirement for officers had been under discussion for some time, before 2000 the PLA assessed that it did not have the resources or training capacity to enforce this requirement. According to the General Political Department (GPD), there were two reasons why the PLA could implement this requirement in 2000: (1) the 500,000-man reduction of 1997 decreased the number of officer billets to fill, and (2) the PLA's increased use of the civilian education system to supplement officer training at military academies alleviated some of the strain on the PLA's PME system and allowed more officers to be trained at one time.[16] On the latter point, because the PLA's military academies have been incapable of providing all of the expertise required to train and educate its officers, the PLA has been required to reach out to civilian universities, and today PME at military institutions is increasingly supplemented through programs at civilian universities.[17]

Data suggests that the PLA is taking this professional military education requirement seriously. According to a recent interview with the director of the General Political Department's Cadre Division, published in *Zhongguo Qingnian Bao* (*China Youth Daily*):

> From 2001, [The PLA] changed the traditional form of directly promoting cadres from outstanding enlisted personnel; instead, the outstanding enlisted personnel are sent to study in military academies . . . and then promoted to be cadres if they meet the standards of training.

At present, only outstanding enlisted personnel who have received the regular training in state-run institutions of higher education can be directly promoted to be cadres.[18]

Addressing Retention Issue. The PLA has addressed retention issues in several ways. First, it has improved officer salaries and benefits. Second, it has standardized and improved its officer evaluation process. These reforms have both helped to keep the people the PLA wishes to retain, and, at least where the office evaluation process is concerned, has helped to weed out sub-standard performance and promote more skilled personnel into better positions.

Salaries and benefits. The PLA has also made a concerted effort to retain its best officers by raising salaries. The most recent increase in salary was in July 2006, when the PLA virtually doubled the pay for officers (discussed further below). In addition to pay increases, the PLA is improving officers' living conditions. Examples include building new barracks, providing better housing subsidies, and better mess halls and meals.[19]

The officer evaluation process. The PLA has recognized the need for an evaluation process that accurately reflects its goals and allows the "right people" to get into the "right positions." It also furthers the PLA's goals of retention as the "best and brightest" perceive that they are undergoing a fair and accurate evaluation and promotion process, as well as helps the PLA better identify who should be promoted and rewarded. As one General Political Department Cadre Department official recently stated when asked about the reasons behind recent reforms in cadre evaluations and appointments:

Currently, the quality of some cadres . . . is not well suited to the requirements of [our] new situation. It is necessary to adopt the systems and mechanisms that can promote the cultivation of a large number of outstanding personnel and promote the enhancement of the cadres' capability and quality . . . In particular, the methods of evaluating cadres are still too simple and not comprehensive enough, are too qualitative and lack the necessary quantitative standards.[20]

The *Active-Duty Officer's Law* and the subsequent *Regulations on the Appointment and Dismissal of Officers in Active Service* took steps to standardize the officer evaluation, selection, and appointment process. Officers are subject to performance appraisal by senior level officers and the unit's political officer, and peer reviews, including the use of opinion polls among officer peers, are also part of the evaluation process. Unit Party Committees are instructed not to select or to promote officers who are disliked or disapproved of by the masses.[21]

Data suggests that the PLA is attempting to address the lack of quantitative basis for officer evaluations. In June 2006 the PLA's General Department issued a new "Circular on Selecting and Appointing Deputy Regiment Leading Cadres by Means of Combining Appraisal with Examination in all PLA Combat Units." Following this, in July 2006 the *PLA Daily* reported that officers at the deputy regiment commander level in all combat units would be evaluated through a combination of both performance and examinations in relevant subjects such as military technology, foreign languages, and computer science.[22] Six months later, *Qianwei Bao* (*Vanguard News*), the Jinan MR's newspaper, reported that the Jinan MR would also select and appoint officers at the deputy regiment level through a combination of exams and appraisal by senior-level officers and the unit's party committee.[23] It is unclear whether this will also be required for officer evaluation at higher levels in the PLA in the future.

NONCOMMISSIONED OFFICERS (NCOs)

With an overall goal of recruiting, training, and retaining more personnel with advanced technical skills, the PLA is currently implementing a number of initiatives designed to diversify NCO selection channels and raise the education level of the NCO corps. The amendment in 1999 of the *Military Service Law of the People's Republic of China* (*zhonghua renmin gongheguo bingyi fa*, 中华人民共和国兵役法), which shortened the conscription process to 2 years and the revision of the *Regulations of the Chinese People's Liberation Army on the Active-Duty Service of Enlisted Personnel* (*zhongguo renmin jiefangjun xianyi shibing fuyi tiaoli*, 中国人民解放军现役士兵服役条例), heralded many of the changes underway in the NCO corps today. The latter regulations formally established the standard 30-year career path that exists for NCOs today.[24] In establishing a professional NCO corps, the PLA has sought to standardize and codify basic practices such as assignment and appointment; selection and recruitment; training; education; evaluation; salaries and benefits; and retirement.

Many of the areas under reform in the NCO corps reflect the PLA's overall goal of transforming into a more technologically capable and better educated force, and thus mirror areas of reform in the officer corps. For example, requiring education and training for NCOs is something the PLA is focused on in both the officer and NCO corps. In the case of NCOs, this is to address the need for better educated and more skilled personnel to compensate for its shortcomings on the conscription side of the force and take some of the burden off of officers, as well as to create a more effective NCO corps in a more modernized military. In 2005, the PLA's four general departments issued the "Opinions on Strengthening the Noncommissioned Officer Corps," which stipulated that individuals selected as NCOs must have a specified level of education and must go to military academies for training.[25]

The NCO selection and promotion process has also undergone significant change since 1999. The *Military Service Law*, the *Regulations of the Chinese People's Liberation Army on the Active-Duty Service of Enlisted Personnel*, and the 2001 *Regulations on the Management of Noncommissioned Officer in the People's Liberation Army* (*zhongguo renmin jiefangjun shiguan guanli guiding,* 中国人民解放军士官管理规定) represented an effort to standardize the procedures for selection into and promotions within the NCO corps, including presenting more stringent requirements and a strict quota system for NCO selection and assignment.[26]

This area appears to still be a work in progress. A recent article in *Zhanshi Bao* (*Soldiers' News*), the Guangzhou MR's newspaper, outlined NCO selection and promotion procedures and stated that "this issue is being widely and closely watched by grassroots officers and soldiers."[27]

PLA OFFICER AND NCO PERSONNEL MANAGEMENT

Administration and Implementation.

Whereas the previous section provides an overview and outlines the major ongoing reforms to PLA officer and NCO personnel management, this section will present the key institutions responsible for PLA personnel tasks. It will also describe the process for implementing each of the following three PLA officer and NCO personnel tasks:

- Evaluation and promotion.
- PME and training.
- Salaries and benefits.

Key Institutions and Tasks.

Task 1: Evaluation and Promotion. Within the PLA, the two organizations primarily responsible for managing the evaluation and promotion process for officers and NCOs are the GPD Cadre Department and the General Staff Department (GSD) Military Affairs Department.

GPD Cadre Department. The GPD Cadre Department and Cadre Departments in military region level headquarters down through the regimental level are responsible for handling cadre (officer) work (*ganbu gongzuo*; 干部工作), defined by the PLA as all tasks relating to PLA officer personnel management.[28] Cadre Departments' responsibilities include:

- Maintaining officer personnel files and managing officers' career paths.[29] Officer personnel files include all information concerning an officer's history and background such as biographical data, original enlistment form, Party membership application, date(s) of previous promotion, and current grade and rank.[30]
- Managing officers' career paths through their supervision of the selection, evaluation, promotion, and demobilization of all PLA officers.[31]

- Evaluating all officers at the military region level and below prior to their selection, promotion, transfer, and demobilization.

GSD Military Affairs Department. The General Staff Department Military Affairs Department (*junwu bu*, 军务部) and Military Affairs Departments located in MR headquarters down to the regiment level are responsible for implementing guidance from the Central Military Commission (CMC) on the management of the NCO Corps.[32] Staff officers (*jiguan renyuan*, 机关人员) within these Military Affairs Departments at all levels are responsible for compiling and managing NCO personnel files.[33] Military Affairs Departments' responsibilities in terms of NCO evaluation and promotion include:[34]

- Formulating the procedures and methods for NCO evaluations and promotions, in accordance with CMC guidance.
- Recruiting, selecting, assigning, promoting, and transferring NCOs.
- Compiling NCO personnel files, which form the basis for evaluation and promotion.

Figure 1 summarizes Cadre Departments' and Military Affairs Departments' responsibilities in terms of officer and NCO evaluation and promotion.

Administrative Organization	Tasks
GPD Cadre Department	Maintain officer personnel files and manage officer career paths.
GSD Military Affairs Department	Maintain NCO personnel files and manage NCO career paths.

Figure 1. Key Institutions Managing Officer and NCO Evaluations and Promotions.

Officer Evaluation and Promotion Process. The 2000 revised *Active-Duty Officer's Law* states that responsibilities for evaluating officers are divided between the headquarters staff (*jiguan*, 机关), commander (*shouzhang*, 首长), and the political department (division) on all levels.[35] As stated above, in 2006, the PLA reformed the pre-promotion evaluation process for officers to include quantitative written examinations in addition to assessing an officer's moral character. These evaluations and examinations form the primary basis for promotion to or removal from posts, and an officer may not be promoted or dismissed without first being evaluated. Officers are assessed as either "outstanding," "competent," or "incompetent," and must be informed of their assessment score. Military officers assessed as "incompetent" are demoted to a lower level post or transferred to other work.[36] According to anecdotal evidence, the evaluation process also includes a 360 degree review of the officer's superiors, peers, and subordinates.[37]

Rank and grade in the PLA. The concept of ranks and grades is vital for understanding what a "promotion" means in the PLA. The PLA assigns all personnel a rank (lieutenant to general) and one of 15 grades. The U.S. military also assigns ranks and grades to all personnel, and each rank corresponds with a specific grade. In the PLA however, most grades have 3-year minimum service requirements, while most ranks have 4-year minimum.

The 2000 *Active-Duty Officer's Law* states that officers are promoted on the basis of their job experience, education level, and their ability to complete the training required for the next higher level.[38] Unit Party committees and Cadre Departments share responsibility for identifying, recommending, and evaluating officers for promotion.[39] The Cadre Department managing the officer promotion depends on the officer's grade as depicted in Figure 2.[40]

Officer Grade	Cadre Department Overseeing Promotion
Grade 3: Military Region Leader	General Political Department
Grade 4: Military Region Deputy Leader	
Grade 5: Corps Leader	
Grade 6: Corps Deputy Leader	
Grade 7: Division Leader	Military Region Headquarters
Grade 8: Division Deputy Leader and Brigade Leader	Political Department
Grade 9: Brigade Deputy Leader and Regiment Leader	
Grade 10: Regiment Deputy Leader	Corps Headquarters Political
Grade 11: Battalion Leader	Department
Grade 12: Battalion Deputy Leader	
Grade 13: Company Leader	
Grade 14: Company Deputy Leader	
Grade 15: Platoon Leader	

Figure 2. Cadre Department Responsibility for Officer Promotion by Grade.

The PLA has also codified minimum time-in-rank and time-in-grade requirements for officers before they are eligible for promotion to the next rank and grade.[41] For all ranks except second lieutenant and first lieutenant, the time-in-rank requirement is 4 years. However, the time-in-grade requirement is only 3 years.[42] This creates a staggered relationship between rank and grade promotions, as shown in Figure 3.

Rank	Cadet	2LT/ENS	1LT/LTJG	CPT/LT	MAJ/LCDR	LTC/CDR	COL/CAPT	
	(3-4 Years)	(2 Years)	(4 Years)	(4 Years)	(4 Years)	(4 Years)	(4 Years)	
Grade	Cadet	Platoon Leader	Company Deputy Leader	Company Leader	Battalion Deputy Leader	Battalion Leader	Regiment Deputy Leader	3 Years Minimum to Each Next Higher Grade
	(4 Years)	(3 Years)	(3 Years)	(3 Years)	(3 Years)	(3 Years)	(3 Years)	

Figure 3. Rank and Grade Promotion Cycle.[43]

While the regulations stipulate a minimum time-in-grade before an officer may be considered for promotion, exceptions to this rule can be made. For example, if an officer has particularly outstanding qualifications or high-demand skills, an officer may be promoted early, and may be promoted more than one level (*yuezhi jinsheng*, 越职 晋升).[44] Additionally, certain officers posted in hardship regions may also be eligible for early grade promotions.[45]

NCO Evaluation and Promotion Process. Within the PLA, an NCO's career is divided into six graded service periods, each of which last for a fixed period as depicted in Figure 4. At the end of each service period, NCOs have the option of being demobilized or applying for promotion to the next higher grade service period. A third option exists for grade-1 NCOs, who may also apply for officer training. Promotion to the next level is by no means guaranteed, and those NCOs not selected for promotion are demobilized from active duty.

Grade	Service period and Years per period	Rank
(dengji, 等级)	(fu xianyi de nianxian, 服现役的年限)	(junxian, 军衔)
Junior NCO	1st Period (3Years)	Grade-1 NCO
	2nd Period (3 Years)	Grade-2 NCO
Mid-Level NCO	3rd Period (4 years)	Grade-3 NCO
	4th Period (4 years)	Grade-4 NCO
Senior NCO	5th Period (5 Years)	Grade-5 NCO
	6th Period (9 Years)	Grade-6 NCO

Figure 4. NCO Service Periods.

NCO promotion procedures are identical to those for selecting NCOs from conscripts.[46] Promotion decisions are made each year in November and take effect on December 1. Promotions are discussed and approved at different organizational levels in the military depending on the NCO's rank as shown in Figure 5 below:[47]

Promotion	Approval Level
Junior NCO (Grade 2)	Regiment- or brigade-level commanding officer
Mid-Level NCO (Grades 3 and 4)	Division- or brigade-level commanding officer
Senior NCO (Grades 5 and 6)	Corps-level; also subject to approval by the GSD Military Affairs Department

Figure 5. Administrative Levels Overseeing NCO Promotions.

There are two processes for evaluating NCOs prior to promotion: annual efficiency reports and pre-promotion evaluations.

- **Annual efficiency report**: All NCOs who have been in their billet for at least 6 months are evaluated no less than once per year by their immediate supervisor in an efficiency report.[48] These efficiency reports become part of the individual's personnel file. The annual efficiency reports provide the foundation for all reward and promotion decisions.

- **Pre-promotion evaluation:** Headquarters, Political, Logistics, and Equipment Department staff personnel conduct an additional evaluation of all NCOs applying for promotion.[49] Headquarters Department personnel focus their investigations into the candidate's military abilities, managerial competence, and cultural knowledge. Political Department personnel evaluate the candidate's political ideology. Logistics staff personnel evaluate the candidate's physical fitness.[50] Equipment Department personnel evaluate candidates based on their professional and technical knowledge.

Task 2: Professional Military Education and Training. Within the PLA, there are several administrative organizations that share responsibility for managing PME and training for officers and NCOs. Those organizations include:
- GPD Cadre Department.
- GPD Propaganda Department.
- GSD Service Arms and Training Department.
- GSD Military Affairs Department.
- Reserve Officer Selection and Training Offices.
- Centers for Military Academy Coordination.

GPD Cadre Department. In the PLA, cadre work also includes overseeing the education and training of both officers and NCOs.[51] One critical component of cadre work is to oversee the recruitment and approve the selection of all officers for attendance at PLA academies and schools. While the GSD decides how many and which types of instructors, students, and researchers are required, the Cadre Department determines which specific individuals are selected to fill these billets. The Cadre Department also coordinates with the GSD Military Affairs Department in drafting the service regulations (*fuyi tiaoling*, 服役条令), which stipulate the number of officers to be trained each year. Finally, the Cadre Department is also responsible for assigning officer cadets to billets after graduation.

GPD Propaganda Department (*xuanchuan bu*, 宣传部). This department oversees political education in military academies and schools. It also directly oversees several academies dedicated to producing political officers.[52]

GSD Service Arms and Training Department (*bingzhong he junshi xunlian bu*, 兵种和军事训练部). The Service Arms and Training Department's responsibilities for PME and training include:[53]

- Deciding which level of academy teaches which type of officers.
- Establishing and evaluating training standards and methods.
- Providing guidance on PME curricula and course content.
- Coordinating with the GPD Propaganda Department to approve new academic specialties and select instruction material for general use throughout the PLA.

GSD Military Affairs Department. Military Affairs Departments are responsible for overseeing the training of all NCOs.[54]

Offices for Reserve Officer Selection and Training (*houbei junguan xuanba peixun gongzuo bangongshi*,

后备军官选拔培训工作办公室).[55] These are military organizations that reside in some civilian institutions of higher education. These offices are mainly focused on managing the PLA's National Defense Scholarship (*guofang jiangxuejin*, 国防奖学金) program including the recruitment, selection, and training of National Defense Scholarship Students (*guofang sheng*, 国防生). Finally, these offices are responsible for coordinating the activities of active-duty officers selected to pursue graduate studies at civilian academic institutions.[56]

Centers for Military Academy Coordination. These Coordination Centers serve as a link between the GSD, GPD, and the actual PME institutions. They pass on higher-level guidance and promote cooperation among the various academies, military institutes, and research institutes within a particular "district."[57]

Figure 6 summarizes these administrative organizations' responsibilities in terms of officer and NCO PME and training.

Officer PME and Training Process. The 2000 *Active-Duty Officer Law* established a system of PLA officer promotion based on training.[58] This law stipulates that all officers must undergo training prior to promotion to the next grade.

As noted above, in addition to relying on PLA academies and schools, the PLA is sending an increasing number of officers to study at civilian higher education institutions. According to GPD Cadre Department Deputy Director Shi Yuhua (石宝华), between 2003 and 2007, the PLA sent more than 200,000 officers to civilian schools.[59] During this time period, the PLA sent increasing numbers of officers to civilian schools to complete PhDs and masters degrees.[60]

Administrative Organization	Tasks
GPD Cadre Department	Oversee officer and NCO education and training.
GPD Propaganda Department	Oversee political education in military academies and schools.
GSD Service Arms and Training Department	Establish and evaluate training standards and methods; Provide guidance on PME curricula and course content.
GSD Military Affairs Department	Decide the exact number of instructors, students, and researchers for each academy.
General Logistics Department General Equipment Department	Formulate policy and guidelines for equipment officer; logistics officer, and technical specialist training.
Reserve Officer Selection and Training Offices	Manage the recruitment, selection, and training of National Defense Students; Coordinate the activities of active-duty officers studying at civilian universities.
Centers for Military Academy Coordination	Coordinate between the GPD, GSD, and PME institutions.

Figure 6. Key Institutions Managing Officer and NCO PME and Training.

NCO PME and Training Process. The 2001 *Regulations for the Management of NCOs* state that NCO candidates must receive the requisite training prior to entering the recruitment and selection process.[61] As noted above, in 2005 the four General Departments issued new requirements aiming to raise all junior NCOs' educational level to high school equivalency (*zhongzhuan*, 中专), and all senior NCOs to the level of 3-year college (technical school) graduates (*dazhuan*, 大专) or higher by 2008.

Additionally, the regulations stipulate that mid-level and senior NCOs should undergo regular intervals of refresher training instructing them how to handle new situations, ordnance, and equipment.[62] Units at or above the corps-level formulate unified training plans for implementing this refresher training at military academies, training organizations, factories, research institutes, civilian educational institutions, or study at foreign institutions. Regiment and brigade-level units are responsible for organizing on-the-job training for NCOs to raise their skill levels and meet units' needs for skilled individuals.[63] Units also encourage all NCOs to continue their education through correspondence courses, television courses, and self-study and examination courses.

Task 3: Salary and Benefits. Within the PLA, there are several administrative organizations that share responsibility for managing officers' and NCOs' salaries and benefits. Those organizations include:

- GPD Cadre Department.
- GPD Organization Department.
- GLD Finance Department.
- GLD Capital Construction and Barracks Department.

GPD Cadre Department. Cadre Departments oversee officer salaries and benefits through their management of the "Cadre Welfare and Salary System" (*ganbu gongzi fuli zhidu*, 干部工资福利制度).[64] This system governs both active-duty and retired officer salaries, allowances and subsidies, and welfare.[65]

GPD Organization Department. Organization Departments are responsible for conducting ideological education for NCOs, issuing rewards, approving NCOs' marriages, providing NCOs' families with accommodations in military units, finding schools for their children, and overseeing compensation for the families of deceased NCOs.[66]

The GLD Finance Department. Within the four General Departments, the General Logistics Department's Finance Department (*caiwu bu*, 财务部) is responsible for formulating policy in conjunction with the CMC and issuing guidelines for both officer and NCO salaries and benefits. Logistics departments on all levels are responsible for ensuring that NCOs receive their wages, allowances, subsidies, food, clothing, lodging, welfare, medical care, labor protection, disability considerations, and insurance, and for guaranteeing that NCOs' families receive medical care.[67]

The GLD Capital Construction and Barracks Department. The GLD Capital Construction and Barracks Department (*jijian yingfang bu*, 基建营房部) is responsible for formulating policy in accordance with CMC guidance and issuing guidelines governing officer and NCO housing.

Figure 7 summarizes these administrative organizations' responsibilities for managing officers' and NCOs' salaries and benefits.

Administrative Organization	Tasks
GPD Cadre Department	Manage officers' salaries and benefits.
GPD Organization Department	Manage NCOs' marriages and benefits for their dependents.
GLD Finance Department	Formulate and implement policy governing both officer and NCO salaries and benefits.
GLD Capital Construction and Barracks Department	Formulate policy on officer and NCO housing.

Figure 7. Key Institutions Managing Officer and NCO Salary and Benefits.

Officer Salaries, Subsidies, and Benefits. In July 2006, the PLA increased the wages, living expenses, and pensions for its officers and NCOs. Reportedly, all

PLA officers and NCOs received pay increases ranging between 80 and 100 percent.[68] For example, prior to the 2006 salary increase, a PLA colonel earned 2,000 RMB (USD 256) per month.[69] Following the salary increase, a PLA colonel now earns 4,200 RMB (USD 539) per month. By comparison, a U.S. military colonel earns about USD 9,000 (70,200 RMB) per month.

Grade	RMB	USD
Corps Leader	¥8,000	$ 1,025
Division Leader	¥5,600	$ 718
Regiment Leader	¥4,200	$ 539
Battalion Leader	¥3,200	$ 410
Company Leader	¥2,600	$ 333
Platoon Leader	¥2,200	$ 282

Figure 8. Base Monthly Salary for Officers after July 2006.[70]

The Cadre Department manages officer salaries, allowances, and subsidies including:[71]
- Base Salary (*jiben gongzi*, 基本工资). This is determined according to the officer's grade, rank, billet, and time in service.
- Servicemen's Professional Allowance (*junren zhiye jintie*, 军人职业津贴). This is an allowance provided to officers who provide certain duties and tasks in addition to their main responsibilities.
- Grassroots Cadre Billet Allowance (*jiceng ganbu gangwei jintie*, 基层干部岗位津贴). This allowance is provided to all officers posted in battalions, companies, and platoons.
- Regional Allowance (*diqu jintie*, 地区津贴). This is a subsidy provided to officers stationed in

hardship areas. The amount varies based on the level of hardship as determined by the PLA.
- Specialty Subsidies (*zhuanye butie*, 专业补贴). This is a subsidy provided to personnel working in high-demand billets that require special skills such as aviation and naval technical positions, as well as national defense scientific research positions. The amount of the subsidy is determined by the degree of specialization that the position requires.

Active-duty officers are also entitled to a number of welfare benefits including free health care, housing, and support for their dependents. Housing for military officers includes provisions for both public and private housing. Whether officers choose to live in public housing or purchase their own homes, they are entitled to the corresponding housing subsidies and preferential treatment. The PLA pays additional subsidies to officers who endure harsh living and/or working conditions. For example, subsidies for officers stationed in Tibet can almost triple the amount they would receive if assigned to other areas in China.

NCO Salaries, Subsidies, and Benefits. NCOs in the PLA receive a monthly salary which is composed of three parts:[72]
- Base Salary (*jichu gongzi*, 基础工资).
- Grade and Rank Salary (*junxian jibie gongzi*, 军衔级别工资): This salary is divided into six grades (NCO grades 1-6) and between five and ten levels (*dang*, 档) for each grade.
- Time in Service Salary (*junling gongzi*, 军龄工资). This is calculated from the time the NCO joined the PLA.

215

Depending on these three factors, the monthly salary for an NCO in the PLA can vary considerably, even within a single grade. According to a former official in the PLA General Logistics Department, following the July 1, 2006, PLA salary increase, NCO monthly salaries for the following three grades are:[73]

Rank	RMB	USD
Grade-1	¥ 1,540	$197
Grade-2	¥ 1,980	$254
*Grade-6	¥ 3,700	$474
*Estimated value		

Figure 9. Base Monthly Salary for NCOs after July 2006.[75]

Although monthly salaries in the PLA are taxable, they are only taxed if the salary exceeds RMB 1,600 (USD 205). While monthly salaries in excess of 1,600 RMB are taxable, the *1999 Revised Regulations of the Chinese People's Liberation Army on the Active-Duty Service of Enlisted Personnel* and the 2001 *Regulations of the Chinese People's Liberation Army on the Management of NCOs* improved the quality of additional tax-free benefits to enhance the attractiveness of an NCO position.[76] These benefits include a servicemen's allowance based on rank and grade; housing subsidies; food subsidies; and free or subsidized medical care for officers, NCOs, and their dependents. For a list of current tax-free NCO benefits and subsidies, see Appendix II.

Additional NCO Benefits. Similar to the regulations governing officer welfare policies, the 2001 *NCO Management Regulations* also stipulate detailed provisions governing the housing, medical,

216

employment, and education benefits available to NCOs and their dependents. These regulations govern every detail of an NCO's family life including what type of housing they may live in, how frequently NCOs may visit their families or have their families visit them, which families are entitled to what level of benefits, and the procedures for receiving those benefits. For example, the 2001 *NCO Management Regulations* stipulate that except for the time period when their families come to visit them, all grassroots-level NCOs are required to live in military housing.[77] They also stipulate that married NCOs' spouses are permitted to visit the barracks once per year and may reside within the barracks under normal circumstances for a period not to exceed 45 days.[78]

CONCLUSION

Officer and NCO personnel reforms are an important component of a comprehensive reform and modernization program ongoing since the mid-1990s. At that time, the PLA conducted a self-assessment and concluded that it did not possess the right type of soldier — particularly officers — to meet the changing requirements of warfare. The PLA also concluded that despite a series of similar reforms enacted in the mid-1980s, PLA education and training institutions were still failing to produce these "new type" officers.

There is nothing new about the PLA's goals to attract, train, place, and retain a high-caliber officer corps. However, it is only fairly recently (since the late 1990s) that the PLA has managed to gain some traction in this area. Even while the PLA itself becomes increasingly modernized and sophisticated, China's economic growth over the past three decades has created a set of new and growing human and financial resources from which to draw in its efforts to create an educated professional officer corps.

Paradoxically, the same changes in Chinese society that have produced the human capital the PLA desires and the financial capital with which to attract and retain it have also created new challenges to the PLA's personnel goals. China's increasingly vibrant private sector now provides fierce competition for China's best and brightest. Even if the PLA manages to successfully attract, train, and place the "new type" officers it requires, it is by no means certain it will be able to retain them.

Finally, it is difficult to assess the PLA's success in meeting its objectives for reforming its officer corps. Many of the personnel reforms the PLA has undertaken are relatively recent, and many are still ongoing. PLA publications contain a wealth of data on personnel reforms, and numerous regulations and laws have been revised and promulgated to reflect the PLA's reform goals. In addition, many of these publications note progress in educating the officer corps and in reforming the professional military education system to better fit the PLA's modernization program. That said, it remains to be seen if the PLA can effectively transfer written laws and policies into reality, and whether China's socioeconomic dynamics will help or hinder the PLA in building the force it needs to fight and win the high-tech wars of the future.

APPENDIX I

NCO APPLICATION AND SELECTION PROCESS FOR CONSCRIPTS[81]

1. **Individual Application** (*benren shenqing*, 本人申请). To begin the process, conscripts must submit a written application to their unit's Party branch in October of their second year of service, 1 month before NCO selection.

2. **Grassroots Recommendation** (*jiceng tuijian*, 基层推荐). After the Party branch receives the application, the company political instructor (also the Party branch secretary) then gathers information on the applicant's qualifications and job performance, and solicits opinions from the applicant's peers.

3. **Headquarters Evaluation** (*jiguan kaohe*, 机关考核). The headquarters organization at the regiment-level and above carries out an evaluation and physical examination of the candidate and compiles a list of those who pass.

4. **Organizational Examination and Approval** (*zuzhi shenpi*, 组织审批). On the basis of the headquarters evaluation, Party committees at the regiment-level and above hold deliberations to make their final selections.

5. **Fill Out the "NCO Selection Report"** (*shiguan xuanqu baogao*, 士官选取报告). After selection, the NCO completes this form for inclusion in his personnel file.

APPENDIX II

NCO BENEFITS AND SUBSIDIES[82]

- **Servicemen's Allowance** (*junren zhiye jintie*, 军人职业津贴). All NCOs are entitled to an allowance based on their rank and grade.
- **.Grassroots Managerial or Leadership Billet Allowance** (*jiceng xingzheng lingdao guanli zhiwu jintie*, 基层行政领导管理职务津贴). NCOs serving as managerial personnel or leaders in administrative, professional, or technical billets at the grassroots level receive an additional allowance
- **Housing Subsidy and Public Provident Fund** (*zhufang butie he gongjijin*, 住房补贴和公积金). NCOs are entitled to a housing subsidy as well as participation in the state-run public provident fund that provides assistance to military personnel seeking to purchase a home.
- **Food Subsidy** (*huoshi butie*, 伙食补贴). All NCOs receive a ration card for their meals. All personnel in a given unit receive the same amount of food regardless of grade, rank, time in service, marital status, or number of dependents.
- **Subsidized Medical Care** (*gongfei yiliao*, 公费医疗). All active-duty NCOs enjoy free medical care in the military's health care system.
- **Hardship Living Relief Fund** (*shenghuo kunnan jiuji fei*, 生活困难救济费). This fund provides supplemental assistance to the parents of NCOs living in dire straits.
- **Child Care Assistance** (*zinü baoyu buzhu*, 子女保育补助) and Child Education Assistance (*zinü*

jiaoyu bushu, 子女教育补助). Issued to NCOs whose child is qualified to attend a military-run pre-school but does not. This money allows the NCO to defray the high cost of school fees for children living elsewhere.

- **One Child Parent Bonus** (*dusheng zinü fumu jiangli fei*, 独生子女父母奖励费) and **Maternity Leave** (*chanjia*, 产假). NCOs who have one and only one child receive a monthly bonus until the child turns 14. The bonus is 5 RMB (USD .64) if one parent is an NCO and 10 RMB (USD 1.28) if both parents are NCOs. Female NCOs receive 3 months' maternity leave after giving birth to their only child.

- **Hardship Post Allowance** (*jianku diqu jintie*, 艰苦地区津贴). The PLA provides additional monthly allowances to NCOs stationed at hardship posts. These posts include many warehouses, military farms, radar stations, and communications-line maintenance stations located in isolated areas. The amount varies between an additional 20 and 270 RMB (USD 2.56-34.62) per month, depending on the level of hardship involved.

- **Allowance for Harmful Substance and Hazardous Work Duty** (*youdu youhai gangwei baojian jintie*, 有毒有害岗位保健津贴). NCOs whose duty involves work unusual hazards or exposure to harmful substances are provided monthly allowances. The amount varies depending on the nature of the risk involved.

- **Proficiency Pay** (*zhiwu jintie*, 职务津贴). In addition to their salaries, some NCOs are eligible for a supplemental subsidy depending on their duties. For example, squad leaders (*banzhang*, 班

长) and NCOs in technical leadership positions receive additional monthly subsidies.

ENDNOTES - CHAPTER 6

1. In 1993, in response to lessons learned from the 1991 Gulf War and Operation DESERT STORM, the CMC issued the "Military Strategic Guidelines of the New Period" ("xin shiqi junshi zhanlüe fangzhen," 新时期军事战略方针). The coalition's successful use of lethal, precise, mobile, high-tech forces in the Gulf War served as a wakeup call to PLA leaders, who realized that their own military was comparatively far behind. They were galvanized into issuing this new strategic guidance, which reassessed the nature of warfare based on PLA analysis of the Gulf War, and introduced the concept of "local wars under modern high-tech conditions." The Guidelines made winning such wars the goal towards which the entire PLA had to orient itself. For a detailed explanation of the Military Strategic Guidelines, see David Finkelstein, "China's National Military Strategy: An Overview of the 'Military Strategic Guidelines,'" *Asia Policy*, No. 4, July 2007, pp. 53-105.

2. Yao Yunzhu, "The Evolution of Military Doctrine of the Chinese PLA from 1985 to 1995," *Korea Journal of Defense Analysis*, Winter 1996, pp. 57–80.

3. Li Xinliang, "High-Tech Local Wars' Basic Requirements for Army Building," *Junshi Kexue*, November 20, 1998, pp. 15-20; "A Retrospective of Army Building," China Internet Information Center, available from *www.china.org.cn/english/2001/Aug/16861. htm.*

4. Wen Tai, "Accomplish the Foundation Project," p. 3; "Stabilizing Principal Grassroots-level Officers and Strengthening Grassroots Development: Sixth Comment on Better Intensifying Implementation of 'Program,'" *Jiefangjun Bao*, December 9, 2000, p. 1.

5. The PLA's "Talented Military Personnel Strategic Project" ("jundui rencai zhanlüe gongcheng," 军队人才战略工程), issued in 2003, provides a development plan for the military up to 2020. This project aims to obtain commanding officers capable of building informationalized armed forces, staff officers proficient in planning military operations, technical specialists with knowledge of hi-tech weaponry, and NCOs with expertise in using weapons and equipment at hand. See Qiang Pen, "PLA Beefs up Military

Training System," *China Daily*, May 1, 2007.

6. The volume, *Civil-Military Relations in Today's China: Swimming in a New Sea*," David Finkelstein and Kristen Gunness, eds., Armonk, NY: M. E. Sharpe, 2007, provides one of the first comprehensive looks at civil-military relations, socioeconomic change in China, and the challenges the PLA is facing.

7. Maryanne Kivlehan-Wise, "Demobilization and Resettlement: The Challenge of Downsizing the People's Liberation Army," in Finkelstein and Gunness, eds., *Civil-Military Relations in Today's China*, p. 255.

8. National People's Congress, *Active-Duty Officer's Law of the People's Republic of China* (*zhonghua renmin gongheguo xianyi junguan fa*, 中华人民共和国现役军官法), December 28, 2000, Section 7, Article 48.

9. For more information on the PLA's interaction with the civilian university system, see Kristen Gunness, "Educating the Officer Corps: The Chinese People's Liberation Army and its Interactions with Civilian Academic Institutions," in Finkelstein and Gunness, eds., *Civil Military Relations in Today's China*, Armonk, NY: M. E. Sharpe, 2006, p. 187.

10. Allen, Cheng, Finkelstein, Kivlehan-Wise, *Institutional Reform of the Chinese People's Liberation Army: Overview and Challenges*, The CNA Corporation, 2002, p. 6.

11. Wang Yongxiao, "The PLA Second Artillery Corps has a Sufficient Number of Qualified Personnel Adapted to Modernized Weaponry," *Zhongguo Xinwen She*, June 14, 2006.

12. For a discussion of social change in China and its impact on the PLA, see Xiaobing Li, "The Impact of Social Change in the PLA," in Finkelstein and Gunness, *Civil Military Relations in Today's China*, p. 55.

13. Li Xuefei, "Outstanding College Graduates can Directly Become Military Officers," *Zhongguo Qingnian Bao*, November 3, 2006.

14. In this chapter, we have opted to translate grade 5, "*jun,* 军" as "corps."

15. Allen, Cheng, Finkelstein, and Kivlehan-Wise, *Institutional Reforms*, p. v.

16. GPD Cadre Department, "Explanations on the Active-Duty Officer's Law of the People's Republic of China," *Jiefangjun Bao,* January 18, 2001.

17. In 2003 the PLA launched its "Talented Military Personnel Strategic Project" (*jundui rencai zhanlüe gongcheng,* 军队人才战略工程), which lays out a development plan for military personnel to 2020. Included in this plan is a plan for enrolling more high-caliber civilian personnel in the military, and sending more PLA officers to pre-promotion education in civilian academic institutions. See Qiang Pen, "PLA Beefs up Military Training System," *Zhongguo Ribao (China Daily)*, May 1, 2007.

18. Li Xuefei, "Outstanding College Graduates can Directly Become Military Officers," *Zhongguo Qingnian Bao*, November 3, 2006.

19. *China's Navy 2007*, "Quality of Life," p. 61.

20. Zhang Jianguo, "Important Innovation of Cadre Evaluation and Appointment System," *Jiefangjun Bao*, July 20, 2006.

21. "CMC Chairman Jiang Zemin Signs Decree on Promulgation of *Regulations on Appointments and Removals of Military Officers on Active Service*," *Jiefangjun Bao,* January 14, 2002.

22. "Combining Performance Evaluations with Examinations for the Appointment of Leading Cadres at the Vice Regiment Commander Level in all Combat Units as a Measure of reforming the Cadre Evaluation and Appointment System," *Jiefangjun Bao*, July 3, 2006.

23. Liu Pengqin, "Jinan Military Region Selects Deputy Regiment Leading Cadres by Means of Combining Performance Appraisal and Examination for the First Time," *Qianwei Bao*, December 29, 2006.

24. For an insightful look at the changes to the PLA's conscription and demobilization system, see Sijin Cheng, "The Challenge of Conscription in an Era of Social Change," and Maryanne Kivlehan-Wise, "Demobilization and Resettlement: The Challenge of Downsizing the People's Liberation Army," in Finkelstein and Gunness, eds., *Civil Military Relations in Today's China*, p. 235.

25. Wang Dongming, "Armed Forces Introduce Several New Policies to Strengthen NCO Corps," *Xinhua*, March 23, 2005.

26. *PLA Regulations for Managing Non-Commissioned Officers*, Chapter 1, Article 6.

27. "Interview with Guangzhou Military Region Ranking Officer on NCO Selection," *Zhanshi Bao*, November 11, 2005.

28. Li Hezhong, *A Guide to Political Organ Work* (*zhengzhi jiguan gongzuo zhinan*, 政治籍贯工作指南), Beijing: National Defense University Press, September 2003, p. 128; *Active-Duty Officer's Law of the People's Republic of China* (*zhonghua renmin gongheguo xianyi junguan fa*, 中华人民共和国现役军官法), December 28, 2000, Section 1, Article 7.

29. Li Yunzhi, *General Political Department*, in Song Shilin and Xiao Ke, eds., *Chinese Military Encyclopedia* (*zhongguo junshi baike quanshu*, 中国军事百科全书), Vol. 4, *Political Work and Military Logistics in the Chinese People's Liberation Army*, Beijing: Military Science Press, July 1997, pp, 398-400; Li Zengguang, *Political Departments*, pp. 374-375; Shambaugh, *Modernizing China's Military*, p. 136; Wortzel, "The General Political Department," p. 235.

30. Li Hezhong, *A Guide to Political Organ Work* (*zhengzhi jiguan gongzuo zhinan*, 政治籍贯工作指南), Beijing: National Defense University Press, September 2003, p. 128.

31. Li Yunzhi, *General Political Department*, p. 398.

32. *PLA Regulations for Managing Non-Commissioned Officers*, Chapter 1, Article 2. For a more detailed explanation of the GSD

Military Affairs Department's roles and functions, see David Finkelstein, "The General Staff Department of the Chinese People's Liberation Army: Organization, Roles, and Missions," in Mulvenon and Yang, eds., *The People's Liberation Army as Organization*, pp. 122-224.

33. *PLA Regulations for Managing Non-Commissioned Officers*, Chapter 5, Article 35; Yang Zhaoguo, "Persist in Selecting and Assigning Noncommissioned Officers According to Law and Enhance Development of Grassroots Backbone Personnel—Interview with Director Yang Zhaoguo of the GSD Military Affairs and Mobilization Department of Military Region Headquarters on Relevant Issues Concerning the Selection of Noncommissioned Officers," *Zhanshi Bao*, November 11, 2005.

34. *PLA Regulations for Managing Non-Commissioned Officers*, Chapter 1, Article 4.

35. *Active-Duty Officer's Law of the People's Republic of China*, Chapter 3, December 28, 2000, Article 11.

36. *Ibid.*, Article 23.

37. Interviews in Washington, DC, and Beijing.

38. *Active-Duty Officer's Law of the People's Republic of China*, Chapter 3, Article 21.

39. Liu Yongshou and Wang Yongquan, "Military Party Committee System (*jundui dangweizhi*, 军队党委制), in Song Shilin and Xiao Ke, eds., *Chinese Military Encyclopedia* (*zhongguo junshi baike quanshu*, 中国军事百科全书), Vol. 4, *Political Work and Military Logistics in the Chinese People's Liberation Army*, Beijing: Military Science Press, July 1997, pp. 131-132.

40. Dennis J. Blasko, *The Chinese Army Today: Tradition and Transformation for the 21st Century*, New York: Routledge, 2006, p. 56.

41. *Regulations on the Military Ranks of Officers of the Chinese People's Liberation Army*, available from *english.chinamil.com/cn/ site2/special-reports/2006-04/20/content_460089.htm.*

42. *Active-Duty Officer's Law of the People's Republic of China*, Chapter 3, Articles 17 and 18. Note: In the PLA, an officer's time in service begins the first day they arrive at an academy, not the day of commissioning upon graduation.

43. "China's Navy 2007," Office of Naval Intelligence, March 2007, p. 63, available from *militarytimes.com/static/projects/pages/20070313dnplanavy.pdf*. Note that this chart represents the *minimum* time in grade and rank required for promotion. It is unclear whether an officer in the PLA could make promotion to each next higher rank and grade after only the minimum amount of time required.

44. *Active-Duty Officer's Law of the People's Republic of China*, Chapter 3, Article 20.

45. State Council, Central Military Commission, Four General Departments, and Navy Headquarters, *Basic Treatment of Naval Officers* (*haijun junguan de jiben daiyu*, 海军军官的基本待遇), *Tuiyi Junguan Wang*, November 14, 2004, available from *www.tyjg.com/xx.asp?newsid=1872*.

46. See Appendix 1 for a detailed description of the NCO selection process.

47. *PLA Regulations on Military Service of Active-Duty Conscripts* (*zhongguo renmin jiefangjun xianyi shibing fuyi tiaoli*, 中国人民解放军现役士兵服役条例), Chapter 3, Article 21 June 30, 1999; *Zhongguo Xinwen She*, "Chinese Armed Forces to Downsize 200,000 by 2005," November 3, 2003.

48. *PLA Regulations for Managing Non-Commissioned Officers*, Chapter 7, Article 36.

49. *Ibid.*, Article 37.

50. In the PLA, health and medical functions fall under the purview of the logistics system.

51. Li Yunzhi, *General Political Department*, pp, 398-400; Li Zengguang, *Political Departments*, in Song Shilin and Xiao Ke, eds., *Chinese Military Encyclopedia* (*zhongguo junshi baike quanshu*,

中国军事百科全书), Vol. 4, *Political Work and Military Logistics in the Chinese People's Liberation Army,* Beijing: Military Science Press, July 1997, pp. 374-375; Shambaugh, *Modernizing China's Military,* p. 136; Wortzel, "The General Political Department," p. 235.

52. Li Yunzhi, *General Political Department,* pp. 398-400.

53. David Finkelstein, "The General Staff Department of the Chinese People's Liberation Army: Organization, Roles, and Missions," in Mulvenon and Yang, eds., *The People's Liberation Army as Organization,* pp. 122-224.

54. *PLA Regulations for Managing Non-Commissioned Officers,* Chapter 1, Article 4.

55. Note: The PLA uses two terms to distinguish between reserve officers studying at civilian academic institutions and active-duty reserve officers. The former are referred to as *houbei junguan* (后备军官) and have not yet entered active service. The term for active-duty reserve officers is *yubei junguan* (预备军官).

56. These offices' responsibilities also include overseeing military propaganda work at the host civilian institution as well as recruiting non-National Defense Scholarship civilian college graduates into the PLA.

57. *Regulations on Education,* Article 70. While the *Regulations* do not define the "districts" for which a particular Coordination Center is responsible for, they may correspond to military districts. Little information is available about this system of Coordination Centers or their position in the PLA hierarchy.

58. *Active-Duty Officer's Law of the People's Republic of China,* Chapter 2, Article 10; Note: It is unclear how training at civilian institutions of higher education fits into this pre-promotion PME matrix.

59. "GPD: National Defense Students to Comprise 60% of PLA Officer Recruits by 2010" ('zong zhengzhibu: 2010 nian guofangsheng jiang zhan jundui shengzhang ganbu de 60%," 总政治部: 2010年国防生将占军队生长干部的60%), *Xinhua She,* May 8, 2007, available from *www.go81.net/html/200705/2007050810415174.*

htm.

60. *Ibid.*

61. *PLA Regulations for Managing Non-Commissioned Officers,* Chapter 4, Article 20.

62. *Ibid.,* Article 23.

63. *Ibid.,* Article 24.

64. Li Yunzhi, *General Political Department,* pp. 398-400; Li Zengguang, *Political Departments,* pp. 374-375; Shambaugh, *Modernizing China's Military,* p. 136; Wortzel, "The General Political Department," p. 235.

65. Note: The Cadre department deals only with soldiers who have been demobilized (*tuiwu,* 退伍) or retired (*tuixiu,* 退休); it does not deal with officers who have transferred to civilian positions (*zhuanye,* 转业).

66. *PLA Regulations for Managing Non-Commissioned Officers,* Chapter 1, Article 4; Chapter 11, Article 65.

67. *Ibid.*

68. Xu Guanyu, "What's Behind the Military Budget Increase?" *People's Daily Online* (English Edition), March 15, 2007, available from *english.people.com.cn/200703/15/eng20070315_357782.html.*

69. Major General (Ret.) Jiang Shiliang, "China's Expenditures for Military Personnel," briefing presented at the Institute for Defense Analyses, Alexandria, VA, June 20, 2007. Major General (Ret.) Jiang Shiliang is a former director of the General Logistics Department Military Transportation department and is currently a senior advisor at the China Institute for International Strategic Studies.

70. *Ibid.*

71. Chen Shushan, "Cadre Salary and Welfare System," in Song Shilin and Xiao Ke, eds., *China Military Encyclopedia,* Vol. 4, p. 41. Unless otherwise noted, all data in this section come from this source.

72. *Active-Duty Officer's Law of the People's Republic of China*, Chapter 6, Article 39.

73. Blasko, *The Chinese Army Today*, p. 56.

74. *Military Finance*, Vol. 3, *China Military Logistics Encyclopedia*, (*zhongguo junshi houqin baike quanshu*, 中国军事后勤百科全书), Beijing, Golden Shield Publishing House (*jindun chubanshe*; 金盾出版社), Aug 2002, p. 47.

75. Major General (Ret.) Jiang Shiliang, "China's Expenditures for Military Personnel," Briefing presented at the Institute for Defense Analyses, Alexandria, VA, June 20, 2007.

76. While we were only able to identify specific monthly salary data for grade-1 and grade-2 NCOs, Major General (Ret.) Jiang Shiliang's briefing reported that Grade-6 NCOs receive pay equivalent to that of a regiment deputy leader (grade 8) officer. Since we know that regiment grade officers (grade 9) receive RMB 4,200.00 per month, and battalion grade officers (grade 7) receive RMB 3,200.00 per month, we estimated a grade 8 officer's salary as RMB 3,700, the exact median of the salaries for grades 7 and 9.

77. *Ibid.*

78. "Income Tax Cutoff Point Lifted to 1,600 Yuan," *Xinhua*, October 22, 2005.

79. *PLA Regulations for Managing Non-Commissioned Officers*, Chapter 6, Article 33.

80. *Ibid.*, Chapter 8, Article 45.

81. "Flow Chart of NCO Selection Work," *Jiefangjun Bao*, December 7, 2005, p. 6; *PLA Management Regulations*, Chapter 3, Article 17.

82. *PLA Regulations for Managing Non-Commissioned Officers*, Chapter 8, Article 40.

CHAPTER 7

PLA CAREER PROGRESSIONS AND POLICIES[1]

Elizabeth Hague

INTRODUCTION

This chapter discusses the career progression, geographic assignments, and ethnic policies of the Chinese People's Liberation Army (PLA) officer corps. The chapter uses available data to explore how officers are selected for geographic assignments, and how junior, field grade, and general officers move between assignments. It also explores how career progressions differ based on operational, political, logistic, armament, and technical career tracks. While even regulations differ depending on an officer's career track, in general, the *system* is fairly regularized. A regularized system follows a set of rules for training, education, age, and time in position for each officer career track. A fairly regularized system does not mean, however, that individuals' career progressions or promotions to specific positions are predictable. Certain positions make officers more competitive for future promotions, but the desirable positions (and the specific criteria for promotion) can change as the PLA's priorities change.

Out of all of the officers that follow the regulations and do what the system requires, a very small percentage end up making it to the top. When they do not climb to the "top," their careers can still be considered successful: technical officers, for example, rarely rise to the top, but still are considered successful if they receive rewards and recognition for their contributions to the PLA's modernization. When officers do rise to the top, their brand of success is due to a lot more than having fulfilled regulatory requirements. For example, while senior general officers have all fulfilled basic requirements for career progression, most also have fulfilled an additional, very important requirement — making a significant contribution to national security. Because the perception of a "significant contribution" changes as the PLA evolves, current general officers cannot serve as a definitive predictor of whom to expect as future officers. In addition, some have other characteristics that make them more promotable, such as good political connections or personal qualities, such as charisma and leadership, that are difficult to identify. Finally, the chapter touches briefly on the careers of ethnic minorities in the PLA: Does the PLA have Chinese-style affirmative action programs for ethnic minority officers, and do they have unrestricted assignments?[2]

Sources and Methodology.

The author examined openly available PLA sources such as regulations and measured these against case studies and examples. Most regulations relevant to this chapter are openly available, though research did not turn up an actual "affirmative action" policy or regulation. The author compiled a database comprised of biographic data on about 180 officers' career progressions, rank, time in position, service and unit affiliation, and personal information. Basic case study or biographic information is available for general officers, though the data lack consistent detail about specific assignments and education and tends to reveal what PLA publicists want to reveal. PLA newspapers, for example, often publish biographic profiles of officers who have demonstrated a quality worthy of example or received awards. For junior and mid-career level officers, specific biographic information is even more spotty: rarely are all of the biographic fields that the author seeks available for a single officer (unless he is a well-known general officer). At more junior and mid-career officer levels, anecdotal information is available on the types of officers who receive awards—a useful measure of what the PLA values in its officers, but far from a comprehensive overview of career progression. Because the data compiled tend to flow from portraits of successful PLA officers, at a minimum these stories, combined, can give an informative picture of what the PLA views as ideal, model officers.[3] A final caveat: many of the officers for whom we have relatively complete biographic data rose through the ranks over the last few decades. However, the criteria for their promotion decades ago often would not equate to the criteria for those promoted today. The PLA in many cases values different skills and promotes for different reasons now compared to 30 years ago. For this reason, we can draw only limited conclusions from examining high-level officers' careers.

Combining a study of regulations and linear career progression does not factor in the role of connections or other intangible factors in the PLA officers' careers. Both are extremely important factors, though less important than 20 years ago because the PLA standards for promotion are far more institutionalized. While regulations are useful guidelines and career progressions offer useful hints, an outside observer is unable to conduct a detailed analysis of how performance is measured and the relative weight of performance, political correctness, and connections in personnel decisions to promote or not promote.

We also have no way to examine why an officer was not promoted. Nonetheless, the regulations provide a useful framework for analysis.

Career Tracks in the People's Liberation Army.[4] For the purposes of professional development, the PLA has five basic career tracks: operational, political, logistical, armament, and technical specialist.[5] Generally officers adhere fairly closely to one of these tracks, though there are examples of officers who take a dual-track path, such as former (until September 2007) Air Force commander, Qiao Qingchen, who has followed a dual operational/political track. Some younger officers seem to alternate between different types of positions: In the case of Second Artillery operators, about 20 percent reportedly now "know how to do both" operational and logistical work.[6]

Operators consist of the PLA's warfighters: its commanders, chiefs of staff, training and operations specialists, and pilots or infantry men. "Operators," also called "military affairs officers" (*junshi guan*, 军事官) in PLA literature, follow diverse, specialized careers in submarines, surface fleets, armored vehicles, infantry, aviation, and numerous other fields. Political officers take on the important responsibilities of ensuring the political rectitude of PLA personnel and play a critical role in personnel decisions (such as promotions and awards). They also can be "specialized" within their fields, focusing on propaganda work or political work tailored to their unit (especially for political commissars (PCs) in more technical units or offices).

Logistics officers generally do logistics, supply, maintenance support, medical, and financial work, and armaments officers focus on equipment and armaments management and integration — often requiring working closely with both operations officers on training issues and with logistics issues on maintenance issues. Technical specialist officers concentrate in a range of technical areas important to the PLA. All of these officers are subject to a body of PLA regulations regarding their recruitment, training, and promotion. These regulations offer insights into PLA policies for officers at different points in their career (junior, field grade, or flag officers) and, in some cases, different expectations for different specialties. Technical specialists, in particular, have a slightly different set of requirements for how many years they can serve.[7]

PLA REGULATIONS

The PLA has a series of fairly detailed regulations for recruitment, education, examination, appointment, dismissal, reward, promotion, transfers, and retirement of officers throughout their careers. One of the most prominent and basic of these regulations is the Active Duty Service Officer regulation. This regulation provides extensive detail on regulations relevant to officers' careers: the regulations for time required at certain level positions before promotion, type of officer, reward and punishment, remuneration, and withdrawal from service, including the required age of retirement for each type of officer and position. Other regulations provide even further detail on these issues.

Operational, political, logistic, armament, and technical specialist officers can be selected from among outstanding enlisted soldiers and military academy middle school graduates, graduates from civilian higher education institutes, civilian cadres transferring into the military, and personnel outside the armed forces, especially those with specialized technical skills. During wartime, enlisted soldiers, reserve officers, and nonmilitary personnel can be appointed as military officers.[8]

Recruitment and Retention. One of the PLA's greatest challenges is recruitment of educated personnel needed to carry forward its "military construction." The need to recruit, train, and retain high quality personnel is a theme that appears over and over again in PLA writings and seems to drive many personnel decisions, including at the official, regulatory level. In an attempt to attract well-qualified and well-educated personnel in a "socialist economy," the PLA revised active duty officer regulations in 2000 to raise the expectations and incentives for technically skilled and better educated officers; similar revisions were made for noncommissioned officer (NCO) regulations also. At that time, the PLA leadership explained that military officers should "have been trained by a military academy and gained appropriate academic qualifications." Furthermore, enlisted personnel and graduates of specialized middle schools can become officers only after they have graduated from a military academy.[9]

The 2000 regulations also offer a higher rank for entry into the military to better educated and more skilled officers.[10] People with advanced degrees can enter the PLA directly at as high as the major level if one has a Ph.D.; as high as a captain, or else a 1st lieutenant with a Master's; 1st or 2nd lieutenant with a university degree; 2nd or as high as 1st lieutenant with a polytechnic college degree (*daxuezhuanke biye*); and 2nd lieutenant for graduation from military intermediate technical schools. In addition, in some cases, the amount of time in service required for promotion to the next rank is shorter for those with some secondary degrees: for example, for a 2nd lieutenant to 1st lieutenant for an officer with a technical university degree, the time in grade requirement is only 2 years instead of 3 years. Despite these enticements, for many with an M.A., Ph.D., university, or other degree that is competitive in the private sector, a military career is unlikely to be as attractive as a private sector job, at least in terms of remuneration.[11]

Training and Education. The regulations outline required training for officers at various levels. Not surprisingly, the type of training one receives depends on what track the officer is in. Prior to or upon entry into the PLA, officers receive training according to their career track and post assignments. All military officers at the battalion level or below have basic command training. Officers at the regiment and division levels have mid-level command training. When an officer reaches the army level or above, he receives advanced command training. After training, he/she must pass a test in the field of study based on Central Military Commission (CMC) standards. Ratings of excellent, competent, or incompetent form the basis for appointment to and removal from officer positions.[12]

Career progressions seem to follow this pattern of entry-level skills-based training, mid-level command or political professional military education, and advanced command or political education. In particular, training frequently precedes positions or promotions that require certain skills. In the past, a political career could be launched at an officer's mid-level by attending the PLA Political Academy or the Central Party School. The case of General Political Department (GPD) Deputy Director Sun Zhongtong is illustrative. As a propaganda specialist within the political track, he took a propaganda course at the Central Party School upon entry into that specialization and then, years later, took a correspondence course at the Central Party School in economic management before taking over the editorial and then directorship of the *Jiefangjun Bao*.[13] For officers currently rising through the political ranks, this is no longer the case: to be competitive, they must prove themselves early as a political officer and rise through the political system. A technical officer usually has specialized training in a scientific field—probably the most common is the field of engineering.

In addition to professional military education, having a background in military training clearly increases one's chances for promotion in the PLA. This has always been the case, and it is not just a result of the PLA's rapid modernization. The one constant in PLA career progressions is that an overwhelming number of top-level PLA generals in the operational track have served in training departments or operations departments at some point in their career. It was true of the generation of PLA officers that retired 5 years ago, and it remains true of the new crop of successful PLA officers. This remains true as the PLA updates its tactics and operational methods in the course of its modernization. Training is at the core of the PLA's emphasis on "high quality personnel." Officers who make noticeable strides in training issues in their units, particularly using new equipment, are rewarded for their efforts.

As the PLA modernizes and faces different training challenges requiring technical expertise, it strives to improve the quality of units' own training, often by bringing in outside expertise. First, there have been several examples of bringing in technical experts from the outside to train personnel in units. Second, academies and combat units interact more than in the past, and in some cases there is even an "exchange program" between academies and combat units. In one such exchange, a second artillery brigade has a commander with a doctorate and a career that has otherwise been technical and academic (he was an associate professor in his last position). In a shorter-term exchange, a navy commander of a submarine *zhidui* (detachment) with years of experience in submarine navigation taught combined arms tactics at the Navy Command Academy for 6 months.[14]

Appointing and Removing Officers. The authority for appointing and removing officers depends on the level of the unit, with officers being appointed by officers a level or more above them in their chain of command:

- The CMC Chairman appoints or removes the chief of the general staff, the director of the GDP, and commanders of the military regions (MRs) and services or equivalent ranks.
- The heads of the four General Departments and political commissars and commanders of the MRs, services, or equivalent level have the authority to remove deputy division or brigade-level officers, regiment and deputy brigade-level officers, certain staff officers, and high level technical specialists.
- Senior officers of MRs appoint and dismiss regiment (deputy brigade) commanders belonging to MRs.[15]
- Group army-level or other senior officers at the army level appoint/dismiss deputy brigade-level officers, battalion-level officers, or mid-level technical specialist level. Senior-level officers in independent divisions appoint/dismiss battalion-level officers in their units.

- Senior division, brigade, or equivalent-level officers appoint/dismiss military officers at or below the deputy battalion level and junior technical specialists.

Personnel and promotion decisions are discussed by the party standing committee at the level authorized to make these decisions. The promotions are based on fairly institutionalized standards, but having connections or mentors at a couple of levels above one's own rank probably helps as promotions become more competitive. Regulations state that those who do not follow the regulations for appointing and removing officers will be punished.[16]

According to the Regulations on Officer Rank, military, political, logistics, and presumably armament officers[17] can achieve all ranks, up to the rank of full general. Specialized technical officers probably can achieve all ranks except full general. This may change in the future as specialized technical officers are valued more or even cross over into commander positions. For now, however, regulations accessed on the *PLA Daily* in 2007 continue to list two-star as the top rank.[18] Table 1 illustrates PLA ranks at the general, field grade, and junior officer levels.

Three Tiers of Officers	Highest Ranking			Lowest Ranking
General Officer Ranks	Full General	Lieutenant General	Major General	
Field Grade Officer Ranks	Senior Colonel	Colonel	Lieutenant Colonel	Major
Junior Officer Ranks	Captain	1st Lieutenant	2nd Lieutenant	

Table 1. Active Duty Officer Ranks.

The regulations on ranks of military officers also discuss how military rankings match up with positions and responsibilities in Article 29.[19] Ken Allen and John Corbett have discussed the important issue of distinguishing between military ranks and grade levels (closely linked to the number of years served in certain levels of positions) in detail elsewhere.[20]

Age and Term Limits. The PLA active duty officers' law also lays out explicit age and term limits for holding posts at a certain level.[21] The restrictions apply to any position held at that level, meaning that an officer who moves into a lateral post is still considered to be at the same level.[22] At the platoon level, one cannot be older than 30 years. At the company level, one cannot be older than 35; at the battalion level, not older than 40; at the brigade level not older than 45; at the division level not older than 50; and at the army level, not older than 55. An officer at division, army, and MR deputy and command-level posts may not remain at those levels for more than 10 years before they are dismissed. At the MR level, the age limit is 63 for deputy level and 65 at the command level. There are some variations for these age groups by services: the navy allows its battalion- and brigade-level equivalent officers serve 5 years longer—40 and 45 instead of 35 and 40. The Air Force allows military officers at the brigade level to fly until they are 50 years old (instead of requiring a maximum age of 45). In addition, military officers at the division and army level doing work that only a few officers are able to do may, with approval, extend their posts for no more than 5 years or 3 years for deputy army-level posts.

Technical specialists and those in noncombat positions can serve for about 5 years longer than those in combat positions. For noncombat positions, the maximum age for an officer is 50 for brigade-level posts, 55 for division-level posts, 58 for deputy army posts, and 60 for army-level posts. Maximum ages for technical specialists are based on junior-level specialists (40 years), mid-level specialists (50 years), and senior-level specialists (60 years old). Exceptions exist for personnel who are in high demand,[23] but extensions do not exceed 5 years.

Rules for Promotion. Generally an officer must hold junior and mid-level posts (not necessarily the same position) for at least 3 or 4 years each before becoming eligible for promotion, though officers who perform extremely well or are serving in a position above their rank may be promoted sooner.[24] In particular, selection for general officer "depends on the officer's duties, integrity, and contributions to national defense construction."[25] "Duties" likely refer to the officer's job responsibilities; "integrity" probably is a combination of political loyalty, adhering to PLA rules, and morality. The unit party committee, in particular political officers, probably are the deciding voice in judging an officer's "integrity."

"Contributions to national defense construction" appear to be a more subjective measure. The concept likely aligns with contributions to key PLA modernization concepts, such as preparing for informationized warfare, information operations and electronic warfare, blue teaming, joint operations, special operations, and other priorities for the PLA. As priorities change, these also are likely to shift, so that the specialties and achievements of today's high-ranking general officers are not necessarily the same specialties and achievements that will be most highly valued in today's upcoming crop of new military leaders. As priorities change, therefore, the kinds of positions that can set an officer up for future promotion also change. Anecdotes and case studies seem to bear this out. The military's propaganda apparatus apparently profiles and singles out for praise officers excelling in areas that the PLA is attempting to strengthen. Another area that seems to be rewarded is *successful* innovation and leadership under difficult conditions (perhaps punished if innovation is unsuccessful).[26]

Of course, receiving an award is a fairly reliable path to promotion at the junior and mid-career levels. Rewards are given to officers or work units who "make an outstanding contribution or a notable achievement in combat or troop building, or makes a significant contribution for the country and the people. . . ."[27] Rewards can be a commendation, merit citation class III, merit citation Class II; or Honorable Mention. The Honorable Mention is the highest of these awards.[28] Honorable Mention for second class bravery awards are approved at the MR level, whereas Honorable Mention for first class bravery awards are approved by the CMC. A work unit receiving first, second, or third class merit reward receives a reward flag (*jiangqi*, 奖旗).[29]

In fact, the regulations state that rewards can translate directly into promotions. Volunteer soldiers receiving a third class or above merit award can be promoted ahead of schedule. NCOs who receive a second class or above merit award can receive an advance promotion. Officers that receive first class or above merit citation can receive a salary increase either by advance promotion in rank or (for technical specialists) duties; civilian cadres who receive a first class or above citation can receive a salary increase either through advance promotion or (for technical specialists) an increase in their position.[30] Advance promotion is used for privates or officers at the rank of senior colonel or below. It does not apply to general officers.

Short of awards, extensive media coverage and profiles — often appearing in conjunction with awards — are another way to receive recognition and eventual promotion at the junior and mid-career levels. Finally, service during wartime can lead to rapid promotion since time-in-rank promotion eligibility requirements are shorter during wartime.

In addition to the awards mentioned here, the military and State Council both award Science and Technology Progress Awards (S&T) for technological achievements. For technical officers in particular, these awards (given as first, second, and third class awards) acknowledge significant professional achievements and can contribute to future promotions or better funding. They play an important role in recognizing those who are making technological breakthroughs at a time when the PLA is striving to prepare to fight and win "informationized warfare."

Technical specialists/experts who work as "S&T" problem solvers in support of PLA modernization often are profiled. One such example is Major General Zhao Xu, a senior-level air force chief engineer and technical specialist who probably has retired (he is around 70 years old). As "father of China's unmanned drones," he did extensive work on unmanned air drones in the People's Liberation Army Air Force (PLAAF) for years. Zhao Xu received numerous state and army S&T progress awards, in addition to receiving a First Class Meritorious Service Citation from Jiang Zemin himself in 1999 and becoming a member of the Chinese Academy of Engineering in 2001. In his particular niche, he was highly successful and awarded many times for his contributions.[31] The work of technical officers and specialized technical NCOs is increasingly important to the PLA's modernization. As a result, the PLA propaganda apparatus often emphasizes that technical officers can win awards and other incentives in exchange for technical work done well.

We do not always have extensive information on the awards the PLA's top leaders have received in their careers — perhaps the fact that they have made it to the positions that they have is the most important reflection on their particular accomplishments as commanders. By contrast, media coverage of awards and biographic profiles can be quite extensive for technical personnel and other professionals in their fields. These particular individuals often do not rise further to become the PLA's top generals, but the role that they play is critical to the PLA's modernization, and it is often highlighted and awarded. Rewards and publicity highlights seem to be one tool for retaining top-quality mid-level and senior-level officers.

Demotions and Dismissal. Demotion and dismissal of an officer must be done by an officer in an equivalent position to the officer who promoted or appointed the officer to his/her current position. This can occur if an officer does not rise to his responsibilities and is assigned to lower-ranking duties, in which case a new rank will be assigned that corresponds with the duty assigned.[32] It also can occur if an officer has committed a crime, in which case an officer is stripped in his rank (if he must continue service after completing the term of punishment, then the rank when he returns is determined by his unit head as if he were entering the service).[33] Once demoted, officers must start at the beginning of their new rank for purposes of counting time in rank before eligible for promotion. However, this period of time in rank can be shortened if they have "corrected their violation or make good contributions to their work or wartime effort."[34] Second lieutenants cannot be demoted.

PLA Navy (PLAN) Deputy Commander and Chief of Staff Ding Yiping is an excellent example of an officer who has both been demoted and redeemed. Following the 2003 *Ming 361* submarine incident, Ding Yiping, along with all Navy officers directly above his chain of command including the Navy commander and political commissar (PC), was removed from his position as commander of the North Sea Fleet and concurrent deputy commander of the Jinan MR. He was then assigned to be deputy chief of staff — a position one level lower than his previous position. Three years later in 2006, however, he was promoted to chief of staff and then deputy commander of the Navy headquarters.[35]

In recent years, there have been a couple of high-profile examples in which officers are either dismissed from their posts or demoted. This is a departure from the past because some of these incidents have been public. The best example was in the Navy incident described above, when the entire chain of command from the North Sea Fleet up were either removed from their posts or demoted. Even Navy Commander Shi Yunsheng (who was due for retirement soon anyway) and the PC were removed. In addition, the Air Force in 2006 had a couple of accidents in the Nanjing MR, one of which caused the deaths of 40 people. According to press reports, personnel were disciplined — the commander and political commissar of the Nanjing MR Air Force each received a "major demerit," and other personnel was punished or even dismissed. In contrast to the Navy incident, however, the Air Force's top leadership was not punished.[36]

Separation from Service. There are regulations stipulating the minimum number of years an officer must serve before reaching retirement age, ranging from 8 years for a platoon commander to 20 years for a brigade commander or above. Exceptions exist for officers who must withdraw from service due to illness or injury; who have not passed examinations for a post and are not suitable for a different post; have committed a serious wrongdoing; or are subject to force reductions or adjustments. An officer who has reached the maximum age for his level also must withdraw.

Analytically, looking at the age of a commander or political commissar is one of the most effective and predictable ways to assess how much longer he has left in his position or career. In general, these regulations are strictly adhered to. There are exceptions, but they are uncommon and therefore notable: Deputy Chief of the General Staff Xiong Guangkai remained in his post for a couple of years past 65, probably because the PLA was trying to decide who could replace him. Likewise, former Air Force Commander Qiao Qingchen remained in his post long past the usual retirement age before his replacement by Xu Shiquan a couple of weeks before the 2007 17th Party Congress. Though technically CMC members have no mandated retirement age, it has become common for its members to retire between 65 and 70. Reaching retirement age is probably the most common reason for MR commanders and deputy commanders to move on; promotion opportunities to the center even for exceptional commanders are limited, especially due to the age requirements. As the third column of Table 2 demonstrates, at a certain age, one must be promoted or retire from positions throughout the PLA chain of command. As mentioned above, retirement from noncombat positions generally occurs 5 years after retirement from combat positions.

	Authority to Assign/ Dismiss	Maximum Age (Combat Officers)	Maximum Age (Noncombat, AF, Navy)	Minimum Years in Post Level (before Promotion)	Minimum Years Required in Peacetime (before Eligible for Retirement)	Maximum Years at Level before Dismissal	Exchange Required after xx Years at One Post
Platoon	Principal Senior Official of Division/Brigade Level Unit	30		3	8		4 years (non-combat 5 years)
Deputy Commander	Principal Senior Official of Division/Brigade Level Unit	35		3	10		4 years (non-combat 5 years)
Company Principal	Principal Senior Official of Division/Brigade Level Unit			3	12		4 years (non-combat 5 years)
Deputy Battalion	Principal Senior Official of Division/Brigade Level Unit			3	14		4 years (non-combat 5 years)
Battalion	Principal Senior Official of Division/Brigade Level Unit	40	45+	3	16		4 years
Regiment/ Deputy Brigade-Level Principal	Principal Senior Official of Division/Brigade Level Unit	50 (45)		3	18-20		4 years
Division Deputy/ Brigade Principal	General Department or MR Principal	45	50*+^	3			4 years
Division Principal	CMC Chairman(?)	50 (55)	55*	3		10	4 years, in unit 25 years
Deputy Army			58*				? 5 years

Table 2. PLA Regulations Affecting Number of Years in Post,
by Rank (for Military Affairs Political Logistics and Armaments Officers)

Army (GA)	CMC Chairman	55	60*	3		10	5 years, in unit 30 years
Military Region Deputy	CMC Chairman	63					
Military Region/ Service/ General Dept Principal	CMC Chairman	65				10	
General Staff, Political Dept Principal	CMC Chairman						
Central Military Commission							
Technical Specialist (Officers)							
Senior Technology Specialist	GSD, GPD Head		60		20		
Mid-level Technology Specialist	Group Army or Equivalent Principal		50		16		
Junior-level Technology Specialist	Principal senior Official or Division/ Brigade Level Unit		40		12		

*Noncombat only
+Navy
^Air Force

Table 2. PLA Regulations Affecting Number of Years in Post,
by Rank (for Military Affairs, Political, Logistics, and Armaments Officers) (Concluded).

CAREER PATH SKETCHES OF PLA OFFICERS, JUNIOR THROUGH SENIOR RANKS

Military Affairs Officer (Operator).

Generally an operator's career begins with training in the skill that he (almost without exception "he") will pursue in his career. He then has experience as a commander of progressively higher units usually within the same parent unit (such as Group Army) and additional professional education as he makes his way up through the junior and mid-levels of his career. Once he reaches the senior level, he diversifies his experience, by transferring to a different geographic command or the national level (such as the General Staff Department [GSD]), a different specialty such as an armament department, and/or gaining some managerial or staff experience as a chief of staff.

The Air Force's Xu Qiliang and the Navy's Sun Jianguo, both in the General Staff Department until just before the 17th Party Congress, are good examples of how a career can progress. Xu Qiliang started out with extensive training to become a pilot at a series of flight schools. Sun Jianguo started out with training to become a submariner at the Navy's Submarine Academy. Both rose their way up through the ranks over a span of decades, proving their abilities as commanders of progressively higher-level units, as well as some time as staff officer or chief of staff, then chief of staff or deputy commander in their services' headquarters. Major achievements or rewards also help. As commander of a nuclear submarine that allegedly "broke the record" for longest self-sustaining period of a nuclear submarine (90 days), Sun might have won some kind of reward or recognition.[37]

Xu Qiliang—a full general and promoted to Air Force commander just before the 17th Party Congress and to the CMC at the Congress—is exemplary for the education he received at the junior, mid-career, and senior level to prepare him for subsequent steps in his career. He enrolled in aviation preparatory schools and aviation schools for the first couple of years of his career. As his career progressed in 1982, he likely stood out as a promising mid-level officer (he did not become a major general until 1991), when he was selected to attend the Air Force Academy and, subsequently, the NDU Basic Department. He returned to NDU to attend a course for generals in 2001. General Xu also is exemplary for his political achievements—he was an alternate member of the Central Committee as early as the 14th Party Congress (1992) and a full member by the 16th Party Congress.

Army officers follow a similar path of education, good political background, promotion, rewards, and further promotion. Liu Zhenwu, the former Guangzhou MR commander who was promoted to Deputy Chief of the General Staff and full general in June 2007, is a good example. Liu's background as a specialist in training and operations, and his procession through a variety of positions including staff officer, chief of staff, and commander, all are typical of a general officer who makes it to the top of the operational officer ranks. Liu Zhenwu is actually unusual, however, in that he remained in the same MR—the Guangzhou MR—for 45 years of his career, until he became full general this year. While little is known about his education, he has had a spotless political record, being PLA delegate to the National People's Congress as early as 1993, and an alternate member of the 15th Party Congress, full member of the 16th Party Congress, and delegate to the 17th Party Congress. Interestingly, Liu Zhenwu was elected neither a full nor alternate member of the 17th Party Congress—perhaps because Central Committee membership has become tied to position, and his current position does not require membership. Liu Zhenwu was a sharp-shooter who rose through the ranks of the 42nd GA in the Guangzhou MR, taking on positions as commander, staff officer, chief of staff, and expert on military training and operations at different level units. He attended the National Defense University just before becoming the commander of the 42nd GA. He commanded the unit that later became the PLA Hong Kong Garrison and lead it during the handover of Hong Kong. He later became the deputy commander and, in 2002, the commander of the Guangzhou MR, where he remained for 5 years before becoming deputy chief of the general staff this year. He has had little recorded foreign travel. At 63 years old (he was born in April 1944), he still has a couple of years left as a full general and deputy chief of the general staff. Based on his public appearances so far, he apparently continues to work on training issues for the PLA.[38]

Increasingly, experience abroad and higher levels of education are valued in younger officers. Foreign travel in most cases still does not occur until one is a general, but this is changing as younger officers participate in working-level or technical delegations. Profiles of the "model" marine brigade commander Chen Changfeng give some insight into what the PLA's propaganda department has promoted—and encourages the PLA to continue promoting—as a model, up-and-coming PLA officer.[39] Chen Changfeng, now a Navy captain and commander of the 1st Marine Brigade belonging to the South Sea Fleet, spent 2 years in Germany receiving an MA in military science. Previously, he had received a degree from a navy academy. He is profiled as an officer who not only braves severe weather conditions in exercises, but also incorporates simulations into training and education, participated in amphibious exercises in the Shanghai Cooperation Organization multinational organizations, speaks German, has a good grasp of Western military theories and operations, has written over 30 articles on military issues—several of which have received prizes—and has participated in cross-training with other services. He has personally briefed Hu Jintao on his military exercises. He is the kind of officer that the PLA may wish to have more of in the future and is not the only young officer highlighted with experience abroad.[40]

In the Air Force and Army, also, qualities that tend to be highlighted in profiles of younger officers include innovation and adaptability to new equipment. The PLA emphasizes the role of operational, armament, and logistic departments' ability to incorporate training, innovation, and maintenance of new aircraft or equipment into the unit. Units that are able to cultivate training of their own personnel to use and maintain such equipment also are highlighted.

One such Air Force unit, which was profiled as a model unit in the *Jiefangjun Huabao* (*PLA Pictorial*), brought in technicians and experts to train its personnel and sent its personnel on training missions abroad in an effort to integrate its new SU-27 aircraft. The commander of the air force unit had spent some time embedded as a group army deputy commander, learning about Army arms, weapons, tactics, training, and even driving armored vehicles, helicopters, and light and heavy weaponry. In particular, his stint in the group army apparently intended to sensitize this Air Force officer to potential Army-Air coordination during island-landing operations and infantry deployments. His initial success as an officer probably had derived from his role commanding and instructing all-weather flights, an area that the PLAAF is striving to improve. He was a lead pilot for four models of aircraft and has had joint experience early in his career, both admirable qualities. The director of the same unit's armament department also is praised for his ability to incorporate new maintenance procedures. The division claims to take pride in its promotion of officers based on ability, not age or seniority. Thus, it is not surprising that the armament director, at 34 years old, is young for the position he is in.[41] This one unit exemplifies desirable young officers who meet the PLA's training and equipment needs.

Political Officer.

Political officers' careers are in some ways similar to party cadres' careers, even if they are military officers. Political officers who are now at the top of the PLA's political system did not necessarily start out as political officers, though most members of the new generation of political officers do, due to intense competition. In some exceptional cases, such as that of former Air Force Commander and Air Force Political Commissar Qiao Qingchen, they do not adhere strictly to the political track. Usually they become strictly political officers, however. Connections probably are more important for a political officer than for a commander—though information is not available to prove this empirically.[42] In some cases, a technical specialty in addition to being a political commissar is useful—particularly for those political commissars who are serving in areas heavily dominated by officers with specialized skills or with a large number of technical specialists. Political officers, like operators, have training at the mid-level and senior levels, often at a political academy or at the Central Party School. Not surprisingly, they tend to have exceptionally good political records, joining the CCP early and serving first in offices carrying out political work and later in party committees, discipline committees, organization departments, and eventually, even on the Central Committee if they become truly top-level senior officers.

Most political officers go through a fairly predictable route of promotion throughout their careers as secretaries, cadres, political instructors, political department directors, and deputy political commissars and political commissars at various levels. Like operators, political commissars often have a specialty. GPD Deputy Director Sun Zhongtong, who has served as a propaganda officer for much of his career (discussed above) is a good example.

Like most PLA officers, political commissars are transferred to a different geographic location as senior officers, particularly if they work closely with MR operators. An excellent example of this kind of career progression is that of Liu Yongzhi, now deputy director of the GPD. He began his career as a soldier and squad leader, not as a political officer. He was a radio operator and worked in a wireless communications company before becoming a political instructor about 15 years into his career. He then served as director of a regimental political office, then the regiment's political commissar. It was at this point — as a late mid-career officer about 25 years into his career — that he attended the PLA Political Academy. Upon graduation, he became the deputy political commissar of a division, the political department director and then political commissar of that division. At this point, he was already a senior officer. As a senior officer, he transferred twice. His first transfer was to the Jinan MR to be political department director of the 20th Group Army (later he was the political commissar of the 20th Group Army). At this time, he attended a correspondence course given by the Central Party School—a fairly common move for senior-level political officers. A few years after this was completed, he was transferred again, to become the deputy political commissar of the Nanjing MR. He received additional cadre training at the National Defense University before being transferred once again to become political commissar of the Lanzhou MR about a year later. This was his last position in the MRs before becoming a deputy director of the GPD in December, 2004. Altogether, Liu Yongzhi received at least three transfers in his years as a senior officer and three occasions of professional training, also at the late mid-level and senior-level point of his career. Until he became a GPD deputy director, he remained affiliated with MR commands. He is the only GPD deputy director with a MR background, indicating an attempt to diversify backgrounds and specializations at this very high level of leadership (other deputy directors have air force, navy, propaganda, and other backgrounds).[43]

Some political commissars also are technical experts. Chi Wanchun is the political commissar of the General Armament Department (GAD)—and a full general. He clearly has had a successful career as a political commissar, almost exclusively within what is now the GAD. His route to success has been exemplary. He attended the Harbin Military Engineering Academy, a school well known as an institute for children of the elite, during the Cultural

Revolution — probably escaping its effects — in 1965-70. There, he most likely cultivated some important contacts. After graduation with a major in aerospace weaponry, he worked for years at various testing and training bases before entering the Nanjing Political Academy in 1980-81 — again, about 15 years into his career. The Nanjing Political Academy is an important training ground for future political commissars and political leaders in the PLA. Following this training, Chi was a political instructor, political office director, and political commissar at various training and testing sites, including two of the most prestigious in what later became the GAD system of bases — the Xichang Satellite Launch Center and the Taiyuan Satellite Launch Center. A series of appointments at key GAD facilities and his promotion to general officer followed his participation in the NDU Basic Course for senior level officers in 1989-1990. He was a Deputy Director of the political department at COSTIND, the organization that preceded the GAD. After this he was a PC of the National Defense University of Science and Technology and, in 2002, became a full 16th Central Committee member (he remains a member of the 17th Central Committee in 2007). He became the PC of GAD 3 years later and was promoted to full general during the June 2006 round of promotions. As a full general at 61, he still has a few years left before he is required to retire. He is an interesting case study as a successful political commissar due to his combination of elite schooling and probable connections, specialized knowledge, political training and track, and periodic training for further professional development.[44]

Increasingly, the political track, like other tracks, is experimenting with integration across the services, especially in its most senior, GPD-level positions. In recent years, the GPD leadership has included Navy and Air Force political commissars. In December 2005, an Air Force PC (Liu Zhenqi), who had been the Assistant to the GPD, was promoted to the post of GPD director.At the same time, a Navy PC (Tong Shiping) was appointed to the post of assistant to the GPD. The Air Force GPD deputy director has a long history in Air Force bases, including as a PC of the MR air force and an MR deputy PC. He has no experience in Air Force headquarters. The Navy GPD assistant director had wide-ranging experience as a deputy PC in Navy headquarters, a PC in a fleet, and deputy PC of a MR before his posting to the GPD. Just before the 17th Party Congress, he was appointed the political commissar of National Defense University.[45]

Logistics Officer.

Logistics officers progress through their careers to become managers of maintenance, logistics, finance, and health.[46] The logistics office director at each level is subordinate to the commander and political commissar of his unit. For example, a MR political department director is subordinate to the commander and political commissar of the MR, also coordinating closely with the chief of staff of the MR. A logistics officer has an area of specialization — usually health, finance, supply and logistics (including in support of operational planning, training, and exercises), and maintenance. It appears that a logistics officer can rise through the ranks either as a leading expert in charge of their subfield or as an officer climbing up logistics offices directly subordinate to incrementally higher-level operational units. In both cases, the officer takes on greater administrative and management responsibilities as he is promoted.[47] For each level of promotion, a logistics officer must go through and pass corresponding training.[48]

The logistics officer in charge of a unit is responsible for understanding the status of the unit's logistics. He makes reports, organizes logistic plans, and suggests improvements to the unit commander, and implements approved plans. Implementation can consist of plans; arranging logistics forces in support of senior officers' force planning; requesting logistics materials and funds; overseeing the financial system; overseeing health care, food, and housing for the unit; training the unit's logistic personnel; and overseeing training and administration (not command) of directly subordinate logistical units.[49]

The General Logistics Department (GLD) is at the apex of the logistic system. While its director, General Liao Xilong, is a career operational track officer, the deputy directors of the GLD represent different aspects of the logistics track—not surprisingly, since the top leaders at the national level generally bring diverse expertise to that level of leadership. GLD Deputy Director Sun Zhiqiang is an example of a logistics officer who has specialized in finance. He studied finance at the Central University of Finance and Economics (*Zhongyang caizheng jinrong xueyuan*, 中央财政金融学院) and entered the PLA 2 years after that, in 1970. His career in PLA finance began just 2 years later, when he was a section assistant to a finance section in a Kunming Military District logistics department. After this, he rose through the ranks of the Kunming Military District's units as a logistics finance officer. Fifteen years into his career, after serving as the head of Kunming Military District Finance Department, he was transferred to the PLA GLD finance department as a deputy director and, in 1991, as the director of that department. He remained in that position until 1999, when he became the deputy director of the GLD and a party committee member of the GLD. He was a full member of the 16th Party Congress Central Committee, but not of the 17th Party Congress. He probably will retire soon: he is already 63 years old – the maximum age for a GLD deputy director.[50]

GLD deputy director Wang Qian also has had a specialized but fairly typical career as a logistics track officer in the medical field. He is the top GLD officer in the medical field, having risen all the way up the ranks in this field. Li Maifu, the third GLD deputy director, has risen through the ranks as an air force deputy director. He represents the fairly recent (last 5 years) trend of incorporating officers from across services into the general departments.[51]

Armaments Officer.

Armaments officers progress through their careers to become managers of equipment integration, testing, and suitability.[52] The armament track was added in 1998 with the creation of a fourth general department, the GAD, and armament departments at all levels to parallel counterpart operational (headquarters), political, and logistic departments. It therefore made sense to create a new career track category to administer officers working within this new system. As the GPD explained:

> With the development of the military's modernization construction, especially in regard to the renovation of armaments, officers engaged in armaments management have not only increased in number, but have been playing, and will play, an increasingly important role in the construction of the military and in any future high-tech war. After the establishment of the

GADand armament departments at all levels, officers engaged in armament management work have already come to constitute a new category under the new administration system.[53]

Prior to 1998, responsibilities for armaments issues had mostly fallen under the General Staff Department and the Commission of Science, Technology, and Industry for National Defense (COSTIND). Because the career track is so new, some ambiguity remains about officers' career progression in this track: high-ranking GAD officers probably were categorized earlier in their careers as military affairs officers in staff positions or even as technical specialists. For this reason, the outside observer can find it difficult to discern boundaries distinguishing the careers of military affairs officers (especially staff officers), technical specialists, and armaments officers — not the least because increasingly officers in these roles play multiple roles. However, regulations do define the responsibilities of armaments officers.[54]

Like most tracks, armaments officers develop subspecialties. As officers rise through the ranks, they become managers of armaments issues in progressively high levels of their area of specialty, such as space testing. Alternatively, officers rise by climbing up the armament system as director of armament departments supporting MR or service parent units. An armament department director is subordinate to the unit commander and political commissar and coordinates his work through the unit's chief of staff.

An armament officer in either a support or a specialized unit, such as space launch testing center, is expected to have an understanding of the unit's armaments issues. The officer formulates plans for armaments work; makes reports and recommendations to senior officers; and implements any armaments plans for the unit. Implementation includes organizing operational and operational training for relevant armaments and technical personnel, organizing training to ensure the armaments department's support role, carrying out inspections, overseeing relevant technical officers, maintaining equipment and armaments, and ensuring spare parts are available and issued to the appropriate troops.[55]

As noted above, the GAD is at the apex of the armaments system. Like the GLD director, the GAD director until 2007, Chen Bingde, and his successor, Chang Wanquan, both are career operators, not armaments specialists. Like the GLD deputy directors, the four GAD deputy directors all are career armaments specialists. GAD Deputy Director Li Andong, who is the only deputy director who also is full general, is only 61. He remained an alternate member of the 17th Party Congress Central Committee. Li Andong has had a long career in the General Armament Department's predecessor doing planning for the PLA's equipment needs, first for aerospace, and then more generally in the comprehensive planning department. He probably worked closely with the vice chairman of the CMC until November 2007, Cao Gangchuan. His career resembled that of a staff officer in the General Staff Department, although he specialized in armament and equipment issues. Deputy Director Zhang Shiming is from the Nanjing MR, where he was the director of the armaments department (he is 63 years old and likely to retire around the 17th Party Congress).[56] Deputy Director Zhu Fazhong is a career specialist in space, satellite, and testing issues and the former director of the Taiyuan launch testing center. Deputy Director Zhang Jianqi also is a career specialist in space launch

264

testing and was formerly the director of the Jiuchuan space testing center.[57]

Increasingly, in many cases the functions and responsibilities of armaments officers (and it seems to a lesser degree those of logistics officers) overlap with those of operational officers. Operational or political officers have also taken on roles that seem to fall within the armament track. Nanjing MR Deputy Commander Xu Chengyun has been an operational commander for his whole career except for a brief stint as the director of Nanjing MR's armament. In his case, it is likely that serving as director of the armament department was advantageous to his career—a rotation that broadened his experience as a commander.[58] Some heads of MR logistics or (more often) armaments departments have been promoted to deputy commander of the MRs. [59] In 2004, there were at least five or six MR chiefs of staff or deputy commanders with direct experience with armaments.[60]

Technical Specialist Officer.

Traditionally, the technical track has been less attractive than the operational, political, or other tracks to many ambitious officers. In recent years, however, the PLA has tried to attract more technical specialist officers—and technical NCOs—to further the PLA's modernization. The value placed on these technical specialists in a rapidly modernizing PLA is increasing, and technical specialists of all kinds (engineers, missile technicians, navy technicians, academics, and doctors) are profiled regularly in the *Jiefangjun Huabao* (*PLA Pictorial*). Mid-level technical officers now can retire at 50 years old rather than 45 years old in recognition that it can be difficult to find a job in the civilian sector after retiring in one's late 40s.[61] In addition, the PLA promulgated regulations on providing rewards and allowances to technical experts in March 2006.[62] In the run-up to the 17th Party Congress, the *PLA Pictorial*, CCTV, and other official media outlets profiled notable military delegates to the 17th Party Congress, including many technical specialists.[63]

Technical specialist officers are present in all parts of the PLA. They wear their own insignia[64] but generally are subordinate to the range of PLA operational, logistical, and armaments units or tasks that they support. In tactical units, "technicians" are in charge of maintaining an intimate understanding of how equipment is used and maintained; provide guidance in its use, maintenance, and repairs; regularly inspecting and testing technical equipment; and providing technical training within the unit.[65] Technical NCOs, not technical officers, are responsible for many of these duties at the unit/tactical level. Compared to technical NCOs, technical officers probably have more specialized responsibilities requiring a greater level of expertise, such as testing, engineering knowledge, and establishing maintenance and repair routines. They are included in many units, particularly those that are in the process of integrating new equipment and technology or requiring innovation. For example, technical officers are important to testing and developing missiles and their components in the Second Artillery and command and control systems throughout the PLA. Technical NCOs take on more routine responsibilities, especially once equipment is integrated and routines for maintenance, repair, and supply are established.[66]

The number of technical specialists has increased, including the number trained in civilian engineering programs and other technical fields. However, there are still instances of engineers graduating only to try to seek operational commands, even in technical units.[67] One technical unit tried to lure technical officers into the technical field by providing them opportunities to command units and move between command and more technical responsibilities.[68] Technical specialists continue to be subject to a different set of regulations for the purposes of retirement and promotion than other officers. As noted above, in contrast to operational and political officers, the highest rank of a technical specialist still appears to be that of a two-star, not three-star, general. This may change, but so far, except for making allowances for more awards and retirement age for technical officers, neither PLA regulations nor the PLA culture encouraging promotion of operational and political officers over technical officers, seems to have caught up with the increased importance placed on technical specialist officers.[69]

Profiles of technical officers are fairly common, but generally they focus on the achievements of the officer rather than his/her career progression. By the time the officer is profiled, he/she is clearly a leading example in their field. Usually it is unclear what training and experience equipped them for their achievements, though technical specialists, like other officers, are trained and assessed throughout their careers. Innovation, especially overcoming critical technical obstacles to PLA modernization, is awarded through a system of awards discussed elsewhere in this chapter.

Several particularly successful technical specialist officer were delegates to the 17th Party Congress. One such technical specialist officer and 17th Party Congress PLA delegate, Wu Jiangxing, excelled during his 30-year career "from soldier to academic" as a specialist in communications equipment. According to

Chinese press, he developed indigenous technologies that decreased China's reliance on Western technology for communications systems. He received a number of prestigious awards for his achievements. Little is known of his background, training, or career progression, except that, according to China's military press, he was born into a revolutionary military family and is politically reliable and nationalistic.[70]

GEOGRAPHIC ASSIGNMENTS

For all tracks, it appears that most PLA officers continue to spend the entry-level and mid-level portions of their careers in a parent unit situated in a relatively distinct geographic location. Officers may serve in the same province or MR as their ancestral home, and many do. It is difficult to find reliable data on both an officer's ancestral home and location of assigned unit. However, amongst officers whose biographic information is available, it appears to be rare—if not explicitly forbidden in regulations—for an officer to work in units actually located in one's ancestral home. However, to avoid a conflict of interest (such as the potential for corruption as a commander in charge of local conscription), officers may not command the Military Sub-district (MSD) or the People's Armed Forces Department (PAFD) in their ancestral home. This does not apply to officers serving below the command level or in operational group army, division, and brigade units. The regulations read: "No officers may hold the post of the principal commander of the military subcommand (or garrison command at the division level) or the people's armed forces department (PAFD) of the county, municipality or district under the jurisdiction of the municipal government in his

268

or her native place."[71] Similar regulations involving conflicts of interest apply for spouses, immediate family, marriage, or relatives within three generations working in the same unit.

As an officer progresses in his career, and especially as he reaches the general officer level, he is expected to transfer units. As mentioned above, this usually means also changing one's geographic location. It does not have to be a transfer between different MRs or military districts, however; it can also be a transfer to a general department or academy, and this often occurs. Interestingly, four out of five of the deputy commanders in the Nanjing MR as of September 2007 spent almost all of their careers in the Nanjing MR. The two that did not are the concurrent Nanjing MR deputy commander and Nanjing MR Air Force commander, who is from Dalian, and a deputy commander who worked on armaments issues at the national level before joining the Nanjing MR. Former Guangzhou MR Commander Liu Zhenwu spent his entire career in the Guangzhou MR before he was finally transferred to the General Staff Department in June 2007. More often than not, however, officers transfer once they reach group army level or above.

ETHNIC POLICIES: DOES AFFIRMATIVE ACTION EXIST IN THE PLA?

Identifying the number of ethnic minorities in the PLA is difficult because this information is not readily available, and most Chinese minorities have names that could be either Han or minority Chinese.[72] Uighurs and Tibetans are the clear exception. Overall, it appears that ethnic minorities are significantly under-represented in the PLA. In the run-up to the yearly National People's

Congress meeting, the PRC announced a plan to elect around 360 minority deputies of a total of 3,000 deputies to the 11th National People's Congress (NPC) next year, or about 12 percent of all delegates (the 10th NPC has about 15 percent minorities). The PLA will provide about 265 deputies to the 11th NPC, but it is unknown how many of those will be minorities.[73] Of the 249 PLA delegates slotted to attend the 17th Party Congress, only seven were minorities—a paltry 2.8 percent of PLA deputies (there were 23 women, or 9.2 percent of the total). Ethnic minorities comprise about 8 percent of China's total population.[74] The actual percentage of ethnic minorities in the PLA is unknown, but given the relative lack of ethnic minority representatives to the 17th Party Congress, it seems that ethnic minorities are under-represented in military leadership positions.

The PLA has made active efforts to recruit minorities in Tibet and Xinjiang. Military districts and subdistricts in these areas have instituted policies favorable to minorities in some cases (such as education). In other cases, policy emphasizes recruiting outstanding enlisted soldiers with nonmilitary university degrees in "remote areas with difficult conditions" to "open up wasteland" in Xinjiang and Tibet. This particular policy is aimed at combat units below the division level. The targets of recruitment are not necessarily minorities, but there is a provision that minorities working in difficult areas can become officers up to a year later than other candidates, at the age of 27. Candidates must have received a bachelor's degree from a 4-year college, be a Communist Party member, be devoted to national defense, be in the PLA for at least 2 years; and be designated an outstanding enlisted person. Those who have received certain types of awards or graduated from engineering colleges are selected first.[75]

Certain military districts and subdistricts in Tibet and Xinjiang also have education policies to promote more university and graduate level education to minority officers. In the Tibet Military District as a whole, the goal of the program is to provide bachelor's degrees to all minority officers and master's degrees to 3 percent of all minority officers within the next 5 years. This goal is more consistent with goals for officers in the PLA, many of whom are now encouraged to have bachelor's degrees. It includes sending 30 minority cadres to Tibet University every 2 years. As of April 2006, there were 39 ethnic minority entry-level officers beginning a 2-year bachelor's program in the Tibet MR. Since 2003, over 90 minority cadres have undertaken military postgraduate studies in majors in demand in the PLA, such as computers, communications, information, and management. Some have studied at the National Defense University of Science and Technology and the Nanjing Political Academy. Of all officers in this program, 37 have already completed their studies and begun as entry-level PLA officers.[76] In a related measure, the Tibet Military District also seems to be trying to make a point of granting party member status for some of these soldiers—necessary for career advancement in the PLA. Of 26 being granted this status in 2005, only eight had a middle school education, so efforts were being made to provide them with Mandarin language training and specialized training (such as computers) at the junior college level or above.[77] The Xinjiang Military District also has made some similar efforts. They include tuition assistance and a stipend, and as of 2004, one Xinjiang Military District sub-district claimed that 85 percent of its minority cadres had at least a junior college education, with 26 being rewarded for outstanding contributions and promoted to higher-level organizations.[78]

These are but scraps of information on PLA ethnic policies. In particular, there are no known regulations, though the above information offers evidence of official efforts to promote the service of ethnic minorities in the PLA or their education, particularly in Xinjiang and Tibet. There is enough information to make some preliminary assessments, but the lack of information is such that most of these assessments are anecdotal rather than definitive.

While information on ethnic minority officers is limited, several — though not all — Tibetans and Uighurs who have made it to general officer in the current generation seem to be located in Military Districts close to their native province, rather than in other PLA units, like MR headquarters or units, or at the national level. Evidence presented above suggests that the more restive Uighur and Tibetan minorities are needed in their native areas and are less well integrated into the PLA as a whole. Certainly most of the officers in the *PLA Personalities Directory* with Uighur names are posted in the Lanzhou MR's Xinjiang Military District. There are at least four serving in the Xinjiang Military District's headquarters as Major Generals. In addition, others serve in subordinate military districts; of these, only one is actually a commander. That commander, Senior Colonel Saimaiti Maimaiti, commands the Xinjiang Military District's Turpan Military Subdistrict and also is a representative to the 17th Party Congress. At the junior officer level, there are some "minority" units, also located close to the native area of the minorities. Reporting suggests a conscious effort to recruit minorities (most likely Uighurs) to serve in the Xinjiang Military District.[79] One article claims that the Lanzhou area has over 1,200 officers from minority groups, with 244 as leading officers at the army, divisional, or regimental levels—this is up from 137 leading officers in the same area claimed in 1996.[80]

In this context, it is important to remember rules about geographic location of PLA units. Officers generally do not serve in their own hometown, and explicitly are banned from command PAFD units in their county or municipal seat—but it is possible to serve in the same province. As noted above, the PLA regulations do stipulate that there can be exceptions to these rules "if their work is especially needed." Although it is not clear whether there are exceptions for minorities since there is not much information on both the officers' place of birth and specific location of service (usually just one or the other), it is likely that some exceptions are made, especially if the ethnic minority's home town is located in "remote or difficult areas." Uighurs and Tibetans appearing in the press often serve in Xinjiang and Tibet (or Qinghai), respectively, areas where their ethnicity is concentrated.[81]

Overall, however, it appears that the PLA is doing as much (or more) to control ethnic minorities as to promote their service. The use of minorities, particularly Uighurs, in restive minority areas could be one indication of this.[82] Organizationally, the most obvious evidence of reinforcing control of the region in the PLA is the dual appointment of the Tibet Military District and Xinjiang Military District commanders as deputy commanders in their respective MRs. This link between military district and MR is not duplicated anywhere else in the PLA except for the Beijing Garrison, whose commander also is a deputy commander of the Beijing MR. While the ethnicity of these commanders is not certain, most likely they are Han Chinese, not minorities.[83]

CONCLUSIONS: LOOKING AHEAD

What will a PLA officer's career path look like in years ahead? Understanding the general patterns of promotion is fairly easy: there are basic requirements that PLA officers must meet, and in general officers progress through their careers according to a well established set of regulations, helped along by connections, if they have them, and rewards, if they make what are considered to be significant contributions. Several indicators remain constant for assessing the progress of an officer's career. Not surprisingly, it is easiest to identify these milestones and indicators for a senior-level PLA general. Membership in the Central Committee, foreign travel, NDU capstone courses, and transfers to other organizations (in particular MRs, service headquarters, or national-level organizations such as the General Staff Department or academies) are all indicators of a successful officer. At an intermediate level, enrollment in mid-level training is a sign of probable further promotion. At the most elementary levels, party membership, which tends to occur early in one's career, further training, and rewards are indicators of success. They also are the most difficult for an analyst to track early in an officer's career.

Beyond the constant indicators of success and turning to the criteria for success, a capable PLA officer is promoted based on needs of the PLA and its modernization goals. Because these goals will change, criteria for advancement of the most outstanding PLA officers also likely will change. What might we see in the future? A PLA officer rising to senior levels may be encouraged to have "joint" experience. Already we have seen a significant increase in Air Force or Navy officers taking on positions traditionally reserved for Army officers, in particular at the senior levels. For example, in 2006, two Air Force deputy commanders took over two such positions: Ma Xiaotian took over as the commandant of National Defense University (in 2007 he was assigned to yet another position traditionally reserved for army officers: deputy chief of the general staff). Li Maifu moved to a GLD deputy director position (where he remains as of December 2007). These kinds of movements could become more widespread throughout the ranks as part of career progression. This has not happened on a large scale yet, but it could in the future. So far there have been few instances of these kinds of "joint" movements below the highest levels of leadership. There have been a couple of examples of cross-service training exercises and even cross-service postings. For example, Navy North Sea Fleet Deputy Chief of Staff Zhang Xuezeng became deputy commander of the Nanjing MR's 31st GA in 2006; it appears that a Jinan MR army officer was named South Sea Fleet deputy chief of staff for several months before returning to serve as deputy commander of the Jinan MR's 20th GA. So far these initiatives have been experimental, not systematic.

While the PLA long ago moved beyond the days of field army affiliations outlined in William Whitson's tome, of course, connections help promotions also. Many of the general officers now in significant positions likely have been helped by their connections or former mentors. These relationships can be strengthened by decades-long shared affiliation in a parent base, group army, or fleet unit, though at the national level, most positions are drawn from a diverse set of different units. In the military as in the civilian world, relationships can be formed by acting as secretaries, especially in the political track. For example, Sun Dafa, recently promoted full general, was once a secretary to former General and veteran Li Desheng—in some senses, his career as a political commissar bears some similarities to that of a Chinese Communist Party civilian cadre.

At less senior levels, concerns may be much more local, or specialized—but still are considered an integral part of PLA modernization as a whole, just on a more tactical, local, and less grand a scale. Thus NCOs as well as general officers are hailed for their contributions to PLA modernization, even if NCOs, junior officers, and technical officers serve in a narrower, micro sense. The emphasis on the officer's or NCO's contribution may be on his ability to fix a mechanical problem key to operating new equipment or incorporating new tactics, for example, rather than his ability to think out strategies for joint operations. Military District careers are more likely to remain fairly local in emphasis and scope, until the officer transfers out of his region. PLA careers represent "hierarchies" of important missions for the PLA and more tactical or local concerns. Service, local, or technical concerns of junior and mid-career officers are recognized as critical to PLA modernization. Senior or even top leaders demonstrate achievements at a more strategic level that grow over the course of a career out of these specialized or operational concerns.

ENDNOTES - CHAPTER 7

1. The author wrote this paper while she was employed at RAND. However, the paper represents the views of the author and not the views of past or present employers.

2. The paper does not address women in the PLA, though this is an under-researched topic.

3. The author compiled a database based on information from newspaper articles, Chinese on-line information (one fruitful source of these were found at China Military Affairs New Observer Forum, at *xinguancha.bbs.xilu.com/*), the Open Source Center (OSC) articles, and other open source information. The database contained fields on the officer's position, organization, date of position, rank, name, military specialty (career path), prior positions and geographic assignment of those positions, education, and other data such as when the officer joined the PLA. Where possible, the author also tried to fill in more personal information, such as the officer's ethnicity, birthplace or ancestral home, and foreign travel. In most cases, the information for all of those fields simply is not available. Taken as an aggregate, however, this data can offer insights into PLA career progressions at a range of officer grades and specialties. More information is available for senior officers than for junior or mid-career officers.

4. The author is indebted to Dennis Blasko, John Corbett, and David Finkelstein for crucial comments on this section. Any mistakes are the responsibility of the author.

5. Article 2, "Full Text of PRC 'Officers on the Active List' Law," *Xinhua Domestic Service* in Chinese, December 28, 2000, in OSC CPP20001228000194; and Question 3, "PLA General Department's Explanations on PRC's Active-Service Officers Law," *Jiefangjun Bao* in Chinese, January 18, 2001 ,in OSC CPP20010118000048.

6. "Di er daodan lü 80% daodan hao shou neng zuo zhan hui baozhang 二炮导弹旅80％导弹号手能作战会保障" (80% of second artillery brigade operators can do logistic work). The story appeared in the *PLA Daily* and was accessed in September 2007, at *www.chinareviewnews.com*, dated September 7, 2007.

7. "Full Text of PRC 'Officers on the Active List' Law," *Xinhua Domestic Service* in Chinese, December 28, 2000, in OSC CPP20001228000194; and "Guanyu zhuanye jishu jun xian shouyu he jinsheng 关于专业技术军衔授予和晋升" (On Technical Specialist Rank, Commission, and Promotion Regulations), *PLA Daily*, available in August 2007 at *www.pladaily.com.cn/item/kjrcdw/zczx/xgzc/04.htm*. These regulations still state that technical specialists also can only be promoted to the two-star level, not the three-star level, but this information likely is obsolete because it predates

the formation of the GAD as a full counterpart body to the General Staff, Political, and Logistics Departments.

8. Article 9, Articles 10, 11 and 21, "Full Text of PRC 'Officers on the Active List' Law," *Xinhua* (in Chinese), December 28, 2000, in OSC CPP20001228000194.

9. "China: Bill Submitted to NPC on Revising Regulations Governing Military Officers," *Xinhua Domestic Service*, December 22, 2000, in OSC CPP20001222000111.

10. "Zhongguo Renmin Jiefangjun junguan jun xian tiaoli中国人民解放军军官军衔条例" (PLA Rank Regulations), available from *www.gov.cn/banshi/gm/content_63642.htm* (*accessed August 2007*). This regulation offers more insights and detail than the Active Duty Service Officer regulations on how the PLA determines at what rank an officer will enter service.

11. According to a 2004 source, graduates from civilian universities would receive a monthly salary of "over RMB 1,200 and enjoy the respective benefit of salary increases as their military rank and post grade are promoted by one grade each year." Still, this is far below what most university graduates make in the PRC. "PLA Navy Benefits Rules," *Tuiyi Junguan* (in Chinese), November 14, 2004, in OSC CPP20061005325003.

12. Articles 10, 11 and 21, "Full Text of PRC 'Officers on the Active List' Law," *Xinhua* (in Chinese), December 28, 2000, in OSC CPP20001228000194.

13. China Military Affairs New Observer Forum, available from *xinguancha.bbs.xilu.com/*.

14. Article 12, "Full Text of PRC 'Officers on the Active List' Law," *Xinhua Domestic Service*, December 28, 2000, in OSC CPP20001228000194.

15. China Military Affairs New Observer Forum, available from *xinguancha.bbs.xilu.com/*.

16. This includes bribes, impropriety, and deciding on personnel appointments without a quorum of over half of the

relevant party committee standing committee members present. See "Rules on Punishing Breaches of Discipline in Appointing, Removing PLA Officers," *Jiefangjun Bao* (Internet Version) in Chinese, July 20, 2004, p. 1, in OSC CPP20040720000077.

17. These particular regulations were written in 1994, before the 1998 reforms establishing the General Armament Department and its subordinate armament departments at all levels. The top armament officer almost certainly can be a three-star, though the information on this remains unclear. General Armament Department Deputy Director Li Andong is a full general, and though his career has been focused on managing equipment, some argue that he is a career staff officer and therefore falls into the category of "military affairs officer" rather than armament officer. This is unclear in part because most of Li's career preceded 1998. It is notable that the director of the General Armament Department who sits on the Central Military Commission to date has been an operator or staff officer. All members of the Central Military Commission are full three- star generals.

18. "Guanyu zhuanye jishu jun xian shouyu he jinsheng 关于专业技术军衔授予和晋升" (On Technical Specialist Rank, Commission, and Promotion Regulations), *PLA Daily*, August 2007,available from *www.pladaily.com.cn/item/kjrcdw/zczx/xgzc/04. htm.*

19. The rank regulations were written in 1994, so they do not refer to armament officers and in this sense are probably outdated. However, more recent sources indicate that armament officers are subject to the same rules for ranks as operators, political officers, and logistics officers. For the rank regulations, see "Zhongguo Renmin Jiefangjun junguan jun xian tiaoli中国人民解放军军官军衔条例" (PLA Rank Regulations), available from *www.gov.cn/banshi/gm/content_63642.htm.*

20. Kenneth W. Allen and John F. Corbett, Jr, "Predicting PLA Leader Promotions," in Andrew Scobell and Larry Wortzel, eds., *Civil-Military Change in China: Elites, Institutes, and Ideas after the 16th Party Congress*, Carlisle, PA: Strategic Studies Institute, 2004, pp. 257-278. See also Dennis J. Blasko, *The Chinese Army Today*, New York: Routledge, 2006, pp. 55-56.

21. "Full Text of PRC 'Officers on the Active List' Law," *Xinhua Domestic Service*, December 28, 2000, in OSC CPP20001228000194.

22. The level is based on a grade system and is distinct from rank. Often an officer at a certain grade can hold a position at, for example, either the major or lieutenant colonel position. For a clear and detailed discussion of this system and its distinction, please see Kenneth W. Allen and John F. Corbett, Jr, "Predicting PLA Leader Promotions," in Andrew Scobell and Larry Wortzel, eds., *Civil-Military Change in China: Elites, Institutes, and Ideas after the 16th Party Congress*, Carlisle, PA: Strategic Studies Institute, U.S. Army War College, 2004, pp. 257-278.

23. Those in demand could include personnel with especially sought-after specialized skills or those posted in certain minority areas or hardship posts.

24. Exceptions can be made for rapid promotion if the officer has "outstanding qualifications, notable achievements, and the work is in demand." If they are particularly outstanding, they can be promoted more than one level. See Articles 17-21, "Zhongguo Renmin Jiefangjun junguan jun xian tiaoli中国人民解放军军官军衔条例" (PLA Rank Regulations), available from *www.gov.cn/banshi/gm/content_63642.htm*.

25. Article 17 Clause 1, "Zhongguo Renmin Jiefangjun junguan jun xian tiaoli中国人民解放军军官军衔条例" (PLA Rank Regulations), available from *www.gov.cn/banshi/gm/content_63642. htm.*《关于修改＜中国人民解放军军官军衔条例＞的决定》修正.

26. The issue of specialty and its association with potential promotions in PLA military regions, in particular, is discussed at length in Elizabeth Hague, "PLA Leadership in China's Military Regions," in Scobell and Wortzel, eds., *Civil-Military Change in China*, pp. 219-256.

27. Article 33, "Full Text of PRC "Officers on the Active List" Law, *Xinhua Domestic Service* (in Chinese), December 28, 2000, in OSC CPP20001228000194.

28. "Zhongguo Renmin Jiefangjun jilü tiao ling 中国人民解放军纪律条令" (PLA Reward and Discipline Regulations), *Chinamil*, October 25, 2004, available from *www.chinamil.com.cn/site1/misc/2004-10/25/content_43969.htm*.

29. *Ibid.*, Article 14.

30. *Ibid.*, Article 15.

31. From Chinese Academy of Engineering website, *www.cae.cn/experts/detail.jsp?id=381*; "Xinhua Backgrounder List Newly Elected CAE Academicians," *Xinhua*, December 12, 2001, in OSC CPP20011212000130; "PRC Paper Details China's Development of Unmanned Drones," *Guangming Ribao* (Internet Version), June 18, 2002, in OSC CPP20020618000086.

32. Article 24, "Zhongguo Renmin Jiefangjun junguan jun xian tiaoli中国人民解放军军官军衔条例" (PLA Rank Regulations), available from *www.gov.cn/banshi/gm/content_63642.htm*.

33. Articles 16 and 28, Officer Rank Regulations.

34. Articles 26 and 27, Officer Rank Regulations.

35. The regulations for the amount of time needed in the new rank/grade for lower levels is clear — one must fulfill the time in rank requirement for that grade. The time in rank requirement at the level of Deputy Chief of Staff of the Navy is not specified in the regulations, but three years is probably a "respectable" time at a lower level position before being reinstated to one's former position. Biographic information on Ding Yiping is gathered from newspapers and from "Jiefangjun zongcan haijun kongjun erpao jiji dajunqu renshi da tiaozheng 解放军总参海军空军二炮及几大军区人事大调整"(Personal Changes in Leadership in the PLA General Staff, Navy, Air Force, Second Artillery, and Military Regions), *Xinhua News Agency*, August 19, 2006, available from *xinhuanet.org/bencandy.php?id=378*; Excerpt from "Zhongguo Renmin Jiefangjun haijun 中国人民解放军海军" (China People's Liberation Army Navy), *Xilu Forum*, June 26, 2007, available from *bbs.xilu.com/cgi-bin/bbs/view?forum=xinguancha&message=34685* (*both accessed August 2007*).

36. "SCMP: 'Eleven PLA Officers Punished Over Anhui Plane Crash That Killed 40,'" *South China Morning Post* (Internet Version) in English, September 8, 2006, in OSC CPP20060908715004; "Hong Kong Journal Profiles PLA Air Force Political Commissar Deng Changyou," *Chien Shao* (in Chinese), No. 191, January 1-31, 2007, pp. 56-59, in OSC CPP20070108710022.

37. Information on Sun's alleged submarine record is based on Hong Kong reports that may or may not be reliable but do reflect a certain "lore" that Sun Jianguo has acquired. See "HK Journal Profiles PLA Deputy Chief of General Staff Zhang Qinsheng," *Chien Shao* (in Chinese), No. 193, March 1-31, 2007, pp. 78-84, in OSC CPP20070314710003; "HK Journal Details PLA Leadership Reshuffle, Analyzes Its Characteristics," in *Kuang Chiao Ching* (in Chinese), No. 389, February 16, 2005, pp. 20-23, in OSC CPP20050218000084; and "Personnel Changes at PLA Navy Headquarters May Involve Taiwan Factor," *Wen Wei Po* (Internet Version), January 11, 2005, in OSC CPP20050111000061.

38. This likely will be his last position, however. Information on Liu is from the author's database. Liu Zhenwu's biographic information also can be found in the China Military Affairs New Observer Forum, at *xinguancha.bbs.xilu.com/*, accessed August 2007.

39. Chen Changfeng is explicitly mentioned in articles by the Navy political commissar and the Navy commander as individuals, even heroes, who should be emulated. He has starred in military media reports for several years, since at least 2002. See "PLA Navy Political Commissar Calls on Renmin Haijun to Promote Navy's Building," *Renmin Haijun* (in Chinese), March 3, 2007, in OSC CPP20070403436006.

40. Much of the content for this paragraph is derived from reports found over a span of years in *People's Daily, Jiefangjun Bao, Renmin Haijun*, and other sources, many of which are available in the Open Source Center. One of the best is derived from a *Renmin Haijun* report, "PLA's South China Sea Fleet Holds Exercise Along Guangdong Coast," *Hsiang Kang Shang Pao* (Internet Version) in Chinese, June 24, 2004, p. B5, in OSC CPP20040624000096.

41. The May 2006 issue of *PLA Pictorial* magazine profiled this AF exemplary unit. Other "experimental units" are profiled in the March 2006 edition of PLA Pictorial. "PLA Pictorial Profiles Integrated Training of Chengdu Theater 'Experimental Units,'" *Jiefangjun Huabao*, in Chinese, March 1, 2006, pp. 40-45, in OSC CPP20060531318002.

42. Political commissar of the Academy of Military Sciences Liu Yuan is probably the best example of the importance of connections and family ties. The son of Liu Shaoqi, Liu Yuan was not even in the military until the 1990s, when he joined the People's Armed Police as a political commissar. Prior to that, he was a cadre. He worked his way up the People's Armed Police political system and then became the deputy political commissar of the General Logistics Department before becoming the political commissar of the Academy of Military Sciences this summer. His ascendance cannot be explained by normal career paths; it is unusual and could be attributed to his background (or perhaps a Tiananmen-era role?).

43. Author database; much of the biographical information is derived from China Military Affairs New Observer Forum, *xinguancha.bbs.xilu.com/*.

44. Excerpt from "Zhongguo Renmin Jiefangjun Zong Zhuangbei Bu, 中国人民解放军总装备部" (PLA GAD), June 27, 2007, *Xilu Forum*, available from *bbs.xilu.com/cgi-bin/bbs/view?forum=xinguancha&message=34684*.

45. Information on both can be found at China Military Affairs New Observer Forum, *xinguancha.bbs.xilu.com/*. Tong Shiping has been listed as political commissar in official press since September 2007, just before the 17th Party Congress.

46. A good overview of logistics officers' responsibilities can be found in Article 34, "'Full Text' of Revised Routine Service Regulations for PLA," *Jiefangjun Bao* (Internet Version) in Chinese, April 1, 2002, pp. 4-8, in OSC CPP20020403000098.

47. *Ibid.*, Article 34,pp. 4-8.

48. Article 10, Active Duty Officers Law, 2000. "Full Text of PRC 'Officers on the Active List' Law," *Xinhua Domestic Service*, in Chinese, December 28, 2000, in OSC CPP20001228000194.

49. Article 34, "'Full Text' of Revised Routine Service Regulations for PLA," pp. 4-8.

50. Although Sun Zhiqiang is still in his position as of November 2007, he will not be for long. As noted in the text, he has reached the maximum age for GLD deputy directors and was not elected to the 17th Party Congress. He also apparently was not a delegate to the 17th Party Congress. An officer with the same name has been selected, but this officer is associated with the People's Armed Police Force (PAPF), not the PLA — it is not the same Sun Zhiqiang. "JFJB Reveals Lists of Elected PLA, PAPF Deputies to 17th CPC National Congress," *Jiefangjun Bao* (Internet Version), in Chinese, July 3, 2007, p. 1, in OSC CPP20070704702001.

51. Unlike Wang Qian, Li Maifu was elected to be an alternate member of the 17th Central Committee. Wang Qian had been an alternate at the 16th Central Committee. They are both approximately 61 or 62 and probably both will remain in their positions for another year or two. The source for the biographic information all of the top GLD officers is the author's database; their biographic information also can be found at "Excerpt from 'Zhongguo Renmin Jiefangjun zong hou qin bu, 中国人民解放军总后勤部" (PLA General Logistics Department), Xilu Forum, available from *bbs.xilu.com/cgi-bin/bbs/view?forum=xinguancha&message=34682*.

52. A good overview of logistics officers' responsibilities can be found in Article 34, "'Full Text' of Revised Routine Service Regulations for PLA," pp. 4-8.

53. Article 2, "Full Text of PRC 'Officers on the Active List' Law," *Xinhua Domestic Service* in Chinese, December 28, 2000, in OSC CPP20001228000194; and Question 3, "PLA General Department's Explanations on PRC's Active-Service Officers Law," *Jiefangjun Bao* in Chinese, January 18, 2001 ,in OSC CPP20010118000048.

54. Some of these regulations include *The Revised Routine Service Regulations for the PLA*, *The Active Duty Officers Law*, and *The Regulation on PLA Equipment, Science, and Technology* (the PLA's

December 2006 White Paper on *China's National Defense* refers to the last of these in its appendix).

55. Article 36, "'Full Text' of Revised Routine Service Regulations for PLA," *Jiefangjun Bao* (Internet Version) in Chinese, April 1, 2002 ,pp. 4-8, in OSC CPP20020403000098.

56. Zhang Shiming was still active in November 2007 right after the Party Congress, but it is possible that he and other PLA officers who were coming of age retired shortly thereafter. The PLA holds an annual meeting in December, and personnel appointments and retirements frequently take place at that meeting and are announced in January or shortly thereafter.

57. Both Zhu Fazhong (born in 1948) and Zhang Jianqi (born in 1946) are likely to remain in their positions for another year or two.

58. Hague leadership database; see also China Military Affairs New Observer Forum, *xinguancha.bbs.xilu.com/*. 徐承云　1945年12月生，安徽肥东人。1992年晋升少将军衔。曾任36师炮兵团司务长，指挥排长，12军炮兵团团长，步兵34师师长，步兵第36师师长，第12集团军副军长、南京军区副参谋长，12集团军长，南京军区装备部部长。2003年1月任南京军区参谋长，2004年7月任南京军区副司令员。

59. For a more lengthy discussion of armaments department directors moving on to serve as deputy commanders in MRs, see Elizabeth Hague, "PLA Leadership in China's Military Regions," in Scobell and Wortzel, eds., *Civil-Military Change in China*, pp. 233-234.

60. Author database.

61. Question #25 in "PLA General Political Dept's Explanations on PRC's Active-Service Officers Law," *Jiefangjun Bao* (Internet Version), in Chinese, January 18, 2001, p. 2, in OSC CPP20010118000048.

62. "Comparison—China's White Paper on National Defense 2006," Beijing *Xinhua Domestic Service* in Chinese, December 29, 2006, in OSC CPP20061229704001.

63. The PLA Pictorial's August issue includes several of these profiles available from *www.plapic.com/txt/200708b/20070807-1b. htm*, last accessed in December 2007. Dennis Blasko brought this to the author's attention in September 2007. The profile series includes six profiles of lower-level officers, including at least two of which could be characterized as "technical officers." CCTV also broadcasted overlapping profiles. See, for example, "OSC Report: PRC TV Reports Profile Selected 17th Party Congress Delegates," October 16, 2007, in OSC CPP20071016050001.

64. Article 85, Section 1, Chapter 6 and Appendix 5, "'Full Text' of Revised Routine Service Regulations for PLA," *Jiefangjun Bao* (Internet Version) in Chinese, April 1, 2002 ,pp. 4-8, in OSC CPP20020403000098.

65. *Ibid.*, Article 48, pp. 4-8.

66. This is the author's assessment of the situation.

67. For an interesting anecdote on a story of a unit's struggle to persuade its many engineer graduates to become technical officers, see "Di er pao bing mou lu peiyang shiyong zhuanye jishu junguan de jingli, 第二炮兵某旅培养使用专业技术军官的经历" ("A certain second artillery brigade's experience in cultivating the use of technical specialist officers"), *Jiefangjun Bao*, February 6, 2006, *mil.news.sina.com.cn/2006-02-06/1602349029.html*, accessed September 2007.

68. See the same example as above. Another such officer in a different unit is a Navy officer highlighted in *Jiefangjun Bao* who graduated from a nonmilitary university, began his career in the military as a logistics ground officer, became a technical officer on a submarine chaser, and finally became a navy frigate captain. "China: JFJB Profiles New-Type Missile Frigate Captain Liu Zhigang," *Jiefangjun Bao* (Internet Version), in Chinese, April 22, 2007, p. 1, in OSC CPP20070423710002. Such cross-over between technicians and operators seems to be particularly valued in the Second Artillery, due to its technical emphasis.

69. In many of the regulations following the GAD's establishment in 1998, there is a distinction between "military affairs,"

political, logistics, and armaments officers" on the one hand and "technical specialist officers" on the other. The distinction used to be between "military affairs, political, and logistics officers" on the one hand and "technical specialist officers" on the other. It appears that some officers who are now armaments officers may have previously fallen into the category of "technical specialist officer" and/or military affairs officer. This is an area that has not been well-researched or documented. It sometimes remains unclear where the line is drawn, or whether the regulations for technical specialist officers are still in transition. "Full Text of PRC 'Officers on the Active List' Law" *Xinhua Domestic Service,* in Chinese, December 28, 2000, in OSC CPP20001228000194; and "Guanyu zhuanye jishu jun xian shouyu he jinsheng, 关于专业技术军衔授予和晋升" (On Technical Specialist Rank, Commission, and Promotion Regulations), *PLA Daily,* available from *www.pla-daily.com.cn/item/kjrcdw/zczx/xgzc/04.htm.*

70. "Wu Jiangxing: From Soldier to Chinese Engineering Institute Academic" [邬江兴：从战士到中国工程院院士], August 30, 2007, available from *www.chinamil.com.cn/site1/xwpdxw/2007-08/30/content_934447.htm;* "An Academic and General with a Passion for Innovation—Dean of Information Engineering Academy, Information Engineering University and Chinese Engineering Academy Academic Wu Jiangxing," [激情创新的将军院士—记信息工程大学信息工程学院长、中国工程院院士邬江兴] *The PLA Pictorial,* August 2007, available from *www.plapic.com/txt/200708b/20070807-1b.htm;* "China Develops Routing Equipment for High-Speed Internet," *Xinhua Domestic Service* in Chinese, August 9, 2001, in OSC CPP20010809000163.

71. Article 31, Active Duty Officers Law, 2000, December 28, 2000, in OSC CPP20001228000194. Thanks to Dennis Blasko for offering useful comments on this section and suggesting the *People's Daily's* own English translation of this article. That translation can be found at *english.chinamil.com.cn/site2/special-reports/2006-04/19/content_459140.htm.* The original Chinese text can be found at *www.people.com.cn/GB/channel1/11/20001229/365771.html.*

72. Ethnicity of officers is not widely discussed and often is inaccurate. For example, Deputy Navy Commander Ding Yiping sometimes is attributed Manchu ethnicity and sometimes Han ethnicity (he was born in Hunan, not exactly a Manchu stronghold).

73. "Xinhua: China To Elect Around 360 Deputies To 11th NPC From Ethnic Minority Groups," *Xinhua* , April 24, 2007, in OSC CPP20070424968141.

74. "JFJB Reveals Lists of Elected PLA, PAPF Deputies to 17th CPC National Congress," *Jiefangjun Bao* (Internet Version), in Chinese, July, 3, 2007, p. 1, in OSC CPP20070704702001. Thanks also to Ivan Szpakowski for coming up with this calculation and much of the baseline research for this section of the chapter.

75. "PRC: Interview With PLA Officer on Recruitment, Promotion," *Zhongguo Qingnian Bao*, November 3, 2006.

76. "Xizang junqu yituo defang peiyang shaoshuminzu ganbu gongcheng qidong 西藏军区依托地方培养少数民族干部工程启动" ("Tibet Military District launches a program to locally educate minority cadres"), *PLA Daily*, April 26, 2006, available from *www.chinamil.com.cn/site1/xwpdxw/2006-04/26/content_463752.htm.*

77. "Xizang junqu mou lü 26 ming shaoshuminzu zhan shi guangrong ru dang, 西藏军区某旅26名少数民族战士光荣入党" ("A brigade in the Tibet Military District is conferring provisionary party membership to 26 minority cadres), *PLA Daily*, May 19, 2005, available from *www.chinamil.com.cn/site1/xwpdxw/2005-05/19/content_208187.htm.*

78. "Xinjiang Boertala jun fen qu guli shaoshuminzu ganbu gangwei cheng cai 新疆博尔塔拉军分区鼓励少数民族干部岗位成才" ('Xinjiang MD's Bortala submilitary district encourages minority cadres to better their position'), *PLA Daily*, September 16, 2004, *www.pladaily.com.cn/gb/pladaily/2004/09/16/20040916001178_zgjs.html.*

79. "Xinjiang Promotes More Ethnic PLA Officers," *Zhongguo Xinwen She*, October 10, 1996, in OSC FTS19961010000081; "China's Lanzhou MR Establishes Program To Promote Minority Officers," *Xinhua*, July 26, 2000, in OSC CPP20000726000137.

80. "China's Lanzhou MR Establishes Program To Promote Minority Officers," *Xinhua*, July 26, 2000, in OSC CPP20000726000137; "Xinjiang Promotes More Ethnic PLA Officers," *Zhongguo Xinwen She*, October 10, 1996, in OSC FTS19961010000081.

81. In a very unscientific survey by the author, of 19 Uighurs profiled, at least 13 were serving in areas with large concentrations of Uighurs (four were in unknown locations); two-thirds of the relatively small number of officers appeared to be in the political track. Few Tibetans were profiled, so it is difficult to make certain generalizations, but at least three out of five identified were serving in their ethnic areas, two in the political track. Again, the sample is small, but it is striking that the other ethnic minorities had a much smaller correspondence between ethnicity and ethnicity of the region they were serving in.

82. Profiles of officers in ethnic minority areas usually focus on their home towns. Themes include Uighur soldiers expressing their gratitude to the PLA's assistance in their hometown, their gratefulness to the PLA, and the "unity" of spirit they experience in the PLA with other ethnic groups, including Han Chinese.

83. Both Tibet MD Commander/Chengdu MR Deputy Commander Meng Jinxi and Xinjiang MD Commander/Lanzhou MR Deputy Commander Qiu Yanhan were still active during the summer of 2007, but they were both born in 1944 and were not reelected to the Central Committee at the 17th Party Congress in October 2007. Dong Guishan, the new Tibet Military District Commander, and Tian Xiusi, the Xinjiang Military District political commissar, also are double-hatted, and both are full members of the 17th Party Congress Central Committee.

CHAPTER 8

EDUCATING "NEW-TYPE MILITARY TALENT": THE PLA'S COMMAND COLLEGES

Nan Li

This chapter examines the advanced (高级) and intermediate (中级) command schools (指挥院校) of the People's Liberation Army (PLA). Specifically, it attempts to answer three analytical questions. First, what are the recent changes with regard to the missions and objectives, curriculums, teaching and learning methods, and faculty development of the PLA's command colleges? Second, what major factors drive these changes? Third, what are the major challenges facing the transformation of the PLA's command colleges?

This study is important and necessary mainly because the extent that the professional military education (PME) system has developed is a major indicator of the degree of military professionalization. This is so for two reasons. First, because of the increasing technological and organizational complexity of the modern military, the specialized knowledge and expertise of the profession can be acquired "only by prolonged education and experience," and their "extension and transmission" require "institutions of research and education."[1] A PME system consists mainly of such institutions.

Second, advanced and intermediate command schools deal with the core specialties and expertise of the military profession, or those that concern "the organizing, equipping, and training of (land, naval, or air) force; the planning of its activities; and the direction of its operation in and out of combat."[2] These specialties and expertise are peculiar and unique to the military profession and as a result mostly absent in nonmilitary professions.

Let us begin by offering major clarifications and definitions concerning this study. First, this study does not examine the PLA's engineering, medical, and other types of professional schools. Neither does this study cover the primary (初级) command schools, or those that are similar to the U.S. military academies and train entry-level officer candidates. Because these two types of schools have also been undergoing important changes,[3] they deserve separate analysis.

Consequently, this essay only examines the advanced and intermediate command schools. Advanced schools refer to those that primarily provide up-to-one-year joint campaign and strategic command education to division or senior colonel and higher-level commanding officers before they are promoted to the next level. So far, the PLA has only one such school: the National Defense University (NDU) in Beijing.

Intermediate command schools, on the other hand, refer to those that mainly provide up-to-one-year single-arm (单兵种) tactical, combined-arms (合成兵种) tactical, service campaign, and joint campaign education to battalion, regiment, brigade, and division or major, lieutenant colonel, colonel, and senior colonel-level commanding officers before they are promoted to the next level (see Table 1 for a list of these schools).[4] Education of battalion-level officers can also be conducted by the primary command schools. Finally, these schools also offer longer-term programs leading to a master's degree for battalion and regiment-level commanding officers and a doctoral degree for brigade and division-level commanding officers.[5]

Schools	Location	Jurisdiction
NDU	Beijing	Central Military Commission (CMC)
Army Command College	Nanjing, Jiangsu	General Staff Department (GSD)
Army Command College	Shijiazhuang, Hebei	GSD
Artillery Command College	Langfang, Hebei	GSD
Engineering Command College	Xuzhou, Jiangsu	GSD
Anti-Chemical Engineering and Command College	Beijing	GSD
Telecommunications Command College	Wuhan, Hubei	GSD
Air Defense Command College	Zhengzhou, Henan	GSD
Army Aviation College	Beijing	GSD
Political College	Xian, Shanxi	General Political Department (GPD)
Logistics Command College	Beijing	General Logistics Department (GLD)
Armament Command and Technologies College	Beijing	General Armament Department (GAD)
Naval Command College	Nanjing, Jiangsu	Navy
Naval Arms Command College	Guangzhou, Guangdong	Navy
Air Force Command College	Beijing	Air Force
Second Artillery Command College	Wuhan, Hubei	Second Artillery

Source: *Liberation Army Daily On-line, available from www.chinamil.com.cn/site1/milschools/yxjs.htm.*

Table 1. Major Command Colleges.

The Chinese names of the primary command schools do not carry the term 指挥 (command). *Shijiazhuang jijiehua bubing xueyuan*, for instance, can be translated as Shijiazhuang Mechanized Infantry Academy. Similarly, *Dalian haijun jianting xueyuan* can be translated as Dalian Naval Combatants Academy. On the other hand, the Chinese names of the intermediate command schools, which are somewhat similar to the U.S. war colleges, mostly carry the term 指挥. *Lujun zhihui xueyuan* in Nanjing, for instance, can be translated as Army Command College. *Haijun zhihui xueyuan*, also in Nanjing, can be translated as Naval Command College. The title of this paper attempts to reflect the type of schools the essay intends to examine. The three levels can also be translated as high-ranking, middle-ranking, and low-ranking.

Finally, major changes of the PME system in China usually take place following the convening of the all-army conference on colleges and schools. Such conferences are usually held sometimes after the endorsement of a new military policy by the Central Military Commission (CMC). The changes of the PME system adopted in these conferences are usually associated with the new military policy and related speeches delivered by key political-military leadership.

The 13th Conference on Colleges and Schools, for instance, was held in 1986 following the 1985 CMC decision to downsize the PLA by a million positions. The 14th Conference was held in June 1999, more or less associated with the 1997 CMC decision to downsize the PLA by another 500,000, and with Jiang Zemin's speech on educating "new-type military talent," delivered at a CMC expanded conference held in April 1999.[6] The most recent, or the 15th Conference, was held in November 2003, following the late 2002 CMC decision to endow the PLA with the "dual-historical task of mechanization and informatization" and to downsize it by another 200,000 positions. It was also related to a CMC expanded conference held in September 2003, where Jiang delivered a speech highlighting again the need for educating "new-type military talent." The *Plan on Implementing the Strategic Project concerning Military Talent* was also endorsed at this conference.[7] This study focuses on post-1999 changes.

The chapter has three sections. The first addresses major changes. The second examines major factors that drive changes. The concluding section discusses major challenges facing the transformation of the PLA's command colleges.

RECENT CHANGES

Recent changes in the PLA's command colleges have become quite apparent in terms of their missions and objectives, curriculums, teaching and learning methods, and faculty development.

Missions and Objectives.

The primary mission of the command colleges is to educate advanced and intermediate-level commanding officers to meet the demand of the PLA for these officers. These colleges are also responsible for "scientific research" on major policy, doctrinal, operational, organizational, and technological issues concerning the PLA. As a result, these colleges are intended to provide effective "personnel" and "intellectual" support for the long-term, general goal of China's military modernization, and the short-term, specific goal of making preparation for "military struggle."[8] While research has been expanded and more institutionalized over time, it is important to note that education is probably still more important than "scientific research" for these colleges. This is because the PLA has various research institutes that are fully devoted to "scientific research."

Because the PLA has been attempting to transform itself from a manpower-intensive, low-technology force to one that is technology-based, not just in terms of mechanized platforms but more in terms of information technologies (IT) and related software, the requirement criteria of the PLA for advanced and intermediate commanding officers have also been changing. The pre-1997 force modernization, for instance, was mainly focused on "mechanization," or acquiring mechanized weapons platforms. As a result, the emphasis of the command colleges was placed on developing relatively narrow technical knowledge and operational ability of commanding officers concerning these platforms. This also means that interdisciplinary and interservice synergy-based leadership training was deemphasized because it was not a central concern.

The gradual shift of emphasis of force modernization from mechanization to informatization since 1997, however, has led to major conceptual change concerning the personnel requirement criteria of the PLA. Rather than training people in narrow technical and operational knowledge of weapons platforms, China's PME is now required to educate "new-type military talent," defined mainly in terms of the compound (复合式) knowledge structure and synthetical (综合) and innovative (创新) abilities.[9] This conceptual change means that rather than specialized platforms operators, the PLA now needs people who receive leadership training and as a result are capable of initiatives and independent decisionmaking.

Educating "new-type military talent" is necessary for the PLA mainly because effective preparation for warfare in the information age requires synthetical integration of diverse knowledge, technologies, command and control, weapons platforms, logistics, and operational units. This is because the battle space has expanded from the traditional domains such as land, sea, and air to outer, electro-magnetic, cyber, and cognitive space. Also winning modern war requires the synthetical employment of military, political, economic, diplomatic, and cultural means. Finally, because political and military competition becomes increasingly fierce and complex, innovative ability is particularly necessary to resolve practical problems and to exploit fast changing circumstances to maximize gains and minimize losses.

For the short-term objective of the PLA, or that to be accomplished by 2010 through command college education, see Table 2. The long-term objective, or that to be accomplished by 2020, is for all regiment and higher-level commanding officers to have a 4-year college degree and to possess diverse service credentials and international experience, and for the majority of them to hold a master's degree. A major implication of accomplishing these objectives, or having PLA officers sufficiently exposed to the educational, operational, and international environment, is for them to become capable leaders who can make good judgments and sound decisions in times of crisis and war.

Levels	Education	Knowledge Scope	Service Credentials
Regiment and higher-level commanding officers	60 percent received 4-year college degree; all attended command colleges for pre-assignment education and high science and technologies education.	Knowledgeable about high science and technologies and military services and arms; familiar with joint operations theory, main battle platforms, and command and control system of one's own unit; organized and commanded military exercises of substantial scale.	Majority had one commanding position assignment within lower two levels, or one staff assignment at higher headquarters, and assignment outside one's own unit; more than one-third of division and higher-level officers had assignments in military schools or other services and arms: more than half of brigade and division-level officers studied or received training abroad; more than one-third of staff officers in relevant general departments come from Second Artillery, Navy and Air Force.
Battalion and lower-level commanding officers	80 percent received 4-year college degree.		Majority held different assignments in commanding, political, and technical positions.
Source: Chen, *Constituting Thoughts*, pp. 70-71.			

Table 2. Objective by 2010.

Curriculums.

To educate the "new-type military talent," curriculums of the command colleges have also undergone major changes. Following the 15th Conference on Colleges and Schools, for instance, the teaching and research components of the command colleges were reorganized. The reorganization in the NDU offers a representative example, mainly because other command colleges share structural similarity with the NDU except for service-based and operational level-based modifications.

As Table 3 shows, new subjects such as joint operations; information operations; operational simulation; services and arms operations; strategic logistics; opinion, psychological, and legal warfare; and new science and technologies have been integrated into the NDU curriculum. Similarly, courses on space operations, cyber-space operations, counterterrorism, military-operations-other-than-war, peacekeeping, and international law have also been added. According to Pei Huailiang, a former NDU commandant, the annual rate of new course addition at NDU is as high as 60 percent, while outdated courses are terminated.[10]

Management	NDU Party Committee; Training Department; Scientific Research Department; Political Department; and University Affairs (logistics) Department.
Teaching and Research Departments (TRD)	Strategy TRD: • Integrating personnel from the old Strategy Teaching and Research Office (TRO), Strategic Research Institute (RI), International Relations TRO, Foreign Militaries and Foreign Languages TRO, Services and Arms TRO, Foreign Officers Training Department and Crisis Management Group.* Campaign TRD: • Military Operations Theory RI. • First Joint Campaign TRO. • Second Joint Campaign TRO. • Services and Arms TRO. • Foreign Militaries' Campaign TRO. • Military Training TRO. Information Operations, Command and Training TRD: • Information Operations RI. • Operations Command TRO. • Strategic Simulation TRO. • Campaign Simulation TRO. • Military Training TRO. • Combat Laboratory. Military Logistics, Science and Technologies and Armament TRD: • Military Logistics and Armament RI. • Strategic Logistics and Armament Maintenance (保障) TRO. • Campaign Logistics and Armament Maintenance TRO. • Military Science and Technologies TRO. • Journal: *Armament Studies.* Army Construction and Military Political Work TRD: • Army Construction RI. • Military Political Work TRO. • Party History and Construction TRO. • Center for Research on Opinion, Psychological, and Legal Warfare. • Journals: *Military Political Work* and *Advisory Report on Opinion, Psychological and Legal Warfare.* Marxism TRD.

*Classical Chinese military thought is an integral part of the curriculum of the Strategy TRD.

Table 3. Post-2004 National Defense University (1).

Besides the classes shown in Table 4, new classes have also been added. As the cross-service assignment (交叉式任职) was introduced, for instance, an up-to-6-month intensive class was recommended to prepare officers before they take up new assignments in other services. This class focuses mainly on issues concerning management, operational organization and command, and logistical maintenance of the unfamiliar services that these officers are assigned to. Adding such a class is also considered an important measure to institutionalize cross-service assignment.[11]

Academic Departments	Classes
National Defense Department (国防系)	• Up-to-6-month class for group army and higher-level commanding officers and provincial governor and higher-level civilian officials on national defense and strategic issues
Basics Department (基本系)	• One-year class for group army-level commanding officers on commanding campaigns. • One-year class for battalion and higher-level staff officers working in group army and higher-level headquarters on staff work before promotion to position of departmental heads. • Two-year class for military school graduates to become instructors at advanced and intermediate command schools.
Advanced Department (进修系)	• Up-to-6-month class for division and higher-level commanding officers, military school commandants and instructors and researchers in intermediate command colleges on new theory, knowledge, weapons systems and technologies.
Graduate School (研究生院)	• Up-to-3-year class for company and higher-level officers who have served for more than 2 years at a specific level, and who work toward master's and doctoral degrees in 13 majors, to become higher-level commanding officers, theoretical researchers, or military school instructors.

Table 4. National Defense University (2).

Finally, deployment of new weapons platforms and force restructuring in operational units leads to new methods of operations, training, and management. As a result, command colleges regularly dispatch investigation and research groups (调研组) to operational units to analyze changes in the demands of the units. The findings in turn are factored into the development of educational plans and curriculums.

The Second Artillery Command College, for instance, established a curriculum committee and sent 15 such groups to the operational units. The new methods of operations and training as a result of the investigation were integrated into the new teaching materials together with the lessons of the Afghan War and Iraqi War. In the meantime, more than 20 outdated textbooks were eliminated from graduate courses, while more than 50 new courses were added, including "Research on Missile Firepower Operations," "Organization and Implementation of Exercises," and

"Computer Network Technologies." Furthermore, more than 20 new disciplinary directions were developed, including joint campaign, electronic warfare, battlefield intelligence acquisition, joint firepower strike under complex electromagnetic conditions, and command automation. Also, 66 assignment-oriented training specialties and 15 "critical demand" training specialties were optimized. Finally, six military theory research centers were established, including one on information operations.[12] All these serve to better meet the demand of the operational units for qualified commanding officers.

Generally speaking, diversification and integration of curriculums are clearly intended to cultivate the "compound knowledge structure" of the students.

Teaching and Learning Methods.

In order to educate "new-type military talent," there have also been major changes in teaching and learning methods. An instructor is now required not just to transmit knowledge and answer questions, but to serve as the organizer, director, and equal participant in small seminars, where issues are identified, analyzed, discussed, and resolved. Case-based instruction has also been adopted to analyze and learn lessons from classical Chinese and foreign cases, as well as those from the PLA's own warfighting experience. Finally, war-gaming has been introduced and extensively employed.[13]

Similarly, students are advised to shift from exam-driven (应试) learning to gaining hands-on experience. Students, for instance, now participate in "joint teaching and training" ("联教联训") programs between colleges and operational units, where they are involved in organizing and commanding exercises of operational units to gain practical knowledge. Such programs have also been introduced among command colleges and between command colleges and civilian universities so that students may take courses and share educational resources in these colleges and universities.[14] The purpose of these changes is to expand the exposure and experience of the students and to foster their innovative and creative abilities.

Finally, a system of "two anonymous reviewers" for a degree thesis has been adopted in command colleges. All students at NDU, for instance, must now be examined by this system in order to graduate.[15] Similarly, a system of separating teaching from examination has been adopted.[16] The introduction of these systems is intended to reduce favoritism and enhance fairness-based competition and quality.

Faculty Development.

To educate "new-type military talent," improving the quality of the faculty has become crucial. As a result, command colleges have introduced reform measures to serve this purpose. First, command colleges have been hiring scholars who are of "disciplinary leadership status," who can "substantially raise the quality of teaching and scientific research," and who are outstanding in research on "high-demand" subjects such as technology-based services and arms operations and information operations. Moreover, retired senior military leaders, party and government officials, diplomats, scientists and scholars, as well as active service unit commanders have been hired as guest or adjunct professors. Furthermore, a substantial number of regiment and division-level commanding officers from the navy, air force, Second Artillery, and army units who have served for more than 2 years in their positions have been appointed as military instructors (教官). They generally compensate for the weakness of regular professors in empirical knowledge.[17]

More importantly, however, intensive efforts have been made to enhance the intellectual and practical knowledge of the regular faculty through continuing education. Faculty members, for instance, have been sent abroad to study and to be visiting scholars. They have also been sent to major civilian universities and research institutions for graduate degree programs.[18]

Moreover, they participate in planning and organizing major military exercises and in investigation and research in lower-level units. They are also assigned deputy positions in operational units and higher headquarters to gain empirical experience and knowledge.[19] Regular teaching and research staff are now required to participate in programs to resolve important but difficult issues in doctrinal innovation, force restructuring, new arms acquisition and deployment, training reform, and systems integration. It is argued that these endeavors can utilize the comparative advantage of command colleges in knowledge and expertise. In the meantime, they help faculty members gain practical knowledge and experience, which in turn enriches their conceptual and theoretical knowledge.[20]

Finally, more "objective" standards have been employed to evaluate the performance of the faculty to determine issues of retention and promotion. Infrastructure and teaching and research facilities have been upgraded. Special funds have been allocated for various allowances for teaching and research excellence. Efforts have also been made by management to resolve practical issues, such as getting access to affordable housing, medical care, and decent kindergartens and schools for children.[21] These measures are generally intended to retain qualified faculty members.

DRIVING FACTORS FOR CHANGES

There are many factors that have contributed to changes in the PLA's command colleges. Four, however, stand out as the most important: security competition, learning and adaptation, central leadership, and technological development of the PLA.

Security Competition.

A product of civil war and social revolution, the PLA had historically been highly involved in the domestic politics of China. It was not until after Deng Xiaoping came to power in 1978 that the PLA was gradually brought out of the class-struggle-based domestic politics. This happened mainly because Deng shifted China away from Mao's project of revolution and class struggle to a nation-building program couched in the notion of four modernizations (modernizing industry, agriculture, science and technology, and national defense).

As the PLA is gradually marginalized in the domestic domain, it has been behaving more like a regular military, whose main concern is the external security of the country. Its discourse, for instance, has become quite similar to the realist argument in the West, namely, that because of international anarchy, self-help is crucial and improving military capabilities is central in enhancing the relative advantage in order to reduce insecurity and ensure the survival of the country. According to PLA analysts, for instance, it is the sense of insecurity associated with the "zero-sum" nature and the high cost of security and military competition that drives major innovations and changes leading to improved military capabilities.[22]

The Gulf and Iraqi Wars demonstrate that a manpower-intensive, low-technology force or even a highly mechanized force proved no match for a force endowed with "information superiority" based on a highly integrated system of command, control, computer, communications, and intelligence (C4I). It shows that the technological gap between the PLA and the world's most modern military is large enough to land China and the PLA in a position of "vulnerability and being beaten up" ("被动挨打").[23] It is this sense of vulnerability that has driven the PLA to embark on a path of "leapfrogging" ("跨越式") development associated with what it calls the "new military revolution."

In this new revolution-driven security competition, human talent is regarded by the PLA analysts as contributing to the core military competitiveness of a country. This is because knowledge and innovation, which are closely associated with human talent, have become increasingly indispensable for accelerating the development of military science and technologies. Also, military competition has shifted from a physical and mechanical-force-based contest to a contest of intelligence and information. Therefore, human intelligence-based judgment and stratagem are crucial in maximizing gains and minimizing losses in the fast shifting circumstances, thus enabling the winning of the contest. Finally, the fighting spirit and the will to win, also human factors, are indispensable to winning the contest against "shock and awe" and other types of information operations of the adversary.[24]

As a result, training "new-type military talent" is of strategic importance to China and the PLA. This is so mainly because such a policy can ensure the survival of China in the fierce international competition for security and military advantages.

Learning and Adaptation.

To PLA analysts, it is quite clear that the best example from which to learn about educating "new-type military talent" is the U.S. military, mainly because it has proven to be the most competent and effective military force in the world. This explains why there has been a large body of Chinese military literature analyzing the U.S. military, including its system to train human talent.[25] Some suggest that the positive comments that such literature has shown toward the U.S. military are an indicator that the PLA is deterred by the splendid performance of the U.S. military in recent wars. This effect is alleged to be particularly pronounced in China's policy shift toward Taiwan from military confrontation to a more conciliatory economic approach and a long-term view.[26]

But China's policy shift may be driven by the Chinese civilian leadership's concern that brandishing military force toward Taiwan may not always deter, but may sometimes aggravate pro-independence sentiment in Taiwan, which may not have much to do with the U.S. military performance. Also, for such an argument to be more persuasive, it may need to demonstrate two things. First, and at least, the PLA has not accelerated its military modernization. Second, and at best, the PLA has embarked on a path of massive unilateral arms reduction, as it did in 1985.

Neither of the two, however, has happened. Instead, the PLA has accelerated its modernization programs, one of which has been discussed in this essay. As a result, alternative explanations may be needed for the PLA's positive evaluation of the U.S. military performance.

A more plausible explanation is the neo-realist theory of international politics, one that argues that major powers imitate the most effective country in military organization and technological development through learning and adaptation. This is because they are concerned about their own survival in an anarchic environment, particularly if they lag behind too far in relative military capabilities. The new PLA policy to educate "new-type military talent" can be understood as the result of such learning and adaptation.

Central Leadership.

The two driving factors discussed so far are necessary but not sufficient if without the endorsement of the central civilian leadership. In this case, the role of Jiang Zemin is crucial. Trained as an electrical engineer and having once served as China's minister of electronics industry, Jiang had been more sensitive to the impact of the information revolution on military affairs than his predecessor, Deng, and the PLA old guards, such as Liu Huaqing and Zhang Zhen, who surrounded him.[27] But it was not until after Deng's death and the retirement of Liu and Zhang from the CMC in 1997 that Jiang felt his power was more secure as the CMC chair. As a result, he began to promote the "new military revolution," including the associated policy of educating "new-type military talent." The move was also intended to show to the PLA generals that he is just as competent in military affairs, if not more so, than his predecessor and the old guards, in spite of the fact that he has never served in the PLA. This should have helped him to enhance his personal image in the PLA and further consolidate his CMC chair position.

Moreover, having served as the CMC chair for many years by the late 1990s, Jiang had largely commanded the obedience of the generals by increasing defense spending and promoting many of them to higher ranks, even though these policies were not solely driven by Jiang's need to consolidate power. On the other hand, Jiang did not want the generals to meddle in the party and government affairs that he presided over, which might have complicated his image and position as an effective leader. So Jiang has endorsed two new military policies since 1998. The first is to order the PLA to divest from its business activities. The second is to promote a "new military revolution" in the PLA, including the associated policy of educating "new-type military talent." Endorsing these policies is clearly intended to confine generals to narrow military-technical tasks so that they stay away from the broad and complex area of civilian politics. It is important to note that in comparison with the Mao and even Deng eras, evidence to show that Jiang employs the military against political opposition from within the party leadership and from society is much more sketchy, speculative and inconclusive.

Finally, as is the case in all other bureaucracies, one major incentive for those working in the PLA bureaucracy is to receive promotion. To the extent promotion is linked to performance and policy accomplishments (政绩), it is natural for PLA officers to be eager to demonstrate their accomplishments to their commander-in-chief by fleshing out and implementing his new policy of educating "new-type military talent." This is particularly so if the commander-in-chief is successful in consolidating his leading position in the party and government and within the PLA. This is because this consolidation enhances his credibility and authority in making decisions concerning personnel appointments and promotions.

Technological Development of the PLA.

Technological development of the PLA may not be an important driving factor mainly because, while the new policy of educating "new-type military talent" was officially endorsed in 1999, the technological development of the PLA was quite modest. The policy was forward-looking, with an eye toward preparing the PLA for its future need for "new-type talent" as technological development accelerates. As shown earlier in the discussion, however, in recent years, deployment of substantial new weapons platforms and force restructuring have begun to influence and modify the educational plans and curriculums of command colleges. It is likely that as the technological development of the PLA quickens and deepens, it may become a major factor driving the need to educate "new-type military talent."

MAJOR CHALLENGES

While some progress has been made in transforming the PLA command colleges in order to educate "new-type military talent," it is still quite preliminary and there are major challenges. First, the progress may be uneven. The 60 percent course turnover rate at NDU, for instance, may reflect a system that runs on constantly obsolete information and one that needs more institutionalization and stability. Also, while cross-service assignment has been introduced, it is still unclear whether the practice has been institutionalized and regularized. It is also unclear how institutionalized the programs to expose faculty and students to operational environment are. Moreover, it is probably easier and less expensive to send younger faculties to acquire advanced degrees in Chinese civilian universities than to foreign institutions. Finally, the critical test on whether the new educational policy is successful is whether the new generation of PLA commanders can use good judgment and make sound decisions in times of crisis and war as well as in times of peace. In a way, these unresolved issues constitute the venues and metrics for further investigation in order to gauge the extent and nature of the progress.

Furthermore, PLA command colleges may need to continue to downsize in order to optimize the use of scarce resources, but major obstacles may exist that are difficult to overcome. Table 3 shows that NDU still maintains two teaching and research departments related to the party and political apparatus of the PLA. Opinion, psychological, and legal warfare are important aspects of information operations, while military political work helps to resolve administrative and morale issues. They generally serve military objectives and enhance the internal cohesiveness of the PLA. But a Marxism teaching and research department seems quite unnecessary. The reason for such a department to survive downsizings may be that it has important patrons at high places.[28]

Finally, as college education is increasingly outsourced to civilian universities and PLA engineering schools are also transformed into comprehensive universities that offer college degrees, primary command schools such as infantry, artillery, engineering, anti-chemical, telecommunications, political, and logistics academies would run low on officer candidates. Therefore it is logical to require these academies to shift their emphasis from degree education to assignment-oriented, specialized training of college graduates. This also implies that their counterparts at the intermediate level, or highly specialized command colleges (see Table 1), should be downsized and consolidated into departments within larger command schools such as Shijiazhuang and Nanjing Army Command Colleges. Such downsizing can not only help to enhance integrated or joint education at higher levels, but also to save money by reducing the number of administrative departments and overheads. One of the reasons why this has not happened is that more bureaucratic positions make it easier to cultivate patronage and to apply for funding. As a result, the PLA general departments that run them want to keep them. It seems that the issue of vertical compartmentalization of the PLA has yet to be fully resolved.

ENDNOTES - CHAPTER 8

1. Samuel Huntington, *The Soldier and the State*, Cambridge, MA: Harvard University Press, 1964, pp. 8, 11-14.

2. *Ibid.*, p. 11.

3. Because these schools offer college degrees and some degree programs are not substantially different from those of civilian universities, the number of these schools may gradually decline over time as college-degree education of officer candidates is increasingly outsourced to civilian universities. The PLA engineering schools would be gradually consolidated and transformed into comprehensive universities offering college degrees (学历教育), while the emphasis of primary command

schools would gradually shift from offering college degrees to post-graduate assignment-oriented education (任职教育) at the primary level. After the 15th All-Army Conference on Colleges and Schools held in November 2003, PLA schools were consolidated from 82 to 67, including 22 college-degree schools, 26 primary assignment-oriented education schools (including four noncommissioned officer schools), 18 intermediate assignment-oriented education schools, and one advanced assignment-oriented education school. In the coming years, the PLA would concentrate resources on developing five degree-education comprehensive universities and 10 primary assignment-oriented education schools as reflected in the PLA general departments' "2110" Project. See Chen Dongxiang *et al.*, eds., *Weilaixing junshe rencai gouxiang* (*Constituting Thoughts on Future-Type Military Talent*), Beijing: Liberation Army Press, 2005, p. 362; Gao Jintao, *Junxiao jiaoyu sixiang yanjiu* (*A Study of the Educational Thought of Military Schools*), Beijing: People's Armed Police Press, 2006, p. 113. Even though under the direct jurisdiction of the Central Military Commission, the National Defense University of Science and Technology in Changsha is a comprehensive university but not an intermediate or advanced command school. As a result, it is not discussed in this chapter.

4. After 4 years of education and training, for instance, a graduate of the Dalian Naval Combatant Academy would be commissioned as the commanding officer of a department or a unit on a naval combatant. In order to be promoted to the position of a ship captain or executive officer, however, he/she needs to receive single-arm tactical command education at the Guangzhou Naval Arms Command College. To reach the commanding position of a flotilla (支队), he/she must enter the Nanjing Naval Command College to receive naval combined arms tactical command education. To become the fleet commanding officer, he/she needs to go to the NDU in Beijing to receive an education on campaign command.

5. See Chen, *Constituting Thoughts*, pp. 266-271.

6. See Jiang Zemin, "Make Great Efforts to Foster and Bring up Large Number of High-Quality New-Type Military Talent," a speech delivered at the CMC Expanded Conference on April 9, 1999, and collected in Jiang Zemin, *Lun guofang he jundui jianshe*

(*On National Defense and Army Construction*), Beijing: Liberation Army Press, 2003.

7. See "An Important Measure to Accelerate the Modernization Construction of Our Army," *Jiefangjun Bao* (*Liberation Army Daily*), September 7, 2003, p. 1. All the *Liberation Army Daily* articles cited in this chapter are acquired from the internet.

8. CMC *Plan on Implementing the Strategic Project concerning Military Talent*, cited in Chen, *Constituting Thoughts*, p. 200. "Military struggle" is the PLA euphemism for a military conflict over Taiwan.

9. Jiang, "Make Great Efforts," p. 373.

10. Pei Huailiang, "Establish and Apply Scientific Development Concept, Advance University Reform and Construction," *Guofang daxue xuebao* (*Journal of NDU*), No. 6, 2006, p. 6. It is reasonable to assume the 60 percent course turnover rate is only associated with a period of experimentation with new materials.

11. See Xu Hua, "Reflections on Improving and Perfecting the Cultivating Mechanisms for Cross-Service Assignment," *Journal of NDU*, No. 2, 2005.

12. See "Second Artillery Command College Reforms and Strives to Educate Talent," *Liberation Army Daily*, July 11, 2007, p. 1. Between October and December of 2006, Naval Arms Command College also sent investigation and research groups to 15 units, organized 22 symposiums, and conducted surveys. See "Naval Arms Command College: Bring up New-Type Qualified Talent," *Liberation Army Daily*, June 7, 2007, p. 9. For similar endeavors, see also "Ability and Quality of Air Defense Command College Students Are in Step with New Arms," *Liberation Army Daily*, July 23, 2007.

13. See Pei, "Establish and Apply Scientific Development Concept," pp. 5, 6; Dong Huiyu, "Accurately Grasp the Essence of Military Case Instruction," *Journal of NDU*, No. 6, 2006.

14. See Pei, "Establish and Apply Scientific Development Concept," p. 6. For an example of "joint teaching and training"

involving the Nanjing Army Command College, Nanjing Military Region (MR) Combined Arms Tactical Training Base, and an armored regiment, see "Joint Teaching and Training in Nanjing MR Resolves the Bottleneck Problems of Unit Training," *Liberation Army Daily*, August 16, 2007. See also "Second Artillery Command College: Let Classroom Link Directly to Battlefield," *Liberation Army Daily*, May 31, 2007. For "joint teaching and training" programs among Second Artillery Command College, Naval Command College, Air Force Command College, and Nanjing and Shijiazhuang Army Command Colleges, see "Second Artillery Command College Reforms and Strives to Educate Talent," and "Five Services and Arms Command Colleges Signed Agreement on Joint Education," *Liberation Army Daily*, December 19, 2006, p. 9.

15. "NDU Degree Thesis Requires 'Two Anonymous Reviewers'," *Liberation Army Daily*, July 23, 2007, p. 2.

16. See "Naval Arms Command College."

17. Pei, "Establish and Apply Scientific Development Concept," pp. 6-7; Yang Weizhan, "Military Colleges and Schools Should Provide Powerful Intellectual Support and Talent Guarantee for Fulfilling the Historical Missions of Our Army," *Journal of NDU*, No. 1, 2006, p. 6; Cadre Department of NDU's Political Department, "An Inquiry on Employing the System of 'Military Instructors' by Assignment-oriented Education Colleges and Schools," *Journal of NDU*, No. 12, 2005. The Artillery Command College, for instance, has hired 50 adjunct professors and more than 40 military instructors. See "50 Commanders Step onto the Lecture Platform," *Liberation Army Daily*, February 1, 2007.

18. Yang, "Military Colleges and Schools," p. 6. The Air Force Command College, for instance, has sent more than 30 faculty members to study in the United States, England, France, and Russia, and more than 40 younger, more promising faculty members and researchers to study for graduate degrees in major civilian universities. See "Air Force Command College: Military Barracks Cultivate Famous Teachers," *Liberation Army Daily*, May 10, 2007.

19. Air Force Command College, for instance, has selected more than 200 faculty members to participate in these activities,

and chosen more than 60 members to take up assignments in operational units. See "Air Force Command College."

20. Zhu Aixian, "A Brief Comment on the Basic Conceptual Contour regarding the Education and Training Transformation of Our Army," *Journal of NDU*, No. 10, 2004, p. 85; Chen Zheluan, "Establishing Joint Training and Education Mechanism between Units and Colleges Is Imperative," *Journal of NDU*, No. 10, 2004, p. 87.

21. See Pei, "Establish and Apply Scientific Development Concept," pp. 6-7; "Second Artillery Command College Reforms and Strives to Educate Talent."

22. Chen, *Constituting Thoughts*, pp. 23-24.

23. Jiang, "Make Great Efforts," pp. 371-372; Chen, *Constituting Thoughts*, pp. 32-35.

24. Jiang, "Make Great Efforts," p. 372; Chen, *Constituting Thoughts*, pp. 57-62.

25. For an example, see Tu Reibin, "The Way the U.S. Military Trains Military Command Talent and Revelations for Us," *Junshi xueshu* (*Military Art Journal*), No. 1, January 2006.

26. Robert Ross, "Navigating the Taiwan Strait, Deterrence, Escalation Dominance, and U.S.-China Relations," *International Security*, Vol. 27, No. 2, Fall 2003, pp. 64-71.

27. Jiang regards the Gulf War as symbolizing an unprecedented new era of warfare which is qualitatively different from that of the industrial age. Therefore, Jiang wants the PLA to transform itself in order to be well prepared for this new era. Liu Huaqing, however, believes that the Gulf War represents an exception to the normative doctrines of people's war and mechanized warfare that he has been socialized into. As a result, he wants the PLA to be selective in learning from the lessons of the Gulf War. For Liu's view on the Gulf War, see Liu Huaqing, *Liu Huaqing huiyilu* (*Liu Huaqing's Memoirs*), Beijing: Liberation Army Press, 2004, pp. 606-613.

28. Apparently for the similar reason, GPD's Military Arts Academy, which trains actors, singers, and dancers, survived both 1999 and 2004 downsizings.

CHAPTER 9

THE CRADLE OF GENERALS: STRATEGISTS, COMMANDERS, AND THE PLA-NATIONAL DEFENSE UNIVERSITY

Paul H. B. Godwin[*]

INTRODUCTION

For three decades, the Chinese People's Liberation Army (PLA) has been undergoing an extensive modernization process. Armaments, support systems, organization, force structure, logistics, officer and noncommissioned officer (NCO) selection and promotion, military strategy, concepts of operations, command and control, training, professional military education (PME), and essentially every other aspect of what is required to be a "modern" military establishment is being transformed. A central question is what kind of senior military leadership is emerging to direct these forces as they modernize and develop the strategy and operations to guide them in future military conflicts? In an effort to answer that question, this chapter assesses the professional military education (PME) China's senior officers[1] receive immediately prior to their appointment to higher staff and command positions. The analysis concludes that the PME they receive is not designed to make them strategists. Rather, the

[*] I gratefully acknowledge the extensive research assistance provided by Ivan Szpakowski of NBR's Washington, DC, office and the University of Maryland.

primary objective is to prepare them to command and staff joint forces. That is, the focus of their professional military education program is far more concentrated on current and future operational issues than it is on abstract principles of strategy. A second objective is to enhance these future military leaders' appreciation of how China's defense policy is an integral component of Beijing's overall security and foreign policies. The PLA's senior officers are expected to understand how defense policy fits into the broader pattern and objectives of China's foreign policy.

China's senior officers do confront demanding tasks. As it modernizes, the PLA is in transition from a ground force-dominated military to a more balanced force structure where naval, air, and missile forces perform missions of equal importance to those of the army. Prior to this change, naval and air forces were seen essentially as adjuncts to the ground forces. Since the early 1990s, the PLA has sought to develop the skills required to employ the synergy created by joint service operations. Developing these skills has been made difficult by advances in technology that have transformed the scope of the battlefield as space operations for intelligence, surveillance, and reconnaissance (ISR) and command, control, and communications join traditional land, air, and sea operations. Precision-guided munitions (PGM) are rapidly improving their range and accuracy, adding yet another technological change to both offensive and defensive operations. Foreign ballistic missile defenses (BMD) are emerging to complicate offensive missile operations and strategic deterrence. Moreover, information operations have joined the "hard attack" capabilities of the armaments wielded by land, air, naval, and missile forces. Developing the skills and knowledge required to implement military strategy and operations for future warfare and to command multifaceted joint forces operations is a challenging task.

China's armed forces, however, prepare for missions in addition to major combat operations, and these are becoming ever more salient as years pass. Among them are anti-terrorism, rescue and relief operations, post-disaster reconstruction, and possibly noncombatant evacuation operations (NEO), all of which require the attention of senior officers. Moreover, the PLA has intensified its military diplomacy by expanding military exchanges, slowly increasing naval port calls and participation in bilateral and multilateral military exercises, and inviting foreign observers to PLA exercises. Thus, military diplomacy is yet another realm where senior officers perform an important role. The PLA's growing involvement in United Nations (UN) peacekeeping operations (PKO) plays an important purpose here as Beijing seeks to enhance China's image as a contributor to global peace and stability. The emphasis on the role of China's defense policy in Beijing's foreign policy can be seen in the section on "International Security Cooperation" found in China's defense white papers.[2]

In preparing its potential senior leaders for these complex tasks, the PLA has two foundations to build upon—the experience officers gain advancing in rank and responsibility over their years of service joined with their exposure to the professional military education required for promotion. Because the PLA has not engaged in major combat since the 1979 invasion of Vietnam conducted primarily by ground forces, the PLA's future senior leaders cannot draw upon any direct combat experience in the conduct of joint operations employing advanced technologies. To compensate for this lack of experience, PLA researchers intensely analyze contemporary military operations, especially those conducted by the U.S. armed forces beginning with the 1991 Gulf War. Although the PLA will not design its operations on a U.S. model, there can be no doubt that the wars fought by the United States are an important component of the PME curricula focused on military strategy and operations. Two drivers suggest this is the case. As numerous articles in China's military journals testify, U.S. armed forces have the most experience employing advanced technologies in combat operations, and they are the most challenging adversary the PLA may have to confront.

In determining how the PLA's top-level professional military education prepares senior officers for a demanding future, the chapter's narrative will first focus on the logic behind the establishment of the PLA's National Defense University (PLA-NDU) in 1985. This will be followed by an assessment of the PLA-NDU's curriculum development and reform since its founding. The analysis will then survey the assignments of officers following their completion of the PLA-NDU's most senior PME program—the National Defense Research course. The chapter will conclude by speculating on what overall qualities China seeks in its future senior military leaders.

THE CRADLE OF GENERALS

As early as 1977, Deng Xiaoping had insisted that rebuilding, revitalizing, and expanding the PLA PME system and research centers was a "strategic" objective within his military modernization strategy.[3] When established by Deng on December 24, 1985, the

PLA-NDU was to be the pinnacle of China's reformed PME system. The PLA-NDU was initially formed by merging the PLA's Military Academy, Political Academy, and Logistics Academy, then the senior PME schools. Known as the "cradle of generals" and reporting directly to the Central Military Commission (CMC) of the Chinese Communist Party (CCP) in the two decades since its founding, the PLA-NDU has become the educational foundation of the PLA's most senior officers.

It is probable that the concept of a National Defense University derived in part from earlier PLA delegations' visits to the U.S. National Defense University (U.S.-NDU). Among these was a 1980 delegation led by Xiao Ke, then Commandant of the PLA Military Academy and Vice Minister of Defense, with responsibility for PME. Nonetheless, PLA delegations also visited PME schools in Europe, so it is quite possible that examples in addition to the U.S. system were influential. Nonetheless, as the PLA-NDU's first president, it was General Zhang Zhen's task to establish the curriculum and research center to support a student body that was to become both joint service and include civilian officials from relevant central and provincial offices. Because this approach to PME was a new venture for the PLA, General Zhang viewed his task to some extent as experimental.[4] The PLA-NDU's future success depended in large part on the foundation General Zhang would build. Because the PLA had little familiarity with joint service PME to draw upon, let alone including civilian officials in the student body, General Zhang combined his own experience as president of the PLA's senior school for ground force officers with an active investigation of major foreign PME centers.[5] Among these, the U.S.-

NDU was of particular interest to him.[6] Although General Zhang did not intend to use the U.S.-NDU as a template for the PLA-NDU, he was most interested in the structure of the U.S.-NDU, the role of its research center—the Institute for National Strategic Studies (INSS); the curricula of its various colleges, especially the National War College (NWC); and the selection of their students, including the foreign officers (International Fellows) to attend the colleges. He viewed the U.S.-NDU as an advanced and experienced example of the kind of PME center the PLA required to prepare its future senior officers for high command and staff positions. Examples of what General Zhang found interesting and incorporated into the PLA-NDU curriculum were the U.S.-NDU "Capstone" course, INSS, and the International Fellows program. In the Capstone course,[7] officers newly promoted to the rank of brigadier general and rear admiral (lower half) are provided not only a compressed course focused on current and future issues in military and international affairs, but also undertake international travel to be briefed by and discuss these issues with U.S. allies and friends. General Zhang's interest in INSS was high, and among his questions was how much of the research undertaken was at the request of higher authorities and how much was self-generated. Because the Academy of Military Science was the long-established PLA research center, it is probable that General Zhang was thinking about how to develop a unique role of the PLA-NDU Institute for Strategic Studies (ISS).

On its founding, the PLA-NDU was closely identified with its predecessor—the Chinese Workers and Peasants Red Army College renamed in 1936 as the Chinese People's Anti-Japanese College of the Red Army, and renamed once more in 1937 as the Chinese

People's Anti-Japanese Military and Political College. The PLA-NDU leadership takes immense pride in the famed military commanders who were students at these schools. Among them were Luo Ruiqing, Yang Chengwu, Xu Shiyou, Hong Xuezhi, Zhang Aiping, Yu Qiuli, Liu Huaqing, and other leading officers, including General Zhang Zhen himself.[8] It is likely that among the several reasons General Zhang Zhen and his political commissar, General Li Desheng, were selected to lead the new NDU, including General Zhang's service as president of the Nanjing Military Academy, was their participation in the PLA's most hallowed tradition—the Long March of 1934-35. The PLA-NDU and its leadership were linked personally to the PLA predecessor's epic march for survival and its most famous leaders. These linkages meant that the NDU's status as the apex of the PLA PME system was unquestioned.

The two decades since its founding have not been easy ones for the fledgling PLA-NDU's maturation. They have encompassed a complex transition within the PLA as it went through the multiple changes required to adjust its reforms and modernization programs to China's shifting security requirements and the impact of technological advances on the conduct of war. At no time in these two decades was the PLA-NDU able to settle on educational programs for more than a few years. When founded in 1985, the PLA was in the midst of its transformation from the sprawling, overstaffed, poorly trained and led obsolescent giant that had emerged from Mao Zedong's maniacal domestic political campaigns, especially his "Great Proletarian Cultural Revolution" of 1966-76. The poor operational performance of the PLA in the 1979 incursion into Vietnam demonstrated that the

PLA's combat capability had eroded to the point it was incapable of conducting modern warfare.[9] Outdated weapons and equipment were not the sole source of the PLA's problems. For more than 10 years, the PLA had not systematically trained for any kind of war, and its doctrine and concepts of operations dated back to the mid-1950s. Establishing the PLA-NDU to be the apex of China's military education system was therefore a critical step in developing an officer corps capable of planning and conducting modern warfare. "Modern warfare," however, was to be a moving target, as were the military security objectives for which the PLA was to prepare.

In 1985, the PLA's military preparations focused on conducting wars on China's periphery limited in geographical scope and political objectives referred to as "local, limited wars." In 1991, the first Persian Gulf War's demonstration of high-technology warfare conducted by joint-service operations led to the PLA being directed in 1993 to prepare to fight and win "local, limited wars under modern high tech-conditions." The shock effect of this war on the PLA was not entirely a consequence of the technologies applied. Equally important were the joint operations employed to exploit these technologies in combat operations that quickly laid waste to the opposing forces. As PLA analysts assessed the war, it soon became apparent that the PLA's operational doctrine was as antiquated as its weaponry. PLA assessments concluded that a revolution in military affairs (RMA) was underway. Information warfare (IW) employed by the U.S. forces was viewed as a central component of this RMA.[10] Thus, "local, limited war under modern high-tech conditions" had major implications for preparing the future officer corps—an importance that continues today as Beijing defines the third step in its three-stage defense modernization as "building an informationized armed forces . . . capable of winning informationized wars by the mid-21st century."[11]

The changing environment of China's strategic deterrent paralleled the changes in the technological and operational requirements for the conduct of conventional war as the United States began developing a national missile defense (NMD) capability following President Reagan's 1983 "Strategic Defense Initiative" (SDI).[12] China's strategic deterrent logic was, and largely remains, based on the belief that even states with overwhelming strategic superiority can be deterred from the threat or use of nuclear weapons when credibly threatened with a punitive second strike. For Chinese nuclear doctrine, such a deterrent does not require nuclear parity; only that sufficient weapons survive a first strike to conduct a retaliatory punitive second strike. SDI threatened to undermine this logic. Even when designed in later years only to defend against a small number of missiles launched by a "rogue" state or an accidental launch, an effective NMD could undermine a strategic deterrent based upon a small number of warheads. China's commitment to the survivability of its strategic deterrent is seen in the development of tactically mobile ground and submarine-based intercontinental ballistic missiles (ICBM). These developments were accompanied by continuing debate within China on whether a strategic deterrent built around a small number of strategic missiles (known in the West as "minimum deterrence") is feasible, given developments in ballistic missile defenses (BMD).[13] China's angst over U.S. BMD continues and includes American development of theater missile defenses (TMD).[14]

Not only did the paradigm of "modern warfare" change, but China's threat assessments also changed over these two decades. The former Union of Soviet Socialist Republics (USSR) was included in the potential contingencies that generated the PLA's 1985 focus on "limited, local war." The Soviet Union's 1991 implosion removed whatever remaining concern Beijing may have harbored about Moscow as a potential adversary. With the unanticipated visit of Taiwan's President Lee Teng-hui to the United States in 1995, Beijing's focus on contingency planning narrowed considerably to a potential confrontation with the United States over Taiwan. When in 1996 the United States dispatched two aircraft carrier strike groups (CSG) to the Taiwan area in response to China's coercive diplomacy employing the launch of a few unarmed short-range ballistic missiles (SRBM) into the waters surrounding Taiwan together with military exercises in the Taiwan Strait area, the PLA's primary tasking was set. It is reasonable to assume that despite other Chinese security concerns, for the past decade the PLA's center of attention has been on a Taiwan scenario. There will be other concerns, such as defending China's interests in the South China and East China Seas territorial disputes and the defense of its sea lines of communication (SLOC). For the immediate future, however, these military security interests will have a lower priority than a Taiwan contingency.

CURRICULUM DEVELOPMENT

Fundamental shifts in threat perceptions, contingency planning, and the demands of modern warfare over two decades could not but affect the curricula taught at the PLA-NDU. Simply designing an NDU in 1985 was hard enough. A *Liaowang* report quotes General Zhang Zhen declaring in 1985 "every step taken with difficulty."[15] General Zhang's observation referred to the reality that prior to the PLA-NDU's founding, China's PME system educated and trained officers (cadres) separately by service and branch as it did officers in the military (command), political, and logistics career tracks. Such training no longer met the demands of modern warfare or the qualities demanded of high-ranking officers. Not only did a modern officer corps have to understand military affairs, logistics, and politics, but its officers also had to be familiar with capabilities of services other than their own. The existing system of education and training of high-level commanders, General Zhang argued, simply did not meet the demands of modern warfare.[16] General Zhang's task was to establish a curriculum focused on developing an officer corps imbued with a joint service culture and a broad understanding of world affairs. Difficult as this was to be in a military culture traditionally dominated by the Army as a direct consequence of the PLA's history, it was but the first step in reform.

The core academic structure of the PLA-NDU has remained in place since its founding.[17] There are five study tracks or courses of study: National Defense Research, Basic Studies, Advanced Studies, Graduate Studies, and Instructor Training. Additionally, the PLA-NDU has conducted a course for foreign officers at a separate location since its establishment. Of these five, the National Defense Research course, also known as the "Capstone" course, prepares the most senior officers (army-level and above) and civilians for future leading roles in China's defense and national security policy arenas. The Capstone course was the most innovative of the courses introduced by General

Zhang Zhen. For the first time, some 24 senior officers and six civilian officials equivalent in rank were to study national security issues in a 3-month common curriculum in the same seminars, and in 1986 travel to Pakistan together on a fact-finding trip.[18] The teaching methodology in this course may also have been innovative for PLA PME at the time. In addition to the expected outside lecturers from Chinese and foreign academic and military institutions, the core methodology was seminar discussion and critical analysis concluding with a student policy paper.[19]

The two-year Basic Studies course is a step down from the National Defense Research course, and draws from group army, division, and brigade commanders and logistic commanders together with Military Region (MR) and above staff officers. The 1-year Advanced Studies course draws from division-level and above military, political and logistics commanders, and provincial officials. The Graduate Studies course lasts 2 to 3 years, drawing from college graduates and graduates of the command academies. The students study for masters and doctoral degrees. Upon graduation, they serve as commanders or conduct research on military theory. The 2-year Instructor Training course prepares command academy and undergraduate technical academy graduates to become mid and high-level command academy instructors. Foreign officers were the responsibility of the Foreign Training Department.[20]

CURRICULUM AND TEACHING REFORM

Whereas curriculum change is to be expected and continuous, major reform of PLA-NDU curricula and teaching was undertaken beginning in 1999.

This series of reforms responded to the CMC issuing the *New Generation Operations Regulations* in January directing the PLA to concentrate on developing joint operations skills.[21] In his January *Jiefangjun Bao* article on the importance of the new regulations, Chief of the General Staff General Fu Quanyou stressed that they affected all facets of PLA war preparations, modernization, training, force structure changes, weapons development, and professional military education.[22] All PLA PME institutions will have used the new campaign-level regulations as the basis for rewriting teaching texts, developing new teaching materials, and revising course curricula. The PLA-NDU party committee initially established five teaching priorities.[23] These focused on practical learning; improving understanding of the advances in military technology in order to grasp the importance of world military developments; enhancing student capabilities in strategic analysis; improving competency in the command of high-tech joint operations; and managing the military in a time when China was constructing a socialist market economy.

Additionally, the party committee developed the "Outline of 21st-Century-Oriented Teaching Reform and Development at National Defense University" as guidelines for future curriculum development. The reforms focused on the importance of building a broad curriculum that went beyond military subjects, but went further in terms of the PLA-NDU's future role in China's armed forces. It sought to build the PLA-NDU into a source of innovation for defense modernization and a center for the exchange of ideas on improving the PME system.

Events in 2002 and 2003, however, were to drive the most sweeping changes in the PLA-NDU's curricula and teaching methods.[24] First, the CMC's 2002 decision directing the PLA to launch a "revolution in military affairs with Chinese characteristics" required specific curricula changes. Second, in 2003 some PLA-NDU professors selected to comment on China Central Television (CCTV) as military experts during the U.S. invasion of Iraq made errors in predicting the war's progress. These errors brought the substance of the curricula and the teaching faculty's capabilities under review.

The revolution in military affairs demanded by the CMC had the objective of "building an informationized armed force and winning informationized warfare." This required the PLA-NDU to explore new concepts in warfare and develop teaching methods to prepare senior commanders for the conduct of informationized operations. The failure of faculty to predict accurately the progress of the U.S. invasion of Iraq brought both the quality and teaching methods at the PLA-NDU into question. The PLA-NDU party committee's investigation of the problem identified two causes behind the faculty's errors. First, the media were selective in what they chose to report, therefore the faculty members were responding to incomplete information. Second, and most important, the faculty had matured in the era of semi-mechanized and mechanized warfare and did not understand informationized warfare. Their erroneous analyses therefore reflected outdated concepts of warfare.

Following the problematic CCTV commentaries, students were critical of the faculty's analytical skills and, perhaps more significantly, the relevance of their courses to the actual needs of the armed forces. The faculty was perceived as too theoretical in its teaching and failing to recognize the new demands on the armed forces. The contemporary PLA confronted complex contingency planning and operations, counterterrorism and peacekeeping missions, the blending of offensive and defensive tactics, precision strikes, and other tasks not approached effectively by the faculty. In short, the faculty was "divorced" from the needs of the armed forces and did not meet student expectations.

Faculty and teaching methods received immediate correction. Thirteen army and division-level commanders from the PLA General Political Department (GPD), the three services, and the Second Artillery were assigned to the PLA-NDU for a 2-year tour of teaching or research.[25] They were to return to their command positions at the end of their tour. In 2007, ship commanders, pilots, and missile launch commanders from the Navy, Air Force, and Second Artillery were assigned to the faculty as instructors. Recruiting experienced commanders from the services continues, and now includes retired senior generals.[26]

Teaching methods were revised to minimize the number of lectures and increase active student participation in their seminars. The instructor now introduces the issues to be assessed and then requires the students to work through the problems themselves. Moreover, the PLA-NDU established cooperative teaching arrangements with major civilian centers of higher education, such as Beijing and Qinghua universities. Similar arrangements were made with the PLA Academy of Military Science and the National University of Defense Science and Technology.

To keep in touch with the current needs of the armed forces, students and faculty now actively participate in PLA exercises. Beginning in 2004, PLA-NDU faculty were assigned to major training exercises organized by the PLA General Departments. They went not as observers but as "combatants." Students assume "battle posts" when taking part in unit combat training. In 2005, students served on ships in a naval training exercise that covered 1,500 nautical miles, and in 2006 students were part of the PLA's first "transregional" exercises where units crossed MR boundaries.[27]

A new General Staff Department (GSD) program designed to enhance the PLA's joint warfare capabilities reflects the continuing role of the PLA-NDU in practical military issues. In June 2007, the GSD Service Arms and Training Department announced the launching of a trial program seeking to improve instruction and training in joint operations.[28] The PLA-NDU has the lead role in this effort joined by five command academies, including the Shijiazhuang Army Command Academy. The objective is to improve the quality of command personnel in joint operations by linking together research in training methods with joint training by units and examining all the requirements for joint operations.

This emphasis on the more practical military concerns of the PLA did not necessarily subtract from the broader focus of the PLA-NDU on preparing senior officers for higher command and staff positions that require knowledge beyond strictly military affairs. A new and evidently technologically sophisticated strategic decisionmaking exercise was introduced, and the number of students traveling overseas to broaden their understanding of world affairs appears to have increased. In 2005, more than 300 students from six classes visited more than 10 countries, including the United States, France, Canada, and Australia, to learn about their views of security and military affairs.[29] The new "strategic simulation system" drew on examples used by foreign militaries to develop a teaching tool for training high-ranking officers in crisis decisionmaking.[30] In the initial exercise conducted on November 29, 2006, the 66 participants fulfilled a variety of responsibilities that included political, foreign affairs, military, and economic roles in developing and implementing a complex strategy. During the exercise, there was continuous broadcast of "virtual" news created in response to students' decisions regarding the situation they faced. The exercise director could and did intervene to create constant pressure on the students, including shifting public opinion and requiring specified students to respond to media questions in news conferences. The purpose of the exercise was to expose the students to the complexities and dynamic process of crisis decisionmaking by role-playing where the different components of China's national security community will be responding in differing ways as the situation evolves.

Curriculum reform extended to the training of foreign officers. The PLA's expanding contacts with foreign military establishments led to a major transition in the Foreign Training Department in 2004, when it became the Institute for Defense Affairs. The institute's purpose is to train senior military officers and civilians from abroad and to promote exchanges with foreign countries. The first class of the new institute reportedly contained 970 students from 40 countries.[31]

STRATEGISTS AND COMMANDERS

Assessing the National Defense Research course's potential role in preparing senior officers to be strategists requires a brief discussion of the source of authoritative military strategy and concepts of operations for China's armed forces. The *Military Strategic Guidelines* promulgated under the name of the CMC Chairman constitute authoritative military strategy for the PLA.[32] Five guidelines have been issued since the founding of the People's Republic in 1949. According to Finkelstein, these guidelines will contain six and perhaps more core components. They include: (1) an assessment of the global security environment and the implications for China's security; (2) The adjustments in the PLA's core strategy of "active defense" required by changes in the conduct of war; (3) A statement of China's broader national objectives, including economic, political, diplomatic, and internal societal goals, in order that the PLA can adjust its missions to support them; (4) Defining the type of war the PLA must prepare for, such as the current directive to "win a war under informationized conditions"; (5) Most importantly, defining where a war is most likely to break out, against what enemy for what national objectives; and (6) The multiple military modernization programs and reforms required to fulfill requirements stemming from the previous five components.

Guidelines are not rigid planning documents. Rather, they are the foundation for a dynamic process that, although directing specific programs and reforms, allows for adjustments over time. Thus, guidelines are modified and the programs they initiated adjusted to meet changes in Beijing's security objectives that do not require a major alteration of the guidelines themselves. Jiang Zemin as CMC Chairman and CCP General Secretary promulgated the current guidelines in 1993 as the *Military Strategic Guidelines for the New Period*. The new guidelines primarily responded to changes in the conduct of war driven by advances in military technology demonstrated by U.S. military operations against Iraq in 1991. The guidelines directed the PLA to change from its 1985 tasking to prepare for "local, limited war" to preparing for "local war under modern high-tech conditions."

In 1999, the *New Generation Operations Regulations* joined the *Military Strategic Guidelines for the New Period.*[33] Like the 1993 guidelines, these new regulations were issued under Jiang Zemin's name as CMC Chairman. They focused on the campaign-level of war to provide guidance for the joint and single-service operations required for the effective conduct of high-tech warfare. Finkelstein judges them similar in function to U.S. Army Field Manuals or the Joint Publications published by the U.S. Department of Defense Joint Staff. The six known regulations are:

- The Essentials of joint Campaigns of the Chinese People's Liberation Army;
- The Essentials of Army Campaign of the Chinese People's Liberation Army;
- The Essentials of Campaigns of the Chinese People's Liberation Army Navy;
- The Essentials of Campaigns of the Chinese People's Liberation Army Air Force;
- The Essentials of Campaigns of the People's Liberation Army Second Artillery Corps;
- The Essentials of Campaign Logistics and Safeguards of the Chinese People's Liberation Army.

In 2002, following assessments of the growing importance of information warfare (IW) in the conduct of war, the PLA's directive to prepare for winning local war under high-tech conditions was modified to prepare for winning "local wars under the conditions of informationalization" — a change reflected in China's 2004 Defense White Paper.[34]

These changes and modifications in CMC directives on military strategy and operations resulted, as noted earlier, in PLA-NDU curricula changes. Unfortunately, there is insufficient detail on what curricula changes the PLA-NDU introduced in response to the CMC's revised regulations for campaign-level war or the 2002 directive that the PLA must initiate a "revolution in military affairs with Chinese characteristics." Moreover, there are few if any details on the substance of the PLA-NDU's National Defense Research course. Given the diversity of officer ranks involved in the five PLA-NDU curriculum tracks, what is known about the PLA-NDU curriculum may not reflect the substance of the National Defense Research course.

The most commonly known PLA-NDU teaching texts were published too early to have incorporated the guidance found in the six operational regulations published in 1999 or the 2002 revision of the guidelines. The PLA-NDU press published *The Science of Military Strategy* in May 1999, *The Science of Campaigns* in May 2000 and *A Course of Study in Combined Arms Tactics* in August 2000.[35] These texts would have taken some two or more years to prepare and receive approval, thus drawing conclusions about the probable substance of Capstone course seminars and lectures from these texts is questionable. Nonetheless, because the PLA-NDU's curricula and teaching reforms were a response to changes in the military strategic guidelines and operational regulations, they can offer some insights into what students were studying.

The curricula and teaching reforms introduced over the years 1999-2003 were designed to orient the PLA-NDU curricula to current operational issues confronting the armed forces. Recruiting faculty from serving commanders in the Army, PLA Navy (PLAN), PLA Air Force (PLAAF), and the Second Artillery was undertaken to correct what was seen as a curriculum too focused on theory. Changing the teaching methods to engage the students in problem solving served the same purpose, as did requiring students and faculty to participate actively in major PLA exercises rather than as observers. As reported, curricula and teaching reforms served more the requirements of joint force commanders than they did preparing military strategists.

The two reported reforms that could serve the National Defense Research course students well were the introduction of a more sophisticated crisis decisionmaking simulation exercise, and the recruiting of retired experienced general officers to serve on the faculty. Neither of these reforms, however, was specifically identified as focused on National Defense Research course students. Moreover, despite the enrollment of civilian officials for the senior course, no mention of their participation was found in the discussion of curriculum and teaching reforms. It is possible that the more encompassing foci of the National Defense Research course designed to broaden the students' understanding of the relationship between defense policy and China's overall foreign policy objectives and strategy were considered effective, and the introduction of current military issues was designed to add balance the curriculum. This, however, is speculation because of the limited information available.

Nor do the curricula reforms suggest any particular concentration on classical Chinese military philosophy or historic texts on military strategy. This could be because traditional Chinese and more modern Western military thought were well-established in the curricula and therefore did not require reform.[36]

Although details of its curriculum are not available, the National Defense Research course does not appear to prepare its graduates to be strategists in the sense that their follow-on assignments are specifically designated for those who develop military strategy. This does not necessarily mean Capstone graduates will not play a role in developing new military strategies and operational concepts for the PLA. The process by which new PLA strategy and operational concepts are developed is not well-understood, but speculation on what is known suggests how Capstone graduates could be involved.

Presumably, when change is required in the military strategic guidelines and operational regulations of the armed forces, the CMC will staff out specific taskings to the PLA Academy of Military Science (AMS), the PLA-NDU Institute for Strategic Studies, and appropriate offices in the General Staff Department and Service headquarters.[37] It is probable that Capstone graduates participate in the formulation of new strategy and concepts of operations when they serve in offices charged by the CMC with this responsibility.

Surveying what is known of the post-graduation careers of Capstone graduates supports the proposition that the National Defense Research course is focused more on improving commanders' knowledge of the PLA's current operational requirements than creating military strategists. Nonetheless, because data on the careers of all Capstone graduates are not available, any conclusion is tentative. Furthermore, a number of senior officers[38] are not National Defense Research course graduates, some attended lower courses, and some appear not to have attended any PLA-NDU course.

For example, in the PLA's most senior ranks, Minister of Defense General Cao Gangchuan,[39] a Politburo member and Vice Chairman of the CMC, attended no PLA-NDU course. General Xu Caihou,[40] a CMC Vice

Chairman and member of the CCP Secretariat, is also not known to have graduated from any PLA-NDU program. General Liao Xilong,[41] Director of the General Logistics Department and CMC member, graduated with the first Capstone class in 1986. General Liang Guanglie,[42] the PLA Chief of Staff and a CMC member, graduated from the Advanced Studies course in 1987.

In the senior joint service research centers, Deputy Commandant of the Academy of Military Science Lieutenant General Ge Dongsheng[43] is a 1988 Capstone graduate. PLA-NDU President Lieutenant General Ma Xiaotian[44] is not a graduate of the senior course, but attended the Basic Studies course in 1993-94. Nevertheless, as an Air Force officer he is the first PLA-NDU president not selected from the Army. His appointment reflects the CMC's commitment to the PLA-NDU's joint service mission. National University of Defense Science and Technology's President General Wen Xisen[45] is not a graduate of any PLA-NDU course.

Among the service commands, PLAAF Commander General Qiao Qinqchen[46] is not a PLA-NDU graduate, but Lieutenant General Liu Chengjun,[47] a deputy commander of the PLAAF, is a 2003 Capstone graduate. Similarly, PLAN Commander Admiral Wu Shengli[48] is not a PLA-NDU graduate, but Rear Admiral Ding Yiping,[49] the PLAN chief of staff, graduated from the senior course in 1996. Lieutenant General Jing Zhiyuan,[50] the Second Artillery commander, attended a senior PLA-NDU course in 2001 — probably the Capstone course.

Similarly, in the MRs, some are Capstone graduates and some are not. General Fang Fenghui,[51] the Beijing MR commander, is a 2001 graduate. Nanjing MR Commander General Zhu Wenquan[52] is a 1996 graduate, and Lieutenant General Song Caiwen,[53] a deputy commander of the Shenyang MR, graduated in 2002. General Wang Jianmin,[54] the Chengdu MR commander, is a 1990 graduate of the Basic Course. Lanzhou MR Commander General Wang Guosheng[55] however, is not known to have attended any PLA-NDU program.

Although the data are far from complete, it appears from follow-on assignments that the Capstone course focuses on preparing its students for higher command and staff positions and not as military strategists. They also suggest that even in the recent past attending the National Defense Research course was not essential for promotion to the PLA's higher command and staff positions. General Wang Guosheng, for example, assumed command of the Lanzhou MR in June 2007 with no public record of any PLA-NDU background. It is difficult to draw firm conclusions from these data, but at this time, graduating from the PLA-NDU National Defense Research course has not been necessary for appointment to senior commands. No doubt attending the Capstone course is a plus when a senior officer is reviewed for high-level appointments, but it does not appear to be essential. Nonetheless, the number of known Capstone graduates in high-level command appointments suggests that attending the National Defense Research course could become a requirement in the near future.

SPECULATIONS AND CONCLUSIONS

Before any conclusions are drawn, there are two potentially significant issues not raised in the sources used for this chapter that should be mentioned. Many of the known Capstone graduates were born in the late

1940s and early 1950s, and joined the PLA in the late 1960s or early 1970s. What was their education level when they entered the PLA?[56] It is unlikely they were graduates of PLA academies. Even if they were, their formal education would be secondary or technical school degrees, not 4-year bachelor's degrees.[57] In 1987, *Xinhua* reported that 25 percent of the officer corps had college education, with 65 percent graduates of "vocational and technical schools."[58] In 1999, *Liberation Army Daily* reported that 65 percent of the officer corps had received a 3-year college education — up from 10 percent in the early 1980s.[59] The PLA's recent quest to have all entering officers be graduates of civilian universities or 4-year military academies confirms that today's senior officers were not well-educated when joining the PLA. Moreover, as junior PLA "cadres" before officer ranks were approved in 1984 and the regulations implemented in 1988, they endured both the disruption and PLA involvement in the chaos created by Mao Zedong's Great Proletarian Cultural Revolution over the years 1966-76. In that decade, student participation in the turmoil marking the era essentially closed down civilian universities, and two-thirds of the PLA schools closed. Those that remained open had their academic period dramatically shortened, and their curricula devoted to politics.[60] Consequently, most officers senior enough to be selected for the National Defense Research course did not enter with a high level of formal education, especially for the first few classes following the PLA-NDU's 1985 founding. Undoubtedly, the level of formal education increased over the years, but many of those even in recent classes would not be well-prepared to understand the implications of technological advances for military strategy and operations. This in part likely explains much of the emphasis on understanding advanced military technology found in the PLA-NDU's curricula reforms. Limited formal education of senior officers, together with their long careers in the PLA before the introduction of modern weaponry and advanced technology supporting systems in the 1990s, may make it difficult for them to fully grasp the complexities of joint operations and the accompanying advanced technologies driving intelligence, surveillance, and command and control requirements.

Second, there was little discussion and no assessment of the role fulfilled by the senior civilian officials attending the National Defense Research course or any other PLA-NDU course. At a minimum, one purpose of having civilian officials participate in professional military education programs is to have each profession understand the other's values. Their inclusion in PME is designed to improve the ability of civilian and military professionals to work together and cooperate in an increasingly multifaceted national security environment that requires the integration of defense policy with the broader concerns of China's foreign policy. A function of the military strategic guidelines is to do just this: authoritatively state China's broader strategic objectives in the economic, political, and diplomatic realms that will shape defense policy and PLA missions.[61] Unfortunately, no evaluation of civilian officials' participation in PLA-NDU courses ever emerged, making it impossible to make any judgment on the success of this aspect of the senior program.

Even with far from complete information on either the National Defense Research course or the officers who have completed the course since 1985, it seems evident that preparing senior officers to be military strategists is not a PLA-NDU priority. There are several reasons why this should be the case. First, military strategy is one of the prime foci of the PLA Academy of Military Science and the PLA-NDU Institute for Strategic Studies. In both institutions, researchers analyze the history of military strategy, research the strategy and operations of foreign defense establishments, and assess the PLA's future strategy requirements. It would be difficult, if not impossible, in a 3-month course to produce military strategists as capable as those found in the AMS and ISS who have dedicated their military careers to the field. The PLA-NDU's educational task is to prepare officers for higher levels of command and staff responsibilities, and prepare more junior officers for teaching and research in the command academies. This does not require a dedicated concentration on military strategy. Certainly, military strategy will be included in the curricula, but to enhance the understanding and knowledge of the officers attending the various levels of courses—not to create strategists.

Second, the distinction between commander and strategist is to some extent a false dichotomy. Ultimately, strategy is implemented through operations conducted by a specific service or services. This is precisely the importance of the 1999 promulgation of the *New Generation Operations Regulations*. They complemented the *Military Strategic Guidelines for the New Period* published in 1993. A major concern reflected in the PLA-NDU curricula reforms over the years was that the officers attending its courses—the PLA's practitioners—understand their tasks in developing and commanding operations capable of supporting the strategy found in the guidelines. To be successful in these tasks, commanders and staff officers must understand the military strategic guidelines. The importance of these operational-level tasks led to a more hands-on approach to learning. Students were to actively participate in PLA exercises rather than attend as observers. Active duty commanders assigned to the faculty were to conduct seminars where the students did not simply listen to and discuss lectures, but were engaged in solving problems introduced by instructors who brought with them their recent command experience. The operational-level issues confronting these officers in their follow-on assignments were the overwhelming focus of PLA-NDU curriculum and teaching reforms over the past decade.

Even with admittedly far from complete evidence, it is plausible to draw an image of the senior officer sought by the PLA-NDU's National Defense Research course. In essence, the PLA-NDU seeks to produce senior officers more competent at two levels than their peers in previous years. First, they are to be more capable of developing and commanding the complex joint operations required by the *New Generation Operations Regulations*. This means they must understand how to employ forces in joint operations entailing complex command and control in a battle area embracing land, sea, air, and space operations, with information operations influencing both the operational and tactical levels of warfare. For armed forces such as the PLA just entering the realm of military operations where ground, naval, air, and missile forces are integrated into operational plans, directing and commanding such an operation is a difficult task. Doing so with technologies equally new to the PLA makes this task even more demanding.

Second, they are to have a more sophisticated understanding of China's place and strategy in world affairs and the role of the PLA in this broader national security strategy, as the military strategic guidelines dictate. Lectures given by important foreign and defense officials, such as those of U.S. Secretaries of Defense William Perry in 1994 and William Cohen in 2000, make a major contribution here. Foreign guest lecturers will enliven seminar discussions of China's foreign policy and strategy, as will the travels abroad undertaken as part of the Capstone course. The knowledge and experience some senior officers bring to the PLA-NDU will also serve to enhance their understanding. The PLA's escalating role in UN peacekeeping operations, increasing participation in bilateral and multilateral combined exercises, and the expansion of military exchanges indicated by the upgrading of the Foreign Officers Training Course to become the Institute for Defense Affairs highlight the reality that the PLA is not nearly as isolated as it was just a decade ago. It is more than just probable that among the senior officers entering the National Defense Research course, a number of them will have direct experience of one or more of the activities bringing the PLA in closer and more frequent contact with foreign defense establishments and international organizations. This enhanced understanding of defense policy's intersection with China's foreign policy will be complemented by the understanding civilian officials gain of the military concerns their counterpart officers. Presumably, this will allow more effective cooperation between senior officers and their civilian equivalents in the formulation and implementation of China's national security policy.

The PLA-NDU was founded in 1985 to create a much-needed new officer corps to lead China's modernizing armed forces. The PLA's warfighting capabilities had begun to erode beginning with the Sino-Soviet dispute of late 1950s — erosion accelerated with Mao Zedong's Great Leap Forward and the turmoil of his Great Proletarian Cultural Revolution. The consequent deterioration of the PLA's capabilities and leadership was fully recognized by most of the PLA's senior leaders. They recognized that the path to modernization was long and difficult, and that the PLA-NDU was to be a core element in rebuilding the officer corps. General Zhang Zhen's 1992 promotion to the CMC suggests the foundation he built was considered successful. Now some 20 years later, the PLA-NDU continues to evolve. The responses the PLA-NDU has made to China's changing defense needs and national security requirements over the years since 1985 strongly suggest that the corps of senior officers prepared by the National Defense Research course will be ever better able to lead China's future armed forces.

ENDNOTES - CHAPTER 9

1. For the purpose of this chapter, senior officer refers to officers at and above the rank of major general and rear admiral.

2. See, for example, *China's National Defense in 2006*, Beijing: Information Office of the State Council, December 29, 2006, pp. 33-37. *Xinhua* translation, December 29, 2006.

3. Deng Xiaoping, *Selected Works of Deng Xiaoping*, Vol. 1, Beijing: Foreign Languages Press, 1982, p. 274.

4. I am grateful to Colonel Alfred D. Wilhelm, Jr., U.S. Army (Ret.) for this insight.

5. Jing Shuzhan, Jia Yong, and Zhou Zhifang, "Generals Arise From Here — Visiting the People's Liberation Army National Defense University," *Liaowang*, May 27, 1996.

6. The following discussion draws on my personal observations from 1987.

7. For a concise description of the U.S.-NDU's Capstone course, see Cynthia A. Watson, *Military Education: A Reference Handbook,* Westport, CT: Praeger Security International, 2007, pp. 28-29.

8. Jing Shuzhan *et al.*

9. See Harlan W. Jencks, "China's 'Punitive' War on Vietnam: A Military Assessment," *Asian Survey*, Vol. XIX, No. 8, August 1979, pp. 801-815.

10. For a succinct analysis of the PLA's early assessments of IW's importance, see James Mulvenon, "The PLA and Information Warfare," in James C. Mulvenon and Richard H. Yang, eds., *The People's Liberation Army in the Information Age*, Santa Monica, CA: RAND, 1999, pp. 175-186.

11. *China National Defense in 2006*, p. 4.

12. For a detailed discussion of China's response to SDI, see Bonnie S. Glaser and Banning N. Garrett, "Chinese Perspectives on the Strategic Defense Initiative," *Problems of Communism*, Vol. 35, No. 2, March/April 1986, pp. 28-44.

13. Pressures to change China's deterrence logic through the mid-1990s can be found in Iain Johnston, "China's New 'Old Thinking': The Concept of Limited Deterrence," *International Security*, Vol. 20, No. 3, Winter 1995/96, pp. 5-42.

14. For an interesting assessment of Chinese responses to U.S. BMD, see Eric A. McVadon, "Chinese Reactions to New U.S. Initiatives on Missile Defense," in Andrew Scobell and Larry M. Wortzel, eds., *China's Growing Military Power: Perspectives on Security, Ballistic Missiles, and Conventional Capabilities*, Carlisle, PA: Strategic Studies Institute, U.S. Army War College, September 2002, pp.169-199.

15. Jing Shuzhan *et al.*

16. *Ibid.*

17. This conclusion is based on comparing my notes from a 1987 1-month stay as a visiting professor and the structure reported in "The Cradle of Generals—The National Defense University," February 8, 2006, in *Pengpeng.com*. *Pengpeng.com* is a web site sponsored by the PLA-NDU as "Pengpeng National Defense Online" (*www pengpeng.com.cn*).

18. "Defense University Graduates First Class," *Xinhua*, December 10, 1986.

19. Personal observation, 1987.

20. This paragraph draws from Jing Shuzhan *et al.*

21. See David M. Finkelstein, "Thinking About the PLA's 'Revolution in Doctrinal Affairs'," in James Mulvenon and David Finkelstein, eds., *China's Revolution in Doctrinal Affairs: Emerging Trends in the Operational Art of the Chinese People's Liberation Army*, Washington, DC: Beaver Press, December 2005, pp. 1-28, for a detailed discussion of these regulations and their significance.

22. *Ibid.*, p. 19.

23. The following discussion is taken from Wang Maorun, "Study and Implement Deng Xiaoping's Thought on Army Building," *Qiushi*, March 1, 1999, pp. 27-29.

24. The following discussion is taken from Li Xuanqing, Wu Tianmin, and special correspondent Lin Peixiong, "Transformation, and What Does It Bring to the 'Cradle of Generals' — An Analysis of the Changes Occurring at the National Defense University, China's Highest Military Academy," *Jiefangjun Bao* (Internet version), November 10, 2006.

25. *Xinhua*, September 1, 2003.

26. See, for example, Zang Jiansheng and Liu Demao, "'New Blood' Injected Into Pool of NDU Teachers," *Jiefangjun Bao*, April 10, 2007.

27. Li Xuanqing *et al.*

28. Liu Feng'an and Li Yun, "(Military Affairs) PLA Launches Trial Project for Joint Instruction and Joint Training," *Xinhua*, June 14, 2007.

29. Li Xuanqing *et al.*

30. "NDU's Research and Development Platform 'Immersion Style' Strategic Confrontation Exercise," *Xinhua*, December 1, 2006.

31. "'Historic Leap' for Foreign Military Trainees," *PLA Daily*, August 9, 2004.

32. The following discussion draws primarily from David M. Finkelstein, "China's National Military Strategy: An Overview of the 'Military Strategic Guidelines," in "Roundtable: Sizing the Chinese Military," *Asia Policy*, Number 4, July 2007, pp. 67-72.

33. The following discussion draws primarily from Finkelstein, "Thinking About the PLA's 'Revolution in Doctrinal Affairs'," pp. 1-26.

34. *China's National Defense in 2004*, Beijing: State Council Information Office, December 27, 2004, p. 5.

35. Finkelstein, "Thinking About the PLA's 'Revolution in Doctrinal Affairs'," p. 19.

36. For example, Peng Guangqian and Yao Youzhi, eds., *The Science of Military Strategy*, Beijing: Military Science Publishing House, 2005, devote chapter 3, "Evolution of Laws and Strategic Theories," to a survey of Chinese and Western military theorists.

37. I am grateful to Dennis J. Blasko for this suggestion.

38. This assessment was undertaken in August-September 2007, and therefore does not reflect the promotions and new assignments announced later that year.

39. People's Online, available from *www.people.com.cn/english/9811/05/target/newfiles/C110.html*.

40. *Xinhua*, available from *news.xinhuanet.com/ziliao/2002-01/21/content_246269.html*.

41. People's Online, available from *www.people.com.cn/GB/shizheng/252/9667/9670/20021129/877930.html*.

42. *Xinhua*, available from *news.xinhuanet.com/ziliao/2004-07/22/content_1626518.html*.

43. *China Military Affairs New Observer Forum*, June 26, 2007, available from *xinguancha.bbs.xilu.com*.

44. "PLA General Staff, Navy, Air Force, Second Artillery, and Military Region Major Personnel Readjustment," *Xinhua*, August 19, 2006.

45. *China Military Affairs New Observer Forum*, June 26, 2007, available from *xinguancha.bbs.xilu.com*.

46. *China Great Wall*, available from *www.cgw.cn/jspd/C_jspd_zgjxx_2002_jiangshailu_info_1873.html*.

47. "PLA Air Force Appoints Six New Leaders," job number 1418-2003, August 11, 2003, *Intelink U*.

48. China Military Affairs New Observer Forum, available from *xinguangcha.bbs.xilu.com*.

49. "PLA General Staff, Navy, Air Force, Second Artillery, and Military Region Major Personnel Readjustment," *Xinhua*, August 19, 2006.

50. "PLA Three Star Generals Series (VI)," job number 5070-2007, March 13, 2007, *Intelink U*.

51. "New Guangzhou Military Region Leaders," job number 2120-2004, May 4, 2004, *Intelink U*.

52. "PLA Three Star Generals Series (V)," job number 5014-2007, January 16, 2007, *Intelink U*

53. "New Lanzhou Military Region Commanders," job number 2102-2004, May 4, 2004, *Intelink U.*

54. *Xilu Forums*, June 27, 2007, available from *bbs.xilu.com/cgi-bin/bbs/view?forum=xinguancha&message=34698.*

55. China Military Affairs New Observer Forum, available from *xinguancha.bbs.xilu.com.*

56. I am grateful to Kenneth Allen for bringing this issue to my attention.

57. For a detailed overview of the long history of PLA educational reforms, see *China's Navy 2007*, U.S. Navy, Office of Naval Intelligence, February 2007, pp. 64-69.

58. "PLA Now Better Educated," *Xinhua*, May 30, 1987.

59. Bo Jinbao, "Civilized Force Marching on the Forefront of Society—10th Roundup of Army Building Achievements Over Past 50 Years," *Jiefangjun Bao*, September 25, 1999.

60. *China's Navy 2007*, p. 66.

61. Finkelstein, "China's National Military Strategy," p. 70.

CHAPTER 10

SHAPING CHINA'S NEXT GENERATION OF MILITARY LEADERS: FOR WHAT KIND OF ARMY?

Ellis Joffe[*]

The new generation of China's military leaders is being shaped first of all by the kind of army that China is developing for missions that the Chinese leadership assigns to it. Until the mid-1990s, these missions had little effect on the development of the Chinese People's Liberation Army (PLA) because it was too technologically-backward to do much more than defend China on Chinese territory. This situation changed radically after the Taiwan crisis of 1995-96 convinced the Chinese leaders that preventing the separation of Taiwan might involve them in a war with the United States. What followed was a decade of intensive military modernization that substantially transformed the PLA's capabilities, but also led to the adoption of a counterveiling American strategy that, in turn, continues to drive China's military modernization. Also driving it is the rise in China's international status, which has awakened the Chinese leadership's dormant long-range external objectives: to make China a great power and to gain regional preeminence. This new connection between military force and external missions is the motive force behind the emergence of a new PLA.

---

* I would like to thank Dennis Blasko and Paul Godwin for valuable comments and suggestions. The responsibility for the final product is, of course, mine alone.

The new generation of China's military leaders is being shaped first of all by the kind of army that China is developing for missions that the political leadership assigns to it. The makeup, mindset, education, and training of these military leaders, as well as their skills and know-how — all these features will derive from the needs of this army. The key questions then are: What missions will the PLA be expected to perform? and What kind of PLA will be needed to perform them?

These missions are determined, first, by the need to defend China and by the leadership's threat perceptions, which identify the enemies against whom China needs to be defended. They are also determined by the short and long range objectives of the Chinese leadership — political and military — in the implementation of which the armed forces have a central role.

Although some of these missions have always shaped the development of the PLA, most did not emerge in their present form until the mid-1990s. This was because at times the leadership sought to achieve certain objectives without using the PLA, while at other times some objectives were dormant. During long periods, moreover, the military mission of the PLA was limited to defending China by relying on a mass-based "people's war," and this did not generate urgent requirements to modernize the PLA. Since the 1990s, however, this connection has become much tighter: The missions of the PLA have become more varied, and their influence on the course of its modernization is much stronger than in previous years.

The new missions have brought about vast changes in the PLA, which have been reflected primarily in three related areas that cumulatively shape its development. First is the leadership's policy of military modernization, which sets the direction and provides the resources for building the nation's military forces. Second are the doctrines that prepare the armed forces for their combat roles. And third is the relationship between political and military leaders, which determines the PLA's influence on military policy and the scope of its professional autonomy.

The new missions of the PLA and the changes they have caused in its development have come together only at the start of this decade. The result has been the emergence of a new PLA. This chapter will examine its evolving missions and their impact.

DEFENDING THE REALM

The most compelling objective that determines the state of a country's armed forces is defense of the realm. Defense preparations are designed first of all to respond to potential threats. Although threats may change, the need to maintain basic defense strategies and minimal force postures is permanent.

The Chinese, of course, are no exception. In fact, they are probably more sensitive to real or imagined threats to their security than leaders of most countries. The memory of imperialist encroachments and humiliations in the 19th and 20th centuries, hostility from the United States and the Soviet Union after the establishment of the People's Republic of China (PRC), and a continuing sense of threat from Washington sparked by the Taiwan issue—all these have made defending China a top priority for all leaderships. However, the strategies of defense changed radically over the years and, with them, the characteristics of the PLA and its leaders who have had to implement these strategies.

When the communists came to power, their backward armed forces were in no state to defend China in the unlikely event of an attack by the United States, and they presumably expected the Soviet Union to deter an attack or, if that failed, to fall back on Mao's "people's war" doctrine to repel it. Before the Chinese could begin to modernize their armed forces, they intervened against the United States in the Korean War. When hostilities ended, they began to modernize the PLA, but this effort was derailed after a few years by Mao's mass-oriented Great Leap Forward and the deterioration of Sino-Soviet relations.

The result for the military was a revival of Maoist doctrine, which based the defense of China on a "people's war." This war was supposed to be fought on China's soil using strategies and tactics which were developed in China's revolutionary wars. It was supposed to be a protracted war of attrition in which the Chinese would trade space for time and would fight short battles of annihilation. This strategy did not require technologically-advanced forces, which, in fact, could actually hamper its implementation. It did require disciplined and highly motivated troops, as well an ideologically-inspired nonprofessional military leadership. Another result was the need to transfer resources from the conventional forces to the development of nuclear weapons which China had to do on its own, without aid from an increasingly alienated Soviet Union.

After the start of Deng Xiaoping's reforms, the Chinese gradually detached the PLA from the burden of depending on Mao's "people's war" doctrine to defend China and adopted a conventional strategy of stopping an invader at the border or beyond. Nonetheless, although major reforms were carried out in the nontechnological sectors of the PLA, its re-equipment proceeded slowly, mainly due to shortage of funds. In the middle of the decade, the Chinese concluded that a major war was no longer a realistic possibility, and they began to prepare elite units in the PLA for short intensive wars outside China's borders. However, the efforts made in this direction were hampered by uncertainty about where such wars would be fought, as well as by the slow technological modernization of the PLA.

This situation did not begin to change substantially until the second half of the 1990s, because until then the Chinese did not envisage a realistic contingency in which they would have to defend the country against outside attack. Although decisions to step up PLA modernization were taken by the leadership in the early 1990s mainly due to lessons of the Gulf War and the fortuitous availability of advanced weapons from Russia, there was no big surge in its capabilities until several years later, presumably for two reasons. First, there is a substantial time gap between the adoption of decisions and their results on the ground. Second, there was no immediate threat and preparations for war had no specific target — until the specter of military conflict over Taiwan and the threat of U.S. intervention became the target for war preparations. This new sense of threat apparently accelerated the implementation of earlier decisions on modernization and led to the adoption of new ones, resulting in a rapid buildup of China's armed forces over the next few years.

RESPONDING TO THREAT PERCEPTIONS[1]

As a rule, defense strategies are bound up with the leadership's threat perceptions that identify the enemies who might endanger the homeland. These perceptions are crucial in shaping the strategies, because different threats require different responses, and these are determined by perceptions of the enemy. In China, however, the situation has been simpler during the Maoist period and for several years thereafter, because the Chinese relied on one all-encompassing non-nuclear strategy — "people's war" — to respond to all threats. Regardless of the threat's origin or severity — whether it was the perceived possibility of an American invasion from the south in 1965 or a Russian invasion from the north in 1969 — the response was the same. And because it was the same, the Chinese did not have to prepare their armed forces for a variety of threats. The "people's army" waging a "people's war" was supposedly capable of coping with them all. Threat perceptions, therefore, were not vitally important to force development during these years.

Their importance began to rise shortly after the end of the Maoist period, when the Chinese abandoned "people's war" in favor of a conventional defense strategy that required modern forces to meet possible threats. It reached new heights in the mid-1980s, when the Chinese for the first time began to consider the possibility of waging short wars at some distance from their borders, which required new kinds of modern forces to cope with a variety of new threats. Nonetheless, these perceptions did not lead to major advances in the establishment of such forces because the Chinese faced no concrete threats. The Soviet Union was on a downward slide and relations with the United States were exceptionally cordial. In addition, funds were short, and the PLA was deeply involved in business ventures.

A dramatic shift in the link between Chinese threat perceptions and force building occurred after the Taiwan crisis of 1995-96. For the first time since the 1960s, the Chinese began to perceive a strategic threat from the United States. This perception emerged after the United States dispatched two carrier groups to the vicinity of Taiwan during the crisis—a new threat that humiliated the Chinese, and to which they had no response. This crisis solidified their belief that the United States would intervene militarily to aid Taiwan if war broke out. What followed was a decade of intensive Chinese preparations designed to provide the PLA with a capability to respond to this threat. It was marked by the procurement of new weapons and the adoption of new doctrines that have substantially transformed China's regional capabilities.

These capabilities aroused serious concerns among American policymakers and defense officials regarding China's military power and intentions. By 2005 many top U.S. officials were voicing these concerns. They were probably best exemplified by remarks made by Secretary of Defense Donald Rumsfeld at a famous 2005 news conference in Singapore. China, he claimed, was "improving its ability to project power" in the Asia-Pacific region and then added: "Since no nation threatens China, one must wonder: Why this growing investment? Why these continuing and expanding arms purchases? Why these continuing robust deployments?"[2]

The reason lies in opposing threat perceptions. Impelled by their belief that the United States will intervene if they try to prevent the separation of Taiwan by military force, and determined to prevent such separation by force if all else fails, the Chinese stepped up the buildup of their armed forces. From their vantage point, it is their right to uphold the "one China" principle by force if necessary and to impede U.S. attempts to intervene. The United States, on the other hand, has perceived China's buildup as aggressive because it threatens Taiwan and poses a long-term danger to U.S. forces in the western Pacific. The *Report on China's Military Power* submitted to Congress by the Department of Defense (DoD) in 2006 warned that China's "attempt to hold at risk U.S. naval forces . . . approaching the Taiwan Strait" potentially poses "a credible threat to modern militaries operating in the region."[3] The 2006 *Quadrennial Defense Review* said that China had "the greatest potential to compete militarily" with the United States and that its buildup "already puts regional militaries at risk."[4]

Is the PLA a "credible threat" to U.S. forces beyond the Taiwan scenario? No one can predict whether the United States, as the predominant superpower, and China, as a rising one, are bound to clash in the future.[5] There is no doubt that the Chinese have begun to view their armed forces as providing essential military backing to China's long-term global and regional objectives. Even if the big buildup of these forces occurred in response to the Taiwan contingency, it is possible that they will be used to advance these objectives.

However, this is a distant future possibility and the Chinese themselves are surely uncertain what role their military forces will play at that time. In the meantime, China's buildup has been oriented toward capturing Taiwan and interdicting U.S. naval intervention. They have pursued a denial strategy for the maritime areas close to Taiwan and their borders, but have not demonstrated an intention of maintaining a dominant presence in the western Pacific. Nor have they demonstrated an intention to challenge U.S. military forces beyond the Taiwan scenario. China's military development in both quality and quantity—submarines and not aircraft carriers, for example—bears this out. Much as the Chinese would presumably like to evict the United States from the region, they know they will have to settle for less—a defensive strategy designed to protect the maritime approaches to China.[6]

The United States, however, views this strategy as a long-term Chinese military challenge and has already adopted a countervailing "hedging" strategy that involves measures to strengthen U.S. military power in the Pacific. These measures include adding at least one aircraft carrier and at least five nuclear submarines to the Pacific fleet over the next decade, which would place half the navy's carriers and 60 percent of its submarines in the Pacific. Other measures include upgrading the U.S. missile defense system, transferring long-range bombers and attack submarines to Guam, stationing stealth bombers in South Korea, redeploying troops to Japan, and establishing new combat headquarters in Honolulu. They also include efforts to strengthen ties and alliances with nations such as Japan, India, and Australia.[7]

The Chinese, for their part, look on these developments as a threat to their security. As one Chinese general put it in 2006: "At present it is not we who pose a threat to others; it is, in fact, others who pose a threat to us."[8] The Chinese government's 2006 *White Paper*, although published at a time of reduced tensions with Taiwan and the United States, nonetheless voiced concern about U.S. activities in the region: "There are," it said,

> growing complexities in the Asia-Pacific security environment. There is a new adjustment going on in the

strategic alignment and relations among major countries in the region, and new changes have occurred in the hotspots in the region. The United States is accelerating its realignment of military deployment to enhance its military capability in the Asia-Pacific region.[9]

A year earlier, the Ministry of Foreign Affairs journal expressed a similar concern:

The United States has taken further steps to build an even tighter strategic ring of encirclement in China's neighboring regions. . . . [It] has significantly strengthened its network of military bases in the Asia Pacific region and its alliance relationship with China's neighboring countries, further strengthened the U.S. Pacific Fleet; and established forward military bases in Central Asia, which is contiguous to China's Western region . . .[10]

This interplay of perceptions and misperceptions almost guarantees that the prophecies of each side will be self-fulfilling. The Chinese are building up their forces — especially air and naval — primarily as a "hedging" strategy against U.S. military might in the western Pacific, which is being expanded as a precaution against what the United States views as China's growing and potentially threatening power, but which the Chinese see as natural if their legitimate interests are properly recognized. As long as these perceptions remain intact, the Chinese can be expected to continue the buildup of their armed forces. The objective will be an ever more modern PLA which, the Chinese hope, will be increasingly capable of keeping the United States away from China and Taiwan.

Beyond Taiwan and the United States, a possible strategic threat that is a source of concern to the Chinese pertains to Japan — first as a U.S. military ally in the context of Taiwan, and, second, as a regional military power driven by the resurgence of Japanese militarism.[11] A possible threat from the West might arise from India—a nuclear power with regional ambitions in South Asia not dissimilar to China's in its nearby neighborhood. Although the Chinese do not seem to have shown undue concern about a challenge from India as a regional power, they began to be apprehensive about U.S. efforts to strengthen military relations with India as part of its "hedging" strategy against China.[12]

In addition to traditional military threats, the Chinese also point to threats that are nontraditional. These include "economic security, financial security, ecological [and] environmental security, information security, resource security, terrorism, weapon proliferation, the spread of epidemics, transnational crime, narcotics smuggling, illegal immigration, piracy, money laundering, and so on. A country's internal problems also come within the scope of national security."[13] It is not clear which of these threats is likely to involve the PLA—aside from border security, anti-terrorist activities, and dealing with social unrest—and which come under the responsibility of other security organs, such as the People's Armed Police or the regular police. In any case, these threats are presumably broadening the missions and functions of the PLA.

For all their importance, the threats faced by China toward the end of the decade are not a clear and present danger to China's security. War over Taiwan has become more remote, the U.S. "hedging" strategy is long-term, the emergence of Japan as a competing military power is far-off, and that of India is even further. China's security environment as of 2007 does not appear to require a rapid and intensive buildup of military forces. So why are the Chinese continuing such a buildup?

The most important reason is undoubtedly defensive. It derives from their belief that the threats to China's national security are long term, and that its armed forces are still far from acquiring the capabilities necessary to effectively cope with these threats. Attaining such capabilities, moreover, requires a major and extensive effort, given the PLA's low base line, its lateness in starting serious modernization, and U.S. capabilities. Therefore, the momentum of modernization that has been gathering force since the mid-1990s has to continue.

Beyond China's security concerns, however, other motives have also become operative. Until recent years, the Chinese had refrained from making a direct connection between their military forces and their long-range objectives in the international arena because the appalling backwardness of the PLA made such a connection irrelevant. However, two trends have started to change this situation. On the one hand, the rapid rise in China's international status, primarily as a result of its economic surge, has given the international ambitions of its leaders a powerful new lift. On the other hand, the PLA's accelerated modernization has held out the possibility that over time the PLA will be able to provide backing for these ambitions. The connection between military force and external objectives has thus become relevant. What then are these objectives?

BECOMING A GREAT POWER

To make China a great power is a basic, long-range, and unalterable objective of the Chinese leadership. However, to the extent that its attainment needs backing by military force, this objective has not been operative at all times. In fact, from the military vantage point, it has been dormant throughout most of the PRC's history, due to the slow and uneven course of China's military modernization.

The essence of this objective is to gain recognition for China as a great power. The specifics of such recognition are vague, but Chinese pronouncements and practice suggest that its attainment entails several conditions: respect for China's national honor; inviolability of its sovereignty and territorial integrity; membership in the exclusive group of major powers that define the workings of the international system; and, perhaps most important, the capacity to act independently in the face of pressure from other countries in matters that involve China's vital interests, as well as the capacity to influence other countries with respect to such interests.

This objective is rooted in powerful forces: geopolitical attributes — territory, population, and geographic location — that endow China with an overwhelming presence and enormous potential; China's soaring economic performance since the 1990s that has already raised it to international prominence; and nationalistic impulses that derive from the past grandeur of the Chinese empire and from imperialist-inflicted humiliations that destroyed it. Leaders nurtured by such sentiments are inclined to react with force to real or imagined threats to interests that arise out of their nationalistic perceptions. And force they reacted with on a number of occasions, but their readiness to do so had not been translated, until the 1990s, into a serious and sustained effort to build up their armed forces.

The first such effort was cut short by the revival of Maoist military doctrine in the late 1950s, which plunged the PLA into a steady decline for 2 decades. This was not because Maoist leaders gave up their aspiration to move China toward a prominent global status, but because they adopted a different strategy, which distinguished between reliance on "national liberation" forces in Third World countries and on China's own armed forces. For a decade, Chinese leaders viewed wars of "national liberation" inspired by the Chinese revolutionary model as the means for this advancement. Alienated from both superpowers, the Chinese decided that disruption of the superpower-dominated world order by many local revolutions was the only way to achieve China's goal. These revolutions were supposed to be carried out by local revolutionary movements without the participation of Chinese forces. In the meantime, the PLA's combat capabilities eroded rapidly, and with them the professional quality of its leadership.

Although the Deng leadership began to modernize the PLA, its global ambitions were not sufficient to generate a major drive to improve the weapons and equipment of the PLA. These ambitions are political and emotional, not strategic, and their absence did not put China's security at risk. This goal, moreover, is long-range, and the Chinese could move toward it without an urgency that required a huge economic tradeoff. And the military effort that is required to bring China closer to great power status in terms of its military capabilities is so gigantic that movement toward it had to be incremental in any case.

There is, of course, no agreed-upon military level that has to be reached in order to qualify China for great power status, but the Chinese are well aware that whatever this level is, it is far beyond China's reach. Although China possesses a large population and territory, as well as a minimal nuclear deterrent, what it sorely lacks are the advanced conventional forces that would enable it to project military power for long periods far from its borders. At a minimum, such forces would presumably need to include aircraft carriers, long-range aircraft, transport aircraft and ships for moving large numbers of troops and supplies, air and sea refueling capabilities, global communications systems, and bases in friendly countries.[14] The Chinese are still nowhere near acquiring such assets in sufficient numbers and at an adequate level of sophistication to enable sustained long-distance force projection. When they accelerated their military buildup in the late 1990s, it was not due to their global ambitions and the buildup did not set its sights on unreachable objectives, which remained limited to regional needs.

This situation is changing. By 2005 a new phrase began to appear in Chinese pronouncements, namely that China has to strive to build "a military force worthy of its international position."[15] This does not mean, of course, that the Chinese have begun to reach for unrealistic objectives. What it does mean is that several factors — the achievements of the buildup and its momentum, China's global economic standing and new international influence — these factors have combined to make advance toward the status of a military great power, however gradual and far-off, a long-term objective of the Chinese leadership. In short, a basic objective that had been dormant in its military aspect, has stirred into action.

The White Paper on China's National Defense in 2006 made this abundantly clear:

> China pursues a three-step development strategy in modernizing its national defense and armed forces . . . The first step is to lay a solid foundation by 2010, the second is to make major progress around 2020, and the third is to basically reach the strategic goal of building

informationized armed forces and being capable of winning informationized wars by the mid-21st century.[16]

These are the long-term objectives that will shape the future PLA and, barring unforeseen economic crises, will ensure its continued modernization not only for current needs, but also to meet needs that lie further ahead.

The most important one probably stems out of China's growing dependence on imported oil, natural gas, and other resources, which will require the Chinese to protect their sea lines of communication, especially from the Middle East; missions that the Chinese navy at present is unable to accomplish.[17] To accomplish them, the Chinese will have to make vast advances in developing a blue-water navy and air support capabilities, and they are not likely to attempt this in the coming years.

ASSERTING REGIONAL PREEMINENCE

On its broad regional aims, the Chinese leadership has been just as vague as on its global objectives and conclusions about them also have to be inferential. The primary aim is to gain a paramount position in the East Asian region — a position from which China will have the final say about what goes on in its extended neighborhood. Or, more importantly, what from China's standpoint should not be permitted to go on — in particular any development in the region that the Chinese perceive as a threat to their security. This means, for one thing, an aggressive military presence of a major power in China's vicinity. It also means the formation of strategic alliances between countries in the region and the United States that the Chinese view as aimed against their interests, such as the alliance between the United States and Japan with respect to the Taiwan issue.

China's regional objectives are driven by the same powerful forces that motivate it on the global scene. However, additional considerations are at work in the region, which make the attainment of China's objectives more imperative.

The most important is security. Whereas China's global aspirations are relevant to its prestige and political standing, its regional objectives are directly connected to defense of the homeland. While China has a variety of instruments, diplomatic and economic, with which to exert influence on its neighbors, in the end it is only military strength that can protect its vital interests and ensure its national security. And, unlike the global situation, building a military force for limited regional objectives is within China's reach.

Nonetheless, when the Chinese faced what they viewed as a direct military threat from the Soviet Union in the late 1960s and early 1970s, they did not rapidly improve their armed forces. The chief reason was that their response took the form of reliance on the "people's war" strategy to meet the possibility, however unlikely, of a limited Soviet invasion. On the political front, they responded to American feelers for a rapprochement in order to break out of the international isolation that was the main external result of the Cultural Revolution.

Even after the Chinese abandoned the Maoist "people's war" doctrine, for more than a decade after the start of military modernization they felt no urgency to substantially improve their conventional forces. The United States did not loom as a military threat, and whatever danger they still perceived from the Soviet

Union was remote and required no rapid improvements beyond the progress made by upgrading weapons and other reforms. From its neighbors, the Chinese faced no military threat, and they were presumably confident that, if a crisis broke out, they could carry out limited military actions beyond China's borders after the adoption of the "local, limited wars" doctrine in the second half of the 1980s.

The move away from preparing for a war that would be fought in China to one waged beyond its borders undoubtedly put new demands on the PLA, and throughout the 1980s the Chinese continued their efforts to raise its professional levels. However, since there was little progress in the improvement of the PLA's weapons and equipment, due to a lack of economic resources, the results of these efforts were limited, especially as more and more officers were turning away from military tasks to economic pursuits. Although modernization was stepped up in the early 1990s, it still lacked the strategic focus that stems from the need to respond to a major security threat. Such a threat arose with the emergence of the Taiwan issue and the belief of the Chinese that the United States would intervene if they attacked Taiwan.

ENTER TAIWAN

From 1950, when the United States created the Taiwan problem by interposing the Seventh Fleet between the mainland and the island after the Korean War broke out, until the mid-1990s, the Chinese acquiesced in the status quo, under which Taiwan made no significant moves towards independence, while China did not press for reunification. In the two crises that the Chinese initiated in 1954 and 1958, they used limited military means to achieve a limited political objective — to interdict trends that they viewed as endangering the "one China" principle. In neither of the crises had the Chinese intended to invade Taiwan.

The Taiwan issue emerged in a new and, from China's standpoint, provocative form after the election of President Lee Teng-hui, who began to make moves toward de facto independence, which, the Chinese claimed, were facilitated by conciliatory U.S. policies and continued arms sales to Taiwan. This sparked a crisis in 1995 that intensified as the Chinese began to fire missiles around Taiwan. It reached a climax during the spring of 1996 in the run-up to elections in Taiwan, when the United States intervened by sending two carrier groups near Taiwan. Tensions were further exacerbated by Lee Teng-hui's 1999 enunciation of the "two state" theory and by his successor, Chen Shui-bian, who continued to push for the de facto separation of Taiwan from China.

The events of September 11, 2001 (9/11) brought about a marked improvement in the relations between China and the United States. Focused on the war on terrorism, the United States adopted a more concilia-tory approach to China, which the Chinese used in their attempt to forge more cooperative relations with the United States. As a result, the Chinese abandoned their previous demand for immediate talks on reunifi-cation and began to focus on one overriding objective: preventing Taiwan's separation from the mainland.

However, this objective appeared unattainable after the reelection of Chen Shui-bian. The Chinese were con-vinced that Chen would continue to move incremen-tally toward independence, while the United States, despite formal declarations, was not doing enough to restrain Chen. By the summer of 2004 Chinese denunciations of Chen and the United States reached a pitch that had not been heard after 9/11.

Tensions did not remain high for long, and within a year or so the overwhelming significance of the Taiwan issue diminished dramatically. The main manifestation of this has been that the specter of a major war no longer hovers over the Taiwan Strait as it had in previous years. This has been due to a combination of reasons — the readiness of China's leaders to acquiesce in the status quo rather than to push for unification as long as Taiwan refrains from declaring formal independence, their belief that economic and other ties will advance the chances for peaceful reunification, the political difficulties of independence-seeking Taiwan President Chen Shuibian and China's expectation that he will not be reelected, and the new U.S. determination to restrain Taiwan from provocative actions.

However, the potential for war has not disappeared. It lies in the irreconcilable positions of the three sides. China considers the reunification of Taiwan with the mainland under the "one-China" principle as nonnegotiable, and has threatened to use force if Taiwan declares independence. The Taiwan government has made significant moves toward independence, and is determined to resist reunification under China's sovereignty. The United States is committed to the peaceful resolution of the issue, but has not ruled out military intervention if China attacks Taiwan.

If the basic positions have not changed, the state of the PLA has changed dramatically. This was because after the 1995-96 crisis, the Chinese began intensive preparations for military action in order to prevent separation. And they had to be preparations for a major war. This was because by the end of the decade, the possibility of U.S. intervention became, for the Chinese, a certainty. Not only did the United States continue to back Taiwan, the "U.S.-led" NATO bombardment of Yugoslavia during the Kosovo crisis was viewed by the Chinese as reflecting U.S. readiness to coerce its adversaries. Foremost among these, as the Chinese saw it, was China, whose efforts to unify Taiwan with the mainland the United States was determined to block.

The conclusion was clear to the Chinese: their armed forces had to prepare for conquering Taiwan and coping with U.S. intervention. This meant that the PLA had to acquire the capabilities to overrun Taiwan rapidly before the United States intervened; to try and deter the United States from intervention by raising its costs; to interfere with the access of U.S. forces to the theater of operations if it intervened; and, if all else failed, to attempt to defeat the United States in combat around Taiwan. A concerted effort to acquire these capabilities, therefore, became the strategic focus of China's accelerated military buildup. Taiwan is the immediate objective of these preparations, but even if the Taiwan issue becomes irrelevant, China's military buildup will continue because China's response to the possibility of a U.S. intervention in a Taiwan conflict has elicited a counter response by the United States that the Chinese view as a strategic threat. It will continue also because China's long-dormant global and regional objectives have become active.

A NEW MILITARY MODERNIZATION POLICY

Military policy provides the link between leadership objectives and the role of the military. It determines the direction in which the leadership wants the military to develop in the light of its objectives and the resources that will be allocated to it. It is closely connected to national policies in other areas. During the Maoist period, with the exception of the mid-1950s, military policy retarded the modernization of the PLA. Subsequently, it provided the essential, if uneven, impetus to military modernization until the mid-1990s and for the rapid military buildup after that.

The post-Korean War military policy was to transform the PLA from the technologically-primitive forces that fought in the war into a modern army, with the indispensable help of Soviet weapons and advisers. One condition for this transformation, as well as its consequence, was the formation of a professional officer corps in the PLA. Another was the acquisition of new weapons, the introduction of regular training methods, and the establishment of advanced organizational and logistics systems. A third was the adoption of modern doctrines by its revolutionary leaders.

These developments were cut short by the revival of Maoist doctrine in the late 1950s, which reestablished the "human factor" as decisive in determining the outcome of war and obviated the need for advanced military technologies and modern operational concepts. The professional progress and weapons modernization of the conventional forces were almost completely frozen, even as the development of China's indigenous nuclear capability was accelerated. The result was enormous damage to the combat capabilities and professional standards of the PLA, which was magnified by the divisive and destructive intervention of the PLA in the Cultural Revolution.

Repair of the damage could begin in earnest only after Mao's successor, Deng Xiaoping, became paramount leader in 1979. However, Deng's military policy made no attempt to rapidly re-equip the backward PLA. It was based on the assumption that China faced no

374

imminent military threat and, therefore, no urgent measures for weapons acquisition were required.

The military chiefs were unhappy about this policy, but accepted it both because of Deng's personal stature in the military and the inherent logic of the policy. They were also reassured by the prospect that large-scale weapons modernization would get under way after the advance of China's economy. The most concrete manifestation of modernization policy has been in the military budget. From 1980 to 1988, the stated budget rose only slightly, but was reduced considerably (by about 8 percent) as a share of the national budget. It is hardly surprising, therefore, that during the first decade of modernization the military not only had little to spare for weapons improvement, but also experienced serious hardships in the daily management of the armed forces.

The substantial annual increase, which raised the budget more than tenfold by 2007, began only in 1989. The initial impetus derived from a combination of factors: the army's role in putting down the Tiananmen demonstrations; the desire of the newly-ascendant paramount leader, Jiang Zemin, to gain the support of the military; the lessons of the Gulf War; and the start of China's economic boom. In the first few years, budgetary increases resulted in the purchase of some new weapons from Russia but a major acceleration of modernization began only after military policy focused on building forces that could prevent the separation of Taiwan by military means if necessary.

THE LONG MARCH OF DOCTRINE

While policy sets the direction for the PLA's development, its activities are guided by doctrine, which has two functions: to delineate the kind war the army will fight in the future, and to prepare it for fighting that war. Accordingly, doctrine has two components: (a) The warfighting component; and (b) The force-building component. Both components have undergone far-reaching changes in line with the PLA's changing missions.[18]

The Warfighting Doctrine.

This component deals with the next war that China will fight: Who will be the enemy and how will China fight the war against it—what will be its strategy, tactics, and operational modes? In conventional warfare, this doctrine has evolved through several stages. From the late 1950s until the end of the Maoist period, it was completely dominated by the Maoist concept of "people's war," which envisaged a long, all-out, and entirely defensive war. The Chinese would fight by drawing the enemy deep into Chinese territory in the first phase, eroding his strength by waging guerrilla warfare in the second, and defeating him in conventional operations in the final phase. To be sure, there was a strong emphasis on offensive operations, but only in the context of a defensive war on the mainland—what the Chinese called "active defense."

Did the PRC fight such a war? No. All the wars that China fought—in Korea, India, and Vietnam—were fought outside China and the "people's war" doctrine was inapplicable, except on the tactical and operational levels in some cases. The exceptions were the firefights with the Soviet Union that occurred on Chinese soil, but these were limited in scope, and the doctrine was irrelevant.

After the end of the Maoist era, the Chinese were able to abandon "people's war" as an unrealistic military doctrine. Of course, they have never said so, and, in fact, they continue to use the term in any instance of mass mobilization for war-related purposes. However, as an operational doctrine that seeks to envisage the next war and to prepare the army for it, abandon it they did. First, because the Chinese did not expect a massive invasion of their homeland, and this assumption was eminently sensible. Second, because in the case of a limited ground invasion, also highly unlikely, China's strategy was not to draw the enemy in and wear him down by guerrilla warfare, but to "meet him at the gate" and stop him by conventional warfare. And third, because more than anything else, China had to prepare for a war outside China's borders. "People's war" gave way to a new modern doctrine.

The new doctrine evolved through several stages. In the first stage, the Chinese detached themselves from Maoist "people's war" by adopting the "people's war under modern conditions" doctrine. In the next stage, they for the first time envisaged the deployment of the PLA outside China's borders under the doctrine of "local, limited wars." In the next two stages, the doctrine was raised to more advanced levels in line with lessons that the Chinese drew from current wars elsewhere and with the development of military technology in China. Accordingly, the doctrine evolved from fighting "local wars under modern high-tech conditions" to fighting "local wars under informationized conditions."

At the same time, two aspects of the "people's war" doctrine have been retained, even as the Chinese for all practical purposes jettisoned it. The first is relevant in the event of a general ground invasion of China, in which case the Chinese will resort to this doctrine.

Although this scenario is apocalyptic and completely unrealistic, it gives the Chinese confidence that they cannot be subdued or conquered.

The second is relevant in the very realistic scenario of massive air strikes on China — if, for example, China invades Taiwan. In this case, the Chinese envisage mobilizing the population for a variety of civil defense tasks to help the people survive extensive bombing and reduce the damage caused by it. This "people's war for civil defense" will enhance China's capability to absorb air attacks and will give Chinese leaders greater freedom and flexibility to take action outside China, which will presumably bring down air strikes on the Chinese homeland, in the belief that the population will be better prepared and more ready to withstand such strikes. The implication of the new doctrine is that it has oriented the PLA toward fighting a modern war beyond China's borders, while its readiness to fight is enhanced by falling back on "people's war for civil defense," which increases China's capacity to withstand air attacks despite defects in its air defenses.

The Force-Building Doctrine.

This component deals with the preparation of the PLA for fighting the type of war envisaged by the warfighting doctrine. In practice, this doctrine is more important than the warfighting one, because the warfighting doctrine can be changed quickly or ignored, whereas the building of forces is a concrete and prolonged process that cannot change direction rapidly. And there is no more convincing proof that "people's war" as a warfighting doctrine is dead than the forces that the Chinese have been building in the post-Mao period and especially since the 1990s. In every important category, these forces are increasingly geared to fighting modern wars: weapons and equipment, institutions and organizations, training and education, and operational modes and doctrines.

At the start of modernization, army building changed faster than the doctrine (although it was slow going for both), because for ideological reasons detachment from Maoist doctrine was cautious. Later, doctrine developed faster than accomplishments on the ground because of the obstacles to military modernization. However, in the last few years, the gap has been closing as the Chinese are modernizing both doctrine and forces.

However, while both the warfighting and force-building doctrines of the PLA are commensurate with its new missions, its capabilities are still limited. China's most modern forces have been developed to respond to the only real threat that China might realistically face in the next few years — U.S. intervention in a war with Taiwan — and it is not at all clear how the PLA would cope with such an intervention. Beyond that, its capacity to carry out complex operations far from its borders is still severely constricted. Doctrine, in short, has outrun developments on the ground. The task of PLA commanders in the coming years will be to catch up with the advanced doctrine that their leaders have enunciated.

CHANGING PARTY-ARMY RELATIONS

At first glance, party-army relations should not be a significant factor in influencing the kind of army that the Chinese will need, because this need should be dictated by external and strategic considerations. However, these relations will undoubtedly be significant in influencing the kind of army that the Chinese will have, because military need alone has never shaped the kind of army the Chinese have had.

As an army that is under the leadership and control of the party, the PLA has always been subject to the intrusion of political preferences and practices in determining its development, doctrines, and duties. The question has always been not whether there is intrusion, which is axiomatic, but to what extent it has interfered with professional military considerations and activities. Although such interference has diminished drastically in the post-Mao period, it continues to be an important factor in PLA development as long as China is a party-state and the PLA, a party-army.

How important depends on party-army interactions. Foremost is the vital relationship between the paramount leader and the generals. This relationship is vital because of the supreme importance of the leader in China's authoritarian one-party system and because of the vital political role of the military in that system. Although the basic framework of this relationship— mutual dependence and support—remains the same, tremendous changes have occurred within it after the passing of Mao and Deng. Unlike changes in military policy and doctrine, most of the changes in party-army relations have resulted from generational transition and new circumstances rather than from deliberate decisions, but this does not detract from their immense importance in shaping the PLA.

The most significant change pertains to the stature of the paramount leader in relation to the military. Mao's stature had been unique. Anchored in past successes, charismatic qualities, and personal ties, he enjoyed unparalleled personal authority. This enabled Mao to intervene freely in military affairs, to mold the PLA in his image, and to use it as his personal power base in elite struggles. Most important, Mao could always rely on the unconditional support of the military chiefs for his position on critical issues, even when they disagreed with him, or in power conflicts, even when they agreed with his adversaries. Given their subordination to Mao, the generals had no significant leverage over him and no influence on policy or budget decisions beyond the limits set by Mao.

Deng Xiaoping's relations with the PLA were both similar and different. Like Mao, he was also a charismatic figure, although he inspired respect more than fear. Like Mao, he had ties with PLA commanders that had been formed over many years, but these ties were built more on collegiality than on sheer loyalty. Like Mao, PLA leaders accepted him as supreme commander, but his position in the military was founded more on equality and cooperation. In the end, Deng dominated the PLA like Mao, but his authority depended more on his achievements than on reflex compliance. For these reasons, the PLA under Deng also did not become a political player in its own right, but it had a broader role. However, there were clear limits to this role as demonstrated by Deng's ability to put restraints on the military budget throughout the decade of his rule.

The position of Jiang Zemin and Hu Jintao is nothing like that of Mao and Deng. Despite the differences between Jiang and Hu, they have been united by several similarities. They are not enveloped in the aura of revolutionary struggle, they did not form ties during that struggle, they had no outstanding achievements prior to becoming paramount leaders, and they are not charismatic. Most significant, upon coming to power, they had no military background and no standing in the military. Both gained overall command of the PLA only by virtue of becoming paramount leaders.

Without personal authority in the military, neither Jiang nor Hu could rely on the unconditional compliance of the PLA as a matter of course in all circumstances. Compliance has become conditional, and the first condition is that the paramount leaders had to gain the support of PLA commanders. This they did by becoming PLA-friendly leaders, whether out of belief or necessity—Jiang much more than Hu, at least more obviously—by granting the military leaders extraordinary professional latitude (which extends to a much less intrusive and more professional role for political commissars as well), supporting military modernization, particularly with generous allocations, and involving them in security policymaking as never before.

This does not mean that the paramount leaders have to constantly curry favor with the generals. Given the basic and long-standing subordination of the military to political authority in the Chinese communist system, the generals will support the paramount leader as a matter of course. And given their professional ethos, the post-Mao generals have preferred to stay out of politics. However, since their support is no longer personal, the post-revolutionary leaders cannot be certain that it will be forthcoming under all circumstances. Consequently, they have to be responsive to the views and needs of the military in a way that was unthinkable for Mao or Deng. And this has worked in favor of military modernization.

A NEW ARMY

The last phase in the modernization of the PLA, which began in the mid-1990s and was stepped up at the end of the decade, has been carried out in exceptionally favorable circumstances in comparison with previous efforts. Impelled initially by the leadership's determination to prevent the separation of Taiwan by military means as a last resort, which entailed coping with American intervention, the drive has continued even as tensions over the Taiwan issue declined — inspired by reawakened external ambitions and responsive political leaders.

Since weapons are the one genuinely quantifiable component of combat capability, the procurement of many new models by the Chinese armed forces since the 1990s has been the most concrete result of PLA modernization. The most noteworthy new weapons have been imported from Russia, and these include advanced Su-27 and Su-30 fighters, *Sovremenny* destroyers armed with deadly anti-ship missiles, *Kilo* submarines armed with sophisticated torpedoes, surface-to-air missiles, and other modern systems.

For the first time since the start of modernization, these imports, augmented by stepped-up indigenous production, especially missiles and J-10 aircraft, have given the Chinese armed forces a small number of weapons that are equal in potential performance to those possessed by the United States. These weapons stand out as an exception to China's vast arsenal of relatively backward hardware, and they still leave the Chinese army nowhere near the United States in military technology. There can be no doubt, however, that the new weapons, if used effectively, have significantly advanced China's capacity to fight a limited modern war at short distances from its borders.

The effective use of advanced weapons depends on a range of "soft" components that are no less important than hardware in preparing an army to fight.

These include training, officer and noncommissioned officer education, organization, logistics, information technology application, and political indoctrination. To the improvement of each the Chinese have devoted a great deal of attention and effort in the last few years.[19]

Guided by what they term as a "revolution in military affairs with Chinese characteristics," the Chinese have reportedly streamlined the army's command structures by reducing staff functions and personnel. They are further reducing the size of the armed forces by eliminating outdated units. They have improved the efficiency of the logistical system by merging myriad support functions into a joint logistical support system and cutting organizations that had been administered by various arms and services. They have likewise improved the military education system by eliminating institutions that are similar to civilian ones, assigning officers to study relevant subjects in these institutions, and focusing on the strictly military ones. At the same time, they are putting much emphasis on raising the educational level of officers and upgrading their expert and command skills. They have made major efforts in assimilating information technology into various command and operational systems. And they have continued to conduct intensive political education among the troops, while emphasizing that its role, as well as that of political officers, is auxiliary in upgrading combat capability.

A potent indication of an army's war preparations lies in its training exercises, which are supposed to be one step away from the real thing. These exercises have been markedly upgraded since the start of the decade. They last longer, encompass more units, and are more complex than before. They seem to focus on elite amphibious units, but are conducted throughout the army in all kinds of terrain and weather. The current emphasis is on "integrated joint operations," which are supposed to combine all combat and support systems, as well as new equipment, into training exercises.[20]

How effective these measures have been is a question that cannot be answered with any certainty because the PLA is not transparent, because it is not known to what extent it has overcome basic difficulties — such as bureaucratic inertia, systems integration, and low technological levels — and because it has not been tested in battle for almost 30 years. There is no doubt that it has made impressive progress in recent years. According to *Jane's Defense Weekly*, "an emerging consensus among long-time PLA observers, including within the U.S. intelligence community, is that the Chinese military has successfully achieved a far-reaching qualitative advancement in its warfighting capabilities since the beginning of this decade."[21]

However, there is also no doubt that this advancement has been far-reaching primarily because of the low base line created by 20 years of damage inflicted on the PLA under Mao, and more than a decade of slow and partially ineffective modernization under Deng. While its capabilities are presumably adequate for defending China, they are uneven, and it has hardly begun to acquire the power projection capabilities that are required for realizing China's long-range global, and even some regional, ambitions.

The PLA, in short, still has a long way to go before it fully reaches the technological and professional levels of modern armies. Its success will depend, at the very least, on the continued advance of the economy, on its ability to obtain adequate funding in the face of competition from other sectors, and on the capacity of China's defense industries to produce modern weapons.[22]

It will also depend on the availability of professionally competent leaders at all levels of the PLA hierarchy. This will require efforts to recruit the "the best and the brightest" into its ranks. And the PLA knows it.[23]

ENDNOTES - CHAPTER 10

1. Some of the material in the next three sections is partially drawn from my article "The 'Right Size' for China's Military: To What Ends?" in Andrew Scobell and Roy Kamphausen, eds., *Right-Sizing the People's Liberation Army: Exploring the Contours of China's Military*, Carlisle, PA: Strategic Studies Institute, U.S. Army War College, 2007, pp. 559-571.

2. *Los Angeles Times*, June 4, 2005.

3. Office of the Secretary of Defense, "Annual Report to Congress: Military Power of the People's Republic of China 2006," Washington, DC: Department of Defense, July 2006.

4. *Quadrennial Defense Review Report*, Washington, DC: U.S. Department of Defense, February 6, 2006.

5. John Mearsheimer, *The Tragedy of Great Power Politics*, New York: W. W. Norton, 2001.

6. See the perceptive article by Bernard D. Cole, "China's Strategy of Sea Denial," *China Brief*, November 22, 2006, available from *www.jamestown.org*.

7. Taipei, *Central News Agency*, July 13, 2005; *Washington Post*, July 22, 2005; *Washington Post*, September 17, 2005; *Asahi Shimbun*, August 11, 2005. See also Roger Cliff, "PLA Modernization And Its Implications For US Force Posture In The Asia-Pacific," in Michael Swaine, Evan Medeiros, and Andrew Yang, eds., *Assessing the Threat: The Chinese Military and Taiwan's Security*, Washington, DC: Carnegie Endowment, 2007, pp. 285-311.

8. Hong Kong *Zhongguo Pinglun She*, Internet edition in Chinese, March 8, 2006, *Foreign Broadcast Information Service* (FBIS) CPP20060316515024.

9. Information Office of the State Council of the People's Republic of China, *China's National Defense in 2006*.

10. Cited in Susan L. Craig, *Chinese Perceptions of Traditional and Nontraditional Security Threats*, Carlisle, PA: Strategic Studies Institute, U.S. Army War College, March 2007, p. 41.

11. *Ibid.*, pp. 58-86.

12. *Ibid.*, pp. 86-97.

13. Guo Xuetong, "Nontraditional Security and China's Rise," *Mao Zedong Deng Xiaoping Lilun Yanjiu*, December 30, 2005; Craig, p. 103.

14. Keith Crane *et al.*, *Modernizing China's Military: Opportunities and Constraints*, Santa Monica, CA: The RAND Corporation, 2005, pp. 200-203.

15. Beijing *Zhongguo Xinwen She*, May 15, 2006; FBIS CPP20060515072002.

16. Hong Kong *Zhongguo Pinglun She*.

17. Liu Jianping and Feng Xianhui, "Going Global: Dialogue Spanning 600 Years," Beijing *Liaowang*, July 11, 2005, FBIS CPP20050719000107.

18. See any of the excellent articles by Paul Godwin on Chinese military doctrine. For example, see Paul H. B. Godwin, "Compensating for Deficiencies: Doctrinal Evolution in the Chinese People's Liberation Army: 1978-1999," in James C. Mulvenon and Andrew N. D. Yang, eds., *Seeking Truth from Facts: A Retrospective on Chinese Military Studies in the Post-Mao Era*, Santa Monica, CA: The RAND Corporation, 2001, pp. 87-118.

19. For an excellent account of these efforts in the ground forces, see Dennis J. Blasko, *The Chinese Army Today: Tradition and Transformation for the 21st Century*, New York: Routledge, 2006; and Dennis Blasko, "PLA Ground Force Modernization and Mission Diversification: Underway in All Military Regions," in Kamphausen and Scobell, eds., *Right-Sizing the People's Liberation Army*, pp. 281-373.

20. Information from Dennis Blasko in a personal communication.

21. *Jane's Defense Weekly*, April 4, 2005. For a superb and comprehensive account and analysis of PLA modernization over 2 decades, see David Shambaugh, *Modernizing China's Military: Progress, Problems, and Prospects*, Berkeley: University of California Press, 2002.

22. Crane *et al.*, pp. 20.

23. *Agence France Presse*, citing the *China Daily*, May 1, 2007.

ABOUT THE CONTRIBUTORS

THOMAS J. BICKFORD currently works for the CNA Corporation. Prior to joining them, he was an associate professor at the University of Wisconsin-Oshkosh, Associate Director of the Wisconsin Institute for Peace and Conflict Studies, and a member of UW-Oshkosh's International and Environmental Studies program. Dr. Bickford is the author of several articles and papers on the PLA and civil-military relations in China. His research interests include Chinese foreign policy and comparative civil-military relations in Leninist and post-Leninist eras. Dr. Bickford holds a Ph.D. in political science from the University of California, Berkeley.

DENNIS J. BLASKO is a retired U.S. Army lieutenant colonel. He was an Army attaché in Beijing and Hong Kong from 1992 to 1996. Lieutenant Colonel Blasko is the author of *The Chinese Army Today: Tradition and Transformation for the 21st Century* (London: Routledge, 2006).

DAVID D. CHEN is a Principal Research Analyst at CENTRA Technology, Inc., in Arlington, Virginia, where he studies economic and security issues in the Asia-Pacific region. He has published in *Space Policy and Space News*, among others, and serves as a reviewer for *China Security*. Mr. Chen earned a Master's degree in Pacific International Affairs at the University of California-San Diego Graduate School of International Relations and Pacific Studies and a B.A. in Public Policy Analysis at Pomona College.

JOHN F. CORBETT, JR., has been an Analytic Director with CENTRA Technology, Inc. since 2001. He specializes in China, Taiwan, and Asian military and security issues. He retired as a colonel after a career in the U.S. Army as a Military Intelligence/China Foreign Area Officer (FAO). His last Army position was as Senior Country Director for China and Taiwan in the Office of the Secretary of Defense for International Security Affairs. During his military career, Colonel Corbett served in a variety of operational, intelligence, and policy positions in the 82d Airborne Division, U.S. Army Pacific, and Defense Intelligence Agency. He also served as an Army attaché in Beijing from 1986-88 and in Hong Kong from 1992-98. He has published articles in *The China Quarterly* and *The China Strategic Review*. Colonel Corbett is a graduate of the U.S. Military Academy, the Armed Forces Staff College, and the U.S. Army War College, and has Masters degrees in International Relations and in Asian Studies from the University of Hawaii.

PAUL H. B. GODWIN retired as professor of international affairs at the National War College, Washington, D.C., in 1998. His research specialties focus on Chinese defense and security policies. Among Professor Godwin's recent publications are "China's Emerging Military Doctrine: A Role for Nuclear Submarines?" in Andrew S. Erickson, Lyle J. Goldstein, William S. Murray, and Andrew R. Wilson, eds., *China's Nuclear Submarine Force* (Annapolis, MD: Naval Institute Press, 2007); "China as a Major Asian Power: The Implications of its Military Modernization," in Andrew Scobell and Larry M. Wortzel, eds., *Shaping China's Security Environment: The Role Of the People's Liberation Army* (Carlisle, PA: U.S. Army War College, Strategic Studies Institute, 2006); "Decisionmaking Under Stress: The Unintentional Bombing of China's

Belgrade Embassy and the EP-3 Collision," in Andrew Scobell and Larry Wortzel, eds., *Chinese National Security Decisionmaking Under Stress* (Carlisle, PA: U.S. Army War College, Strategic Studies Institute, 2005); "Change and Continuity in Chinese Military Doctrine: 1949-1999," in Mark A. Ryan, David M. Finkelstein, and Michael A. McDevitt, eds., *Chinese Warfighting: the PLA Experience Since 1949* (Armonk, NY: M. E. Sharpe, 2003). Professor Godwin is now a consultant and serves as a nonresident scholar for the Foreign Policy Research Institute. He graduated from Dartmouth College with a degree in international relations, and received his doctorate in political science from the University of Minnesota.

KRISTEN GUNNESS currently works as a China advisor on the Navy Staff. Previously she was the Deputy Director of the China Studies Center at The CNA Corporation. She also worked as a business consultant for a well-established American firm based in Shanghai, where she specialized in providing market growth strategies for multinational companies in Asia. In that capacity she spent several years working in China, Taiwan, and Southeast Asia. Upon returning to the United States, she worked as an Asia analyst for the Intellibridge Corporation and also served as the China Country Manager for the U.S. Trade and Development Agency. Ms. Gunness has written extensively on Chinese security, foreign and economic affairs, and is the co-editor of *Civil-Military Relations in Today's China: Swimming in a New Sea* (Armonk, NY: M. E. Sharpe, 2007). Ms. Gunness holds an M.A. in Security Studies from Georgetown University's Edmund A. Walsh School of Foreign Service and is a graduate of the Hopkins-Nanjing Center for Chinese and American Studies. She has studied Mandarin at Beijing Capital Normal University and the Harbin Institute of Technology.

ELIZABETH HAGUE has been a China research analyst at the State Department since October 2007. She worked at the RAND Corporation from 2005-07, when she wrote this paper. Previously, Ms. Hague analyzed Chinese leadership and political-military affairs at the U.S. Department of Defense (DoD). Before joining DoD in 2000, she worked in the Voice of America's East Asia Division and Mandarin Service. She received a B.A. in East Asian Languages and Literatures from Bates College in 1992 and an M.A. in East Asian Studies (China) from Stanford University in 1998.

ELLIS JOFFE is professor emeritus of Chinese studies and international relations at the Hebrew University of Jerusalem and adjunct professor at Tel-Aviv University. He has written two books and many articles and book chapters on the Chinese military.

ROY KAMPHAUSEN is Vice President for Political and Security Affairs and Director of the National Bureau of Asia Research, Washington, DC, Office. Prior to joining NBR, Mr. Kamphausen served as a U.S. Army officer, where his assignments included Country Director for China-Taiwan-Mongolia Affairs in the Office of the Secretary of Defense and intelligence analyst and China Branch Chief in the Directorate for Strategic Plans and Policy (J5), Joint Chiefs of Staff. He served two tours at the Defense Attaché Office of the U.S. Embassy in the People's Republic of China. His areas of concentration include China's People's Liberation Army (PLA), U.S.-China defense relations, U.S. defense and security policy toward Asia, and East Asian security issues. His recent research has embraced PLA modernization, Taiwan defense and security issues, changing U.S. defense policy and posture in Asia, and the implications of China as a "responsible stakeholder" in East Asian security. Mr. Kamphausen received a B.A. in Political Science from Wheaton College and holds a Master's in International Affairs from Columbia University. He studied Chinese at the Defense Language Institute and Beijing's Capital Normal University.

JAMES MULVENON is the Vice-President of Defense Group Inc.'s Intelligence Division and Director of its Center for Intelligence Research and Analysis. A specialist on the Chinese military, his research focuses on Chinese C4ISR (command, control, communications, computers, intelligence, surveillance, and reconnaissance), defense research/development/acquisition organizations and policy, strategic weapons programs (computer network attack and nuclear warfare), cryptography, and the military and civilian implications of the information revolution in China. Dr. Mulvenon's book, *Soldiers of Fortune* (Armonk, NY: M. E. Sharpe, 2001), details the rise and fall of the Chinese military's multi-billion dollar international business empire. He is the author of numerous chapters, articles, and monographs on the Chinese military. Among his professional affiliations, Dr. Mulvenon is a term member of the Council on Foreign Relations, founding member of the Cyber Conflict Studies Association, and a member of the National Committee for U.S.-China Relations and the Association for Asian Studies. He received his Ph.D. in political science from the University of California, Los Angeles, and attended Fudan University in Shanghai from 1991-92.

NAN LI is an Associate Professor at the China Maritime Studies Institute of the U.S. Naval War College. He has published extensively on Chinese security and military policy. Professor Nan Li's writings have appeared in *Security Studies, China Quarterly, China Journal, Armed Forces & Society, Issues and Studies,* and many others. He has contributed to edited volumes from RAND Corporation, Clarendon Press, National Defense University Press, and M. E. Sharpe, and has published a monograph with the U.S. Institute of Peace. He is the editor of *Chinese Civil-Military Relations: The Transformation of the People's Liberation Army* (Routledge, 2006). Professor Nan Li received his Ph.D. in Political Science from the Johns Hopkins University.

EDWARD C. O'DOWD is Professor of Strategic Studies at the Marine Corps War College. He has had extensive experience in the study of Asian military affairs.

ANDREW SCOBELL currently is at Texas A & M University. His previous assignments included associate research professor at the Strategic Studies Institute, U.S. Army War College, and adjunct professor of political science at Dickinson College. Dr. Scobell also has taught at the University of Louisville, Kentucky, and Rutgers University, New Jersey. He is the author of *China's Use of Military Force: Beyond the Great Wall and the Long March* (Cambridge University Press, 2003) and numerous other publications. Dr. Scobell holds a Ph.D. in Political Science from Columbia University.

TRAVIS TANNER is a Senior Project Director and Director of the Pyle Center for Northeast Asian Studies at the National Bureau of Asian Research. Mr. Tanner's interests and expertise include Northeast

Asian regional security, China's economy and foreign affairs, and Taiwan politics. Prior to joining NBR, he was Deputy Director and Assistant Director of the Chinese Studies Program at The Nixon Center. He also worked as a research assistant at the Institute for International Economics in Washington, DC. Mr. Tanner graduated from both the Johns Hopkins School of Advanced International Studies (SAIS) and the Hopkins-Nanjing Center in Nanjing, China, earning an M.A. in international relations. He received his B.A. from the University of Utah in Chinese language and literature.

FRED VELLUCCI is an Asia Security Analyst in Project Asia at The CNA Corporation. Prior to joining CNA, Mr. Vellucci worked as an analyst focusing on Chinese domestic political reform and East Asian security for a number of organizations in Washington, DC, including the National Bureau of Asian Research, Intellibridge Corporation, and the Sigur Center for Asian Studies. In addition to Chinese foreign policy and East Asian security affairs, Mr. Vellucci's research interests include domestic political reform in China and its implications for continued social stability and one-party rule. He studied Mandarin Chinese at the Beijing Institute of Technology, Capital Normal University in Beijing, and the Hopkins-Nanjing Center for Chinese and American Studies. Mr. Vellucci holds an M.A. in Asian Studies from the Elliott School of International Affairs at the George Washington University.